Margaret Durrell was born in India, the privileged child of the British Raj. Following the death of her father in 1928, the family returned to England, settling in Bournemouth. Lured by tales of the magic of Greece, the Durrells uprooted again and moved to Corfu in 1933. Rumours of war forced the family to return to England, but Margo escaped back to Corfu to live with her village friends.

After marriage and extensive travels in Africa, she returned to England again before the birth of her second son. Divorce followed and she married again, but, unable to curb her restless urge to travel, she became a mariner on a Greek cruise ship.

Living in Bournemouth once again, Margo is now a mother, grandmother, and great-grandmother.

WHATEVER HAPPENED TO MARGO?

MARGARET DURRELL

A *Warner* Book

First published in Great Britain
by André Deutsch Limited in 1995
This edition published by Warner Books in 1996

A CIP catalogue record for this book is available from the British Library.

ISBN 0 7515 1673 2

Printed and bound in Great Britain by
Clays Ltd, St Ives plc

Warner Books
A Division of
Little, Brown and Company (UK)
Brettenham House
Lancaster Place
London WC2E 7EN

To my family, who have supported
me in all my adventures

PREFACE

People are always asking me what happened to my sister. I am pleased to report that Margo is still full of beans and that our lives continue to be as entangled as they were during those halcyon days on Corfu. She helped raise my animals; I helped raise her children. She descends upon me frequently at my zoo in Jersey and my house in Provence; I often invade her territory in Bournemouth. We have taken many holidays together – driving through the back lanes of France and arguing about a picnic site or when it is biologically necessary to stop the car; feeding the pigeons in the Piazza San Marco in Venice and watching them (the pink kind) in the tropical paradise of Mauritius. And, yes, sharing again the charms of Corfu, looking for and finding the deserted olive groves and sea caves where we were all so happy.

From the beginning and every bit as keenly as the Durrell brothers, Margo displayed an appreciation of the comic side of life and an ability to observe the foibles of people and places. Like us, she is sometimes prone to exaggeration and flights of fancy, but I think this is no bad thing when it comes to telling one's stories in an entertaining way. I am delighted that she has written down the experiences at '51' and I know you will enjoy them, too.

Gerald Durrell
Jersey, 27 November 1994

Introduction

The year was 1947, the place was suburban Bournemouth and the idea had started with a telephone call from my Aunt Patience, a formidable spinster who had rung the family home in Bournemouth to announce her impending visit.

'How is your dear mother, poor soul – such a handful to bring up all you children alone.' (Mother was a widow.) 'And that clever boy, Lawrence, is still about, well and writing?' (Lawrence was aspiring to be a literary genius.) 'And how is Leslie? Has he got another job yet? For it's high time he had!' (Leslie, with the hint of an entrepreneur and another venture abandoned, had been out of work for some months with no particular career prospects in mind.) 'And dear brother Gerald, is he still away, exposing himself to tropical diseases?' (Brother Gerald, showing a distinctive leaning towards nature from the age of two, was at that moment surrounded by animals in some zoo, observing heaven knew what.) 'And you dear – I trust you are not letting the grass grow under your feet?' I had returned home for a spell, after an adventure both into marriage and exciting travels to faraway countries and now, undecided what to do next, I was, in fact, in limbo.

Satisfied that we were all at least living, Aunt Patience then probed me on the second most important subject – money.

'And how are the finances?' No doubt she had been hoping for a miraculous answer.

'Well I have my inheritance father left me . . . maybe,' I edged uncertainly, not wanting to create too black a picture in case I incurred her imminent disfavour, or too prosperous a one which would possibly kill any generous urges she might have. I imagined the fond smile accompanying her questions turning sour with disapproval at the mention of any impending financial muddle.

'I have been giving you, Margo dear, a considerable amount of thought lately, and I have an idea.' She announced the word grandly then paused ominously, waiting for my gasp of anticipatory pleasure.

'Margo, are you still there?' the voice demanded, sensing the drifting threads of concentration.

'Yes, of course,' I replied quickly and sat down with a silent sigh of resignation, knowing Aunt Patience's ideas required making oneself as comfortable as possible, in order to enjoy a lengthy conversation.

'You really must pull yourself together dear, and work hard for your future prosperity, as I have done.'

It was a lecture all about working hard – something I knew nothing about. Dismayed, I let my mind hastily return to its wandering. I was brought back to the present by a sudden squeak in a tone of urgency. 'It's the only thing to do – don't you agree?'

'Yes!' I gasped, alarmed at my aunt's implications.

'You, dear, will start a guest house. Not a common affair, but something rather superior, something secure – and safe!' The voice rose firm and enthusiastic. 'Marriage is neither secure or safe.' (Aunt was a spinster by design.) 'It will be a sort of anchor for you: at the moment you are like an old boat being tossed about without a rudder.'

Not caring for my Aunt Patience's descriptive values, I reassured myself in the mirror opposite. There was no resemblance to her simile yet but the thought of financial security suddenly lifted my spirits to unquestionable heights. I analysed the situation briefly. Aunt Patience was right; a property, a boarding house. What a good idea! Not that I had any experience in these matters.

'A boarding house? I have never thought of that,' I replied with a growing interest.

'Not a boarding house dear, a guest house – boarding is so common. I was only saying to Mummy yesterday,' Aunt Patience continued, 'what Margo needs now is something solid behind her, not another marriage but a business property, for there's no stability in marriage with her temperament.'

I found myself grinning fondly across the distance into the 'Kensington' room of aquarium greenness straight to my Aunt Patience. The idea was suddenly a challenge. With security so elusive, who was I to treat lightly any suggestion to better myself financially? The rosy life of a landlady floated before me, the proverbial grey cloud with its silver lining was actually within my grasp. Consequently, I blessed my Aunt Patience on this fateful day as I made for the kitchen, a little diffidently perhaps, for there was still the inevitable family comment.

I broke the news of my intended venture to Mother and anyone else who was around at the time, with glowing descriptions of financial gain and life-long security in an atmosphere of quiet refinement. The place wasn't going to be an ordinary lodging house, I explained, chatting on enthusiastically to a row of granite-like expressions, but something on a higher plane: a guest house.

They treated my colourful conclusions with prolonged silence then retired hurriedly behind locked doors to discuss what they called 'this new madness'.

Why must a new venture be treated by my family as if it were only once removed from lunacy, I asked myself bitterly. What could be wrong with becoming a sedate landlady in a respectable town, when backed morally by Aunt Patience – and, possibly, financially if she should have one of her generous urges – and who were they to judge such an important business issue when there wasn't a single commercially-minded one amongst them? I analysed my family's virtues with the jaundiced mind of retaliatory criticism.

Take my mother, for instance: tiny and courageous – yes; indomitable in mother love – yes; but no connoisseur of landladies and certainly no businesswoman. How could she be, with her limited experience, completely engrossed as she was in family affairs: the animals; the garden; concentrating on the delicate art of Indian cooking and the fascinating pages of *Prediction*. How could she possibly interpret the respectable role of a landlady into a Crippen-like drama of unpredictable dangers? Her worries so far had been an impending overdraft and a terror of the white slave trade. She still warned me, her only daughter, against hypodermic syringes administered swiftly in cinemas by dark-skinned strangers and, of course, the perils of not lifting public lavatory seats. Lawrence had not helped the situation either, fostering her fears with his diabolical genius for invention and urging her loudly to put her foot down. Neither had Leslie, that squat, Rabelaisian figure lavishing oils on canvas or sunk deep in the intricacies of guns, boats, beer and women; penniless too, having put all his inheritance into a fishing boat that had sunk even before the maiden voyage in Poole Harbour. He had agreed with every word Lawrence had uttered, illustrating the already imagined horrors with still more graphic accounts of lewd male lodgers, landladies throttled at their posts, questionable births and remarkable deaths. His final pronouncement that 'landladies are born, not made', in a voice suggesting that they had just laid a very dear corpse to rest, upset Mother still further.

Fortunately, brother Gerald's absence had temporarily spared me his comments, which would, no doubt, have equalled anything his brothers had to offer. I shuddered at the recollection of his activities (which did not include the apt handling of a vast business fortune or running a sedate boarding house, I thought with some scepticism), as I re-lived tins filled with beetles, boxes of lizards, evil-smelling bird droppings, stinking snakes preserved in alcohol, corpses splayed grotesquely ready for dissection, the air thick with ether as a maimed animal was skilfully treated and brought back to life, while those with weaker stomachs than his tottered away to readjust themselves. His return would mean confusion and disorganisation, and we would all be enthusiastically forced out, regardless of weather conditions, to scan the countryside for possible properties, where he could, without restraint, create the first nucleus of a dream zoo. Already a lively candidate, a marmoset, a small furry apparition with the face of an old sage, ruled the house in his absence. Perching in strategic spots to relieve the pangs of nature, deeply offended if disturbed, Pavlo would sulk for hours in some inaccessible place while an over-fed Tibetan sheepdog tussled against him for first place in the family's affections. A badly stuffed crocodile, from which a musty odour exuded in strong waves, glared with beady eyes from the top of the bathroom cupboard, and beneath, scrawled across the mirror in red soap (a strong reminder that his absence was only temporary), a warning read, 'Please don't touch', along with a reminder to himself of a dental appointment.

So, who wouldn't want to escape to a landlady's Utopia?

Chapter One

Consequently I left the warm familiarities of well-known surroundings and started weeks of intense house-searching. A new world opened before me; a fascinating world of bricks and mortar, that carried me away on the heady wings of exploration – and I saw everything but the right house! Shuttered windows opened to reveal silent ballrooms; marble pillars spiralled up to ornate ceilings, where lusty rotund cherubs unashamedly chased each other in play; secret stairways laced in cobwebs; attics, breathless in their wealth of waiting shadows; shoe-box bungalows, prim and lifeless; monstrosities in corrugated iron and dull brown paint, alive yet dead; whilst a host of echoes whispered of Aunt Patience's unseen scolding presence ('A most unsuitable property, dear') and brother Gerald's gleeful murmurings ('Look, marvellous as a hippo pond') as another corner revealed a neglected sunken garden. And the margin of suitable houses narrowed alarmingly, forcing me to consider practicalities.

I didn't know what I wanted – then suddenly I did, in one wild unpredictable moment, completely without reason and unbelievably near home. Of course, I'd seen the house before, but never 'felt' its presence, or even noticed who lived behind the yards of dismal maroon curtaining. Now a FOR SALE notice had changed everything, I thought in amazement, as I stood starry-eyed and contemplated my choice in this sedate wide road of large Edwardian houses (our own road, in fact).

The object of my affection, a big comfortable, square house, stood solid on three floors. Wide bay windows broke the solidity of thick walls in the front and between these, small domed windows in bright stained glass added the odd bizarre touch to the somewhat dull colour scheme outside of murky green. High between the chimney stacks, I noted with satisfaction the enticing windows of an attic. A large porch sheltered the front door and lying back from the porch, a stone garage narrowed the entrance to the back garden, a square of unpruned trees and rough lawn surrounded by a high wall, stout fence and a deep privet hedge. A wilderness – but to me, at this moment, it was paradise.

The front door opened to my eager enquiry almost before I reached it and, piercing me with a shrewd look from eyes permanently screwed up in putty-coloured folds, as if they had spent a lifetime in hot sunlight, was a woman of ample proportions and declining years. A voluminous white blouse, sadly yellowed, sloppily topped a threadbare skirt held together on straining seams. The blouse buttons, a solitary two of glass and chipped like crystal rock, hung by a lonely thread, gallantly but vaguely restraining the pendulous breasts which threatened to burst forth; through the grinning gaps a grimy wool vest and cambric framework of ingenious invention fought for first place to freedom. In contrast to the rest of her, a halo of hair shone forth like a message. Plaited in a thick, white rope and circling her head neatly several times, it was skewered to firm immobility. It was as if she wore a silver crown.

I stood, astonished, startled by the ill-assorted appearance. Not wholly confident, I felt the sharp edge behind the soft, gargantuan bulk, whilst my inquisitive eyes glanced past her and examined the hall which, despite the dismal decor of faded mottle beige, was large, with many possibilities; long stained glass windows opening onto the porch reflected shades of bright colour. The centre light was a gloomy contraption, covered by a brown paper shade, an amateurish homemade hotchpotch, and carelessly gummed.

Possibly, at some other time, my first impressions of a grubby interior and peevish inglorious old woman would indisputably have put me off, but now, feeling supremely confident in my choice, nothing would turn me from my task as I was swept along in the wake of something that was not unlike a Cook's tour. For now Mrs O'Grady had become humanly garrulous, interspersing her sales talk with other incongruous subjects, with the dogged playfulness of an elderly bitch long past her prime. She stressed the beauties of the house, repeating the phrase 'newly decorated' constantly, which was a downright lie because it was very apparent that only the woodwork in the most prominent parts had been licked with a brush. She hurried me cunningly from one small patch of fresh paint to the next, hoping to deceive, expanding her stories of life in China – years spent saving souls in a

Mission, along with the demands of an ailing husband – while my curious eyes, missing nothing, noted that there was not a single personal object in memory of a country to which she had given her best years.

The wide staircase, turning gently at two points, led up to an airy landing which overlooked the well of the hall; bright, with a long window in opaque emerald glass, I saw it as a musicians' gallery. Rooms spread out widely around the square. Nothing could depress that airy landing, I thought, not even the evil smell of burning stew bubbling on the gas stove. At the top of the stairs I turned to find with surprise yet another spacious landing and more large and well-planned rooms, including a huge bathroom with a cast iron monster of a bath standing on curved feet, full of dirty crockery. A narrow stairway led up to a long white attic of sloping ceilings and dormer windows. The garden spread out beneath us, melting into a tangle of green shrubs and tall trees, the view stretching out again to rooftops and misty greens rising in a distant line of hills, blurred now in the softening light of the end of yet another day.

It was dusk when I left. Long shadows lay silent across the avenue and the odd light twinkled. Mother's dog Simon scampered down the road in hot pursuit of a ragged cat to the muffled cheers of her ancient Irish neighbour, Miss Brady, who loathed cats even more than dogs.

Battle, I sensed, would now commence, in the legal wrangling for a house – my house – a guest house – tomorrow, and possibly the day after. . . .

Chapter Two

Mrs O'Grady proved to be a hard old nut, just as I had suspected from her shrewd face. Her years in a Chinese Mission supplementing the Lord had not given her a warm or generous nature. She was as crafty as an old jackdaw, lying boldly, haggling like an Eastern vendor in a bazaar, squatting in the midst of her worm-eaten belongings. She prolonged the final purchase as long as possible, endeavouring to muddle the course of red tape and relish a few extra pennies. A born Shylock, she hotly demanded a fair price for what she termed 'scarcely worn fittings' – some curtain rails, green and bent with age, which hung aloft by the grace of a few rusty screws.

I was lost in a sea of incomprehensible depth, not understanding the necessity for so much red tape in buying a house or this greedy, grasping woman. How anyone could argue and haggle over mouldy curtain rails only fit for scrap or how they could bother to creep out after dark and remove quantities of plants, leaving a tell-tale trace of newly turned earth was beyond me.

A rose tree disappeared from the garden, then another, while slowly the boring rigmarole of house-buying was completed. I signed document after document of unfathomable length, and my money – a legacy from my father – dwindled somewhat. I began to doubt the wisdom of my choice, but there was no turning back now.

This momentous decision over the house coincided with Aunt Patience's arrival, an arrival I now regarded as an omen of good fortune, a direct pointer from whence to borrow money if necessary, so I welcomed her with open arms while the rest of the family fled.

Aunt Patience arrived with all the pomp of a mayoral visit, erect and queenly at the wheel of a smooth-purring Bentley, not chauffeur-driven for no one was going to send her to an early grave! A quick glance told me that she carried the usual precautions against the elements: travel rugs and hot-water bottles, a rain cape covering a bulging picnic basket, and a first-aid box, carefully wedged in a strategic position, was ready in case of emergency. A Japanese sunshade threatened to break its way out of the rear window and a sonorous sound came from the depths of the back seat.

A moment's struggle with the door and she was emerging daintily, giggling a little as she untangled herself from behind the wheel, her brown eyes bright, her cheeks like pink velvet. A tan velour cloche snugly covered her neatly waved hair and a waisted travel coat in a mixture of beige and green wool fitted tightly across her stomach, with one large mottled button. A fox fur hung about her neck in an agonised way. From the depths of the back seat, disturbed from their slumbers, followed her usual retinue: yapping Bedlingtons and Pussy, the Siamese cat.

Full of exuberance at our reunion, my aunt

shepherded us, with the aid of the Japanese sunshade, towards the house. A whiff of expensive scent drowned any animal smells and amidst a scurry of animal legs we made for the drawing room.

Smothering my curses at the inconvenience of so many animals in every direction, I hastily locked away Mother's dog Simon, who was growling threateningly at the sight of a glossy, potbellied Siamese making for his chair. I shooed Gerald's marmoset Pavlo up to the top of the curtain rail where it screamed abuse at the intrusion and throwing a tea-towel swiftly over a biscuit tin of mealworm, guaranteed to upset anybody, I settled my aunt comfortably among the opposing smells. Feeling that the scene was now set, I apologised for the temporary absence of the family and unfolded with great detail the story of my own activities, painting a grim picture of Mrs O'Grady and what seemed to me her unreasonable and cunning ways. Giving a glowing account of the house, I took Aunt Patience to the door and pointed out my near purchase and its possibilities from a business point of view.

Aunt Patience heard my story oscillating between cries of dismay, horror and indignation, and praise when she thought I had shown a modicum of business sense and scored a point. I was pleased with her rapt attention and interest in my affairs, and consequently elaborated with intense enthusiasm.

'And what do you think – she wants to force me to buy a lot of old junk!' I complained, coming to the end of my other more important items.

'The wicked old woman!' Auntie beat the arm

of her chair, indignantly. 'Obviously not a churchwoman,' she added.

'Oh, she is,' I contradicted. 'A missionary from China.'

'Never trust one of those, dear.' There was a scornful sniff. 'What you need, Margo, is to cultivate the ability to sum up people, to be able to separate the wheat from the chaff, the rough from the smooth.'

'And she's digging up plants, and carrying them away,' I interrupted plaintively, as I suddenly remembered the missing rose trees and, rather enjoying the uproar with which my words were being greeted, I was unable to resist the further temptation to add more fuel to the already explosive atmosphere.

'Whatever next! She will have to be dealt with!' Scandalised comments filled the drawing room once again.

'So I told her I would see the solicitors about the matter,' I added, in a tone that suggested I had played a trump card.

'Well done, dear. That was the right thing to say.' Aunt Patience then stood up. 'We'll go and settle that woman now,' she announced dramatically.

Horrified at the sudden turn of events, I tried hard to dissuade her, but she was determined. Gathering up her coat she flung herself into it, crushed her cloche rapidly back into place, swung the ailing fur across her shoulders, then, taking me firmly by the arm, she marched me forcibly to battle.

We sailed purposefully down the drive. I followed my aunt apprehensively – things had taken a turn I had not expected. I dreaded the scene which I knew would materialise shortly, with Aunt Patience, in her most ladylike way, demolishing the enemy. I began to feel a little sorry for Mrs O'Grady and hoped she was out. Vainly I tried to postpone the evil moment by calling out a friendly greeting to an elderly, rotund, robin-like gentleman, with cheeks like freshly washed china and frightening false teeth, who was watching with interest his dog about to leave an offering on our front lawn. He had been to tea on several occasions and we had urged Mother, repeating the gossip about his fabulous wealth, to look upon him in a favourable light and replenish the family fortunes (now somewhat diminished since our Corfu experience*) – with the added pleasure of matrimonial bliss – and we tried to outwit the pigeon-like housekeeper who guarded him with vigilance as he tried to attract Mother's attention. Mother said primly 'that she was much too old for that sort of thing, and in any case she couldn't cope with the silly old fool.'

Now I greeted Mr Beetle warmly. Delighted at the welcome, his old eyes sparkled and he answered eagerly, apologising for his dog, remarking on the weather, and asking tenderly after Mother's health – at the same time faithlessly eyeing my aunt with relish, with a view to a possible second best, no doubt. But Aunt

*The Durrell ménage had fled Bournemouth in the thirties to bask in the magic of a Greek island – sun, warm seas and a life of idle bliss had left their mark on each family member. The appealing account by my brother Gerald in *My Family and Other Animals* will surely entice any reader to do likewise.

Patience, as if on a pilgrimage, pressed forward heedlessly to the purpose in hand, leaving him gazing regretfully after her with a speculative glint in his eyes.

Mrs O'Grady met us in a hideous floral dress, on which puce roses glared at yellow daisies while blue lover's knots threaded their way between the screaming flowers. I shuddered at the combination and trembled at the consequence of my exaggeration. My aunt was, of course, master of the situation, her quick mind sensing the weakness in her opponent immediately. Her accurate knowledge of legal proceedings, not to be trifled with at the best of times, was this day as keen as a freshly sharpened stiletto, as she banded intricate lawyers' jargon, defying argument and completely flooring her adversary's attempt to justify herself. Mrs O'Grady reeled uncertainly, like a bull recovering momentarily before the final thrust of the matador. I was impressed by the female brain that could master such technicalities.

Aunt Patience, having made her point, was now satisfied and with a cursory last look and a final pitying 'breeding will out, I always say,' she turned magnanimously – all sweetness now – to a heartfelt chat with Mr Beetle, followed by shamefaced me.

'How right you are, dear Madame,' agreed Mr Beetle. 'A most unChristian, ill-bred woman.'

I couldn't help grinning.

'Quite,' agreed my aunt, warming to the tubby figure.

I glanced around – Mrs O'Grady had fled and I stood suspended between fatuous laughter and genuine horror at the debunking of our fellow man, for which I was responsible. This, I decided, was the moment to change the subject.

'Mother asked after you today,' I said cunningly. 'Quite worried she was about you – said she hadn't seen you for days. Wanted you to go to tea, I think.'

'Really?' Mr Beetle was immediately in a visible flurry. He gave his prospective new love an apologetic look. 'Must dash – best trousers at the cleaners – dear Mrs Durrell – so charming . . .'

'Silly old fool,' my aunt said to the retreating back, in just the way Mother had done. I grinned disarmingly at my aunt in complete agreement.

With Mrs O'Grady and Mr Beetle banished successfully, minutes saw us striding out again to sort out my affairs. The fire was well and truly lit.

Some time later, having achieved our objective, we returned home. My aunt was still prattling. 'Now dear, having sorted out that little matter of the plants with your house agent,' she said graciously, 'I have other things to say to you . . .'

Seeing that my aunt, with what seemed to me a magical wave of her hand, had sorted out my legal affairs, I now listened indulgently to anything that she might have to say.

'The house must run on a thoroughly business-like and respectable basis. There is to be no nonsense.'

'Nonsense?' I asked, surprised. What was nonsense to my aunt was not, as a rule, nonsense to me. 'What sort of nonsense?' I inquired in dulcet tones.

'Nonsense, dear. A squandering of money,

extravagances and that sort of thing. You know you have an irresponsible streak in you, and at times an irrepressible gaiety, that I am not totally in approval of. As I said before, the house must be run on a thoroughly business-like and respectable basis, and remember, you must refer to your people as paying guests. "Lodgers" is so vulgar. And do try and get nice, respectable guests – people of breeding, who pay their rent. No missionaries, of course!' she said meaningfully. Her faith in good breeding was unshakeable.

'Of course Aunt, those are just the sort of people I thought of too,' I agreed hypocritically. I was lying, of course. The idea of boring individuals, religious characters and spinsters, possibly smelling of mothballs, or worse eucalyptus, was not my idea of a jolly household.

'One can hardly have any faith in the family's business acumen,' she complained. 'And after your brother Leslie's foolhardiness and your desire to break free – well!' The subject of Leslie's sunken fishing boat and my matrimonial affairs would, I feared, always be a bitter one.

A large fire now glowed in the grate and Mother presided over her traditional tea, a steaming pile of hot scones and a trolley laden with her best china. The dogs, at the return of their mistress, flew at her, barking joyously and Pussy was waiting to leave.

Aunt Patience soundly kissed everyone, asked a hundred questions, scolded, applauded, gave a lot of good advice, ate a huge tea, then decided suddenly that a liver attack was imminent and driving in the dark would endanger her health. She then herded her flock together and left.

‘Well – that’s that,’ I said, heaving a sigh of relief as the great car, gathering speed, nosed its way out of sight. I was well satisfied at the final turn of events.

With the mass exodus of the O’Grady establishment, No. 51, now silent and shrouded in emptiness, became my constant companion in the following days and my eagerness to prepare the house and install my lodgers was compelling.

In secret moments of disquiet I viewed England with misgivings. After constant travel abroad I was afraid that I might find a continual dose of suburbia irksome. In these moments I could not help wondering if I and my neighbours were not only going to be friends but at times enemies by the sheer incompatibility of our natures. We were a motley crew: the bustling Miss Brady, withered as a tortoise but still hawk-eyed; Mrs Briggs, lusty voiced, good-hearted, incorrigibly inquisitive with her ‘I don’t want to be nosy, mind, *but*’; perky Mr Beetle, ready to swoop gallantly in the light of new love. The liverish huddle of fur, Lady Booth, who passed daily, dragging a permanently yapping terrier, so that I had heard Miss Brady, nerves frayed, threaten to do it in more than once. Methods were discussed openly: a kipper stuffed with arsenic, said the proud owner of a poodle, who encouraged her own dog to scrub about other people’s gardens at least twice a day. Miss Brady said this method was reserved for cats – when all else failed. The matter was dropped. Then there was Lord and Lady Booth, an aloof pair who seldom smiled and whose approach was guaranteed to break up any gossiping party.

The first day of true ownership I crossed the road to my new house trying to look inconspicuous but inconspicuous I was not to be.

'See you're busy then,' Mrs Briggs was at her gate. 'And 'ands full, I see,' she added cheerfully. She reminded me of a chrysanthemum that was just about to fall apart; it was the burnished hair, I decided, wisping out in curved strands. 'Paid a good price for that house, I have no doubt?'

'Yes,' I agreed unwillingly, trying once again to escape.

'Sure, the price of things today, it knocks yer flat.' She beamed sympathetically and then confided, 'You know the woman who owned the house, one of them missionaries, barmy she was – I'm not surprised after living in them foreign parts.'

'Yes,' said I.

'It rots yer, I always say . . .' I agreed, politely. 'Of course you needs plenty of maids in houses like these,' she reflected, gazing up at the house with respect. 'You won't be 'aving any maids, will you?'

'No,' I said, wondering if she was going to offer me her services and if so, how I was going to get out of it.

'You're a good-hearted girl, for all your "blah", I tells my hubby.'

'Really,' I said, feeling more pleased.

And so we chatted. A passing Mr Beetle was summed up in a few words: 'Well, you know what men are! It's all sex with some – never too old – disgusting I call it!'

'Yes,' I agreed.

'Of course, there's snobs around 'ere you know!'

The voice was full of scorn and class distinction reared its ugly head: I eyed the way of escape longingly.

'Of course, you've come down in the world, 'aven't you? Miss Brady and I both agree to that!'

As I was moving such a short distance I supposed it was inevitable that some of my business should be known. I did not have time to find an answer to her last remark, however, for like a bloodhound she was on the trail again.

'You used to 'ave maids and silver and that sort of thing. There doesn't look like much silver among your things now.' The candid observation of my belongings just brought out of store brought a withering look to her countenance.

I agreed, amused at this paragon of backyard gossip, the backbone of every suburban road, a mixture of pure good heartedness and uncrushable tittle-tattle.

'But I really must go, there's a lot of work to do,' I explained, looking for excuses to get away.

'Sure, sure poor you. I pity you.' She shook her head, still reluctant to leave me. ''Aven't you got two children?' she inquired, hovering, curiosity getting the better of her again.

'Yes. They're holidaying with their father – such a good man. Hasn't Mother told you?'

'Oh.' There was a long pause as she digested this bit of news. 'Ah well,' she said, throwing it off lightly, 'ta-ta for now,' and satisfied she bustled away quickly, eager to discuss this interesting titbit with everybody and anybody, no doubt.

My first act on entering the new house had been to reach up from a chair and dismantle the greasy, tatty paper shade hanging in cobwebs and fly dirt. Then, wandering casually about the empty house, fetid with the aromas of Mrs O'Grady, I began to plan – flinging wide the windows, letting the clean sweet air blow lustily through the big rooms, while in darker corners and cupboards, where the shadows of Mrs O'Grady still lurked, I lit sulphur candles until the odour seeped mercilessly out and I was forced to capitulate in my zealous drive against the nauseous staleness of fish stew and embrocation and admit that every vestige of O'Gradyism must now be well and truly dead.

An imminent second visit by my Aunt Patience had been prevented by an epidemic of 'flu. However Auntie, not to be daunted, was still with me in spirit. Making full use of the postal service ('so much more economical than the telephone, dear') I kept her diligently posted with news, and was in turn bombarded with stern warnings, and the announcement that she would hurry down as soon as illness allowed and Pussy was sufficiently recovered to cope with car travel.

The family opposite at No. 52 were curious as to what was now going on at No. 51 and called daily, unable to resist the temptation to give me the benefit of their advice. Mother, remaining a little dubious and unconvinced that I was safe in my new sanctuary, hovered, genteelly brewing constant cups of tea for the various workmen in residence, questioning them closely on the safety of the electricity and gas, probing about in dark corners for the mains, finding them, and then calling me and carefully explaining the dangers of not knowing the position of all these vital points in case of emergency. She stood in the kitchen by the hour to make sure that her much-loved grandchildren, Gerry and Nicholas, who had arrived back from their prolonged stay with their devoted father, were not now starving to death in my hands and concocted special dishes with all the enthusiasm of a witch doctor. The children, overjoyed to see their grandmother and strong in the knowledge that every whim was an immediate victory, made full use of the situation.

In the wake of Mother came my brothers, bustling with energy, aglow with feelings of responsibility for my welfare: Lawrence with uneconomical suggestions for burglar alarms, revolving baths and lavatory walls lined with bookshelves and a concealed radiogram, saying that it was the only place in any family residence where one could be completely private; Leslie, delighted that my scheme appeared to be taking shape, with plans for uneconomical swimming pools, a rifle range and a specially designed bar.

A card arrived from brother Gerald, saying he had heard by devious methods that I was about to replenish the family fortunes and was delighted with the news. I read the brief communication with great mistrust and no enthusiasm: Gerald would just have to realise that I had moved into an area of civilisation and that there would be no animals, or their dung, littering the place, however sweet or however small. (How wrong I was.)

My house now lay in an atmosphere of feverish activity. I had worked hard: disorganised, reorganised, and turned my hand to decorating, slapping on paint and distemper with gusto, mastering the art of working at dizzy heights, taking on furniture moving or housework with equal ease. The children, excited and noisy at their return, embraced the upheaval with glee. They followed the path of an emaciated gas man with rapt interest. They cadged bits of wood from the carpenter, normally a mild man but now irritated to the point of blasphemy, waited for a death fall from the stepladder, encouraging a fatal slip and revelling in the possibility of an ambulance calling or the excitement of the fire brigade. Uninhibited, snub-nosed, tousle-haired, they cheerfully awaited calamity.

The most fascinating distraction was Charlie Hardcastle, the plumber. A sly old rogue, reeking of stagnant beer, withering happily and surveying the world about him with tolerant twinkling eyes. A decrepit cloth cap, set at a crazy angle, usually covered his egg-shaped cranium where a few spare white hairs sprouted like fresh cress. From his top lip, reminiscent of a tattered paint brush, hung a grey moustache, heavily stained with cheap tobacco. A wide grin showed two remaining discoloured teeth in barren gums.

In the morning Charlie invariably arrived late. In the afternoon he always arrived late, slightly intoxicated, his gait a little unsteady as he smacked his thigh, whistling a saucy ditty – an aging Don Juan showing off hugely. His rich Dorset twang rolled amidst his own and the children's appreciative laughter. I couldn't control him at all, in fact after the first attempt I didn't try. He enjoyed this little farce, swaggering dangerously, a little more crazy, a true extrovert. Realising his thirst, I would some days secrete a bottle of beer for him in the airing cupboard where he would go like a child to claim it, and like a child would delight in his find. Later I had cause to doubt my action in aiding and abetting Charlie along the primrose path – but that was later.

One morning, just as Charlie (mercifully sober) and I were coping with a blocked main drain, our heads inquisitively deep into the dark smelly waste where, just maddeningly out of reach what looked like a toy car glimmered faintly in the distance, we were distracted by the purr of an expensive engine, and a lush-looking car rolled to a standstill at the gate. Charlie and I straightened up together to see who the visitor might be, my thoughts immediately rushing to my aunt.

'Money,' Charlie muttered contemptuously, noting the shining chromium plate, and he spat generously with great ceremony into the gaping sewer. I dropped the plunger which Charlie had presented to me as a very necessary part of my future equipment. After a morning spent examining the intricacies of a draining system, I was hardly ready for a visitor, especially a smooth creature with the proportions of a young panther, dangling a grey Homburg nonchalantly from dainty fingers, where a heavy signet ring flashed.

'Major-General Durrell about?' he drawled effectively, leaving his car and measuring me with a too-experienced eye. I hastily manoeuvred Charlie back to the sewer and went forward to join the visitor.

'As far as I know, he has been dead for years,' I answered, keeping my voice cool and a little unfriendly, detesting his manner. He laughed long and loud, as if I had made an uproarious joke. It was no joke however. The only army celebrity I knew of in our family was long dead – my father's brother: a fair, thickset man of medium height, with kindly blue eyes and a crisp moustache. In fact, only the other day, when sorting out an old tea chest of long forgotten memories, I had resurrected a large photograph of him in uniform, with a Sam Browne belt and a chest full of medals – and hadn't we got his heirloom resplendent on the mantelpiece, a monstrous black clock with marble pillars, which chimed the wrong hours at the right intervals, and a little below the ugly face a small silver notice stated the solemn fact. Mother had refused to allow it to go out of the family for sentimental reasons.

'I am afraid you have got the wrong address,' I suggested, eager to get back to my drain as a subterranean rumbling noise and long drawn-out 'Aargh' from Charlie told me that victory was in sight.

'I've come about yachts and boats, you know – things that sail on the jolly old sea,' he explained. 'Luxury class, what?' he ended playfully.

The whole situation suddenly became clear – it was Leslie he wanted. Leslie, with his catalogue mania and nom-de-plume of Major-General, who had obviously given my address. Well, he'd gone too far this time: he would end up in prison for fraudulent impersonation if he didn't look out, and serve him right too, I thought uncharitably. Still, poor Mother would be upset if Leslie went in the dock, though Lawrence and Gerald would probably relish the spectacle 'as a new experience'. Better act quickly, I decided, before Leslie reaped the seeds he had sown and we were all forced to find money for bail. I saw my letting profits visibly vanishing.

'Gout,' I said hastily, and without much thought. 'I'm afraid he's suffering – in great pain – bedridden and can't be disturbed.'

'Bad show,' the visitor was suitably awed. 'No chance of seeing him, then?'

'No,' I answered firmly, with a certain smug satisfaction, 'no chance at all,' for at that moment Leslie was in fact doing a part-time job delivering beer in crates for the tall and robust, good-natured Doris, with a booming laugh: she ran the off-licence at the bottom of the hill. He had passed by only half an hour ago with his small Morris belching black smoke as a signal of protest against the weight. It was hardly the sort of position to be caught in unaware. For a short tubby figure in rough sea-going clothes, struggling with wooden crates marked 'Strongs' from a shabby wreck of a car, was very far removed from a sleek yachtsman with the esteemed title of Major-General.

The visitor, exclaiming deep sympathy as though Leslie was already on his death-bed, took a card out of his wallet. 'Perhaps you can give him this?' he asked respectfully, no longer playful, 'and he can contact us when he is fit again, when we may have the pleasure of meeting . . .' I took the card, promising to deliver it safely.

'The General will ring you,' I said calmly after the retreating slinky figure. 'If he lives,' I added grimly.

Then I hurried back to join Charlie in his triumphant hour, for he was holding aloft a toy car and grinning from ear to ear. Leslie could be dealt with later.

Chapter Three

May found the house ready, with only the lodgers to install. Our house over the road was closed, a reminder that my family had decided, on impulse, to disperse in all directions – though some not far. I had spoken sternly to Leslie over his criminal tendencies in written impersonations but he poo-pooed my warning and assured me that I should be thankful that the situation had been no worse, for it was Gerald I wanted to worry about – he was the one who usually caused the most trouble and I had to admit he was right. And anyway he was moving in with Doris and taking Mother on holiday.

Charlie Hardcastle, the plumber, had been the last workman to go, and as the small, now rather crest-fallen figure had gathered up the tools for his final departure, croaking 'parting be such sweet sorrow' on a breath laden with beer fumes, I had decided to speak to him sternly about the doubtful effects of liquor whilst at work and the trail of cold taps pouring hot water and hot taps pouring cold water. But Charlie was philosophical. Regarding me with a pained look he had answered gravely, 'what will be will be, and what be life without liquor?' There was a chorus of agreement from the children – what could I say?

I left the taps in memory of the craziest, but most lovable plumber of all time.

Leaving my children happily busy over the funeral arrangements of a dead sparrow, I sallied forth to put the finishing touches to my plans and advertise my rooms. Miss Brady, I noticed, was as usual waging the everlasting battle against germs of one sort or the other. In fact Miss Brady spent most of her days in abandoned anticipation, alternating between cleaning for guests that never arrived and galloping between the boundaries of her land, sprinkling pepper to prevent the desecration of her property by animal excreta. Today the blue guest room, already hygienically clean, was disintegrating under the onslaught as the contents of the room appeared to be steadily mounting at the window; the window where for much of the day she surveyed the passing world, for the high fence and laurel hedges that surrounded her house made vision from any other place impossible. She passed the open aperture, a mobcap encasing her head like a sagging pancake, and although she appeared completely absorbed in her work, I knew her sharp beady eyes watched the road from all angles, missing nothing. Then there she was, a perilous leaning structure. 'Shoo, you damned old thing – you'll get a barrel of buckshot up your posterior!' she cried out in a husky warning, her voice dropping easily into a lusty Irish brogue. 'Where it'll hurt most,' she added with certain satisfaction. I lowered my eyes hastily, Miss Brady had a gun.

The cat, the usual product of suburbia, spent his days leisurely, when not panicking the birds to a medley of reproachful twitters, cushioned comfortably on any fresh shoots he could find, bruising the buds that were about to flower so that they withered and died, snoozing for hours with one eye open or painstakingly attending to his toilet with equal leisure, deciding to dig and squat just where a prize bulb had been carefully bedded. Mother had lost quite a few bulbs that way, as had Lord Booth. Wailing ceaselessly through odd hours of the night with a sound that made one's heart leap uncertainly, the cat was also shamelessly polygamous and courted every female in the district. Now he leapt over the gate behind me, as he tore to safer quarters. I followed less swiftly, avoiding the blue eyes of Miss Brady in the window, and crossed the road to miss the tall figure outlined in fur, dragging a shopping basket on wheels and a four-legged powder-puff with a blue bow, meandering on towards the town.

I felt the road with fresh awareness, since I was to become so much a part of it. It was a quiet road with large houses: red brick, grey stone, white- and pink-washed walls mingling tastefully amidst tidy gardens. Once the indomitable stronghold exclusive to retired gentry, the road was changing face, definitely and unrelentingly, as money dwindled. Big houses fell under the hammer and were converted into flats, while homes of various sorts sprang up almost undetected. Amidst these changes the dwindling diehards still strove to maintain their gentle moneyed atmosphere. It was a losing battle I feared, examining the pleasant grey and white building with shady garden which had once been the home of a sprightly, buxom, bridge-playing widow, graciously befurred, and was now a nursing home. The constant comings and goings created an alarming atmosphere of urgency, and starched white cotton and sterility took the place of bridge soirées and fashionable hats.

A home for unmarried mothers, still mentioned only in whispers, had slipped in unnoticed, guarded by high railings and scarcely seen behind the opaque barrage of green foliage. Very occasionally a faint wail gave substance to the rumours, while the know-alls exchanged significant glances. On the brow of the hill, softly framed in thick shrubs and flowering trees, a solid yellow-washed house stood quietly, missing the strong-armed colonel and his nasal peroxide-haired wife, catering now for a feeble throng of senile women awaiting the inevitable handshake with death. How terrible to be old, but to be unwanted – that was unthinkable. One became very conscious of the old in this southern paradise, especially of old ladies – a living graveyard, Lawrence had called it. Of course, there were the lucky ones: Mr Beetle for instance, aging but as chirpy as a cricket; Miss Brady, with the energy of a firefly, glowing with argument and independence (old age would have to reckon with her) and Mrs O'Grady too, that egotistical old hypocrite, still a queen and fighting every inch of her way to the grave.

I hurried down the hill past the ugly rusty railings of the unmarried mothers' home and the tall wire litter basket, past the bench, a resting place for those struggling up the hill usually occupied by one or two middle-aged ladies with overloaded shopping baskets who paused from their nattering to scrutinise carefully any casual passer-by. Today it was empty, however the wire basket was full, I noticed, with sweet papers, newspapers, a cardboard box or two and an abundance of empty gin bottles. Who was the secret gin drinker in our midst who hid his guilt from the dustmen? I was still trying to fit a body to the abandoned bottles, when a hissing noise warned me that the trolley bus approached and I ran to catch it.

For the first time despondence had inexplicably touched me. The idea of being a landlady, up to now such an amusing one, suddenly appalled me. The family were right; I wasn't cut out for this sort of thing, such as demanding rent from strangers. At home on the mantelshelf a pile of rent books, sent to me by aunt, stood as a reminder of the fact. Fright and a sudden dryness made me long for a cool beer – one of Charlie's refreshing draughts. I reached my destination, the office of the local paper, the *Echo*, in a dilemma of mixed feelings. Sitting down listlessly at one of the large and imposing desks, I grabbed the pen provided and, plunging it into the thick congealed ink, I brooded without hope. With what words should I entice my lodgers? 'Delightful residence for cultured persons' – that sounded like Aunt Patience; 'Sunny home for well-bred persons' – that sounded like Auntie too. At length in desperation I scribbled out a form headed 'cosy rooms for comfort', which sounded like Mother. The deed was done.

This was now the inevitable invasion of my privacy, but it was too late for regrets. The whole venture was running along as if on wheels. It was with these sombre misgivings in my mind that I found myself, with great surprise, standing in the quiet, dimly-lit nave of the church nearby. A Catholic church; a trespasser I told myself. Puzzled at my action I turned to go then hesitated; something made me stay, a lone self-conscious figure in the gloom. I slipped quietly into a pew; the polished wood felt hard and secure against my hands, the strange calm steadied me. Relaxing a little I sat back and peered about me in the dappled light. There were three of us, I noticed with a start; another figure, a shabby hunched creature who did not stir at my intrusion. She was not a stranger. I had seen her before, aimlessly wandering through the town, gathering cigarette butts from the gutter and pitifully examining litter baskets for spoil. Was she praying, or like me drawn there for reasons remote, I wondered, sniffing the musty atmosphere and feeling the intense stillness.

I gathered up my bag which had slipped to my feet noiselessly and tiptoed up the flagged aisle. One solitary candle flickered. Dropping a coin into the box, noisily in the stillness, I took a slim candle, lit it carefully, and placed it firmly alongside the other. This small act of faith revived my spirits and I left the church quickly, without a backward glance, for such is human nature.

The boys were astride the front wall watching for my return with eager curiosity; their interest was inexhaustible as they pestered me with questions.

'How did the burial go?' I enquired fondly, kissing them, not willing to be drawn.

'It was very sad but interesting,' Gerry

answered reverently. 'Nicholas was the mourner and I was the priest. It was a moving performance.'

'But we are more interested in your business,' Gerry said noisily. I silenced him quickly.

'Keep your voice down, we don't want everybody in the road to know what we are doing.'

'Why not?' Nicholas piped up. 'We like to talk about our business with everybody, don't we Gerry? And, in fact, we've had quite an interesting morning, haven't we?' he remarked with deep satisfaction to his brother. 'Miss Brady says,' he went on, reminiscing, 'the road's getting into a sorry state – what with animals' you-know-what's all over the place, and the ambulance coming and going at the nursing home, within sight of her very door, it's all enough to give her an acute heart attack she said.' He gave a good imitation of our aged and eccentric neighbour. 'Yep, she was out with the old pepper pot and muttering as usual about the fallen carrying their sins for all the world to see.'

'That's what she said – sins for all the world to see.' Gerry rolled the words round his tongue with relish. 'I suppose that's the unmarried mothers' home. It's a bad word, sin, isn't it Mum?' he asked hopefully.

'Oh, she's talking rubbish,' I answered impatiently. 'I do wish she would mind her own ruddy business,' I grumbled, more to myself than to the children. Now they would get involved with the unmarried mothers' home – with relish no doubt.

'There you are, Gerry,' Nicholas sang

delightedly, 'I knew we should have told her to mind her own business.'

'You never tell grown-ups to mind their own business,' said I quickly, torn between the wish that they had and the knowledge that they shouldn't. It was more than apparent that my children were succumbing very readily to suburban life.

'And what else did the old – the good woman have to say?' I enquired cynically, changing 'old hag' to 'good woman' in the certain knowledge that the statement would most likely be repeated at a later date.

'Well . . .' Nicholas paused, making sure that I was listening, 'she said "and what with people starting to let rooms, things were going from bad to worse." It let the tone of the road down, or something, and Lady Booth blooming well agreed with her.' He enjoyed delivering news that he knew instinctively would cause bad feeling.

I was silent. Any bonhomie I might have felt towards my neighbours was definitely dead, and I suddenly regarded the animal excreta in a new light. 'May the cats, dogs and birds have a long and busy life and may Miss Brady's gatepost rot away!' and I laughed aloud at the thought.

'What are you laughing at?' the enquiry was both puzzled and disappointed that this news had not caused the sufficient amount of havoc intended.

'Just a thought,' I said happily, changing the subject. 'Anything happened while I've been away?'

'There's a man to see you inside.'

'And a funny one, with a straggly beard and

long hair – a sort of medicine man, but he's white.' Nicholas always put the finishing pictorial touches to Gerry's unadorned statements.

How much of our business had fallen into the hands of this stranger, I thought dismayed, as I hurried indoors. It was no wonder they had taken to idle gossip; they were going through a period of acute loneliness with the exodus of all the workmen. The house had subsided into calm, there were no interesting, breathtaking cavities to explore with the removal of floorboards, and the disintegration of the family over the road left them in a state of limbo.

Nicholas's description was very apt, surprisingly enough for he tended to exaggerate greatly, as the stranger, a small figure dominated by colour, unfolding a lean childish body rose languidly from my scarlet drawing room divan to greet me. A pale face, veins finely traced, gave him a delicate look. The aquiline nose was softened by long reddish hair, swept back, and a fiery beard, feathery and unclipped. A flamboyant pink silk shirt, the pointed collar open, was enriched by a muted paisley scarf slotted carelessly through a thick gold ring – an opposing splash of colour against the red beard; his trousers, pale beige cord, were tight – too tight. Swinging a silver-topped cane gently he gave me a generous smile: I noticed a fine set of even teeth.

'Hello there,' he drawled pleasantly. 'Forgive the intrusion – two charming little boys let me in.'

A psychologist too, I was quick to note, for any mother could be won with a soft word about her offspring, however hypocritical. Disinclined to disturb the elusive picture of charm already created by my children, I responded readily while the visitor introduced himself.

'Edward Feather.'

There was no need for him to tell me he was an artist – his appearance had already told me that.

'Have you come about the rooms?' I enquired hopefully, yet feeling an odd stir of apprehension at the thought.

'In a sort of way.' He paused, feeling around for an explanation. 'Somebody told somebody, and somebody else told somebody that there may be something to let here?'

So the children had been having an enlightening gossip with someone, I thought accusingly.

'I need a new studio,' he confessed at last. 'My present landlady and I do not agree – tiresome mundane woman and constantly on the nag.' He was disarmingly frank. 'I have work to do, you see – and it is so difficult to find anywhere suitable here at this time of year, when the holiday locusts are about to storm Bournemouth and brigades of old ladies, swarming out of their winter hibernation, are settling like flies in every available empty nook.'

It was true. The town now awaited the first onslaught of holiday-makers and landladies sat back like watching spiders to await their prey. Unlike the dowagers, closeted in security, there were many impoverished old people seeking out a life on inadequate means. Though welcomed for their rent through the lean months of winter, now at the approach of the summer visitors and higher rents they found themselves unwanted;

chevied, refugees, scouring the papers for fresh accommodation daily, and constantly on the move. It was a sad reflection.

'What exactly do you need?' I faltered, with sneaking unease, for I knew instinctively that this would be one person who would have to be hidden from my Aunt Patience as he obviously transgressed all her ideas of good breeding. His likeable voice, soft and slightly tinged with a northern accent, while falling pleasantly on my ears would have grated like a dentist's drill on the tender eardrums of my aunt. Over some things she was adamant, and good breeding was one. 'No one with an accent is well-bred – the two things just don't go together, dear,' she had said so often with pursed lips and a look that defied contradiction.

'I need,' he told me gravely, watching my facial reactions with more than casual interest, 'just a simple room to paint in: my work takes me into realms of nudity . . .'

'Do you mean you want to paint naked men and women?' I interrupted bluntly as if I had never heard of such a thing.

'But, of course, dear soul. Naked, how else can you show the human form in all its beauty? The essence of innocence is nudity, don't you think? Unfortunately my present landlady forbids it.'

'Well, I don't know.' I was very doubtful, yet wanting to agree if only to outdo the other landlady. But there was Aunt Patience and my mother's reaction to consider, and what about the road!

'You don't agree then?' he asked, keeping me to

the point, and no doubt about to involve me in a technical discussion.

'Oh, it's not that!' I explained lamely, 'I don't think it would work, that's all. I think it would cause gossip trouble in the road and so forth.' I was quite certain now that Aunt Patience would have her first stroke at such a suggestion, and Mother too for that matter. And such goings on wouldn't go unnoticed by the children I felt sure – they would revel in it.

'You see,' I went on, explaining carefully, trying to justify my reasons. 'I personally have nothing against you painting men and woman, but someone might object – neighbours for instance. A scandal might start . . .' I envisaged the scene with perfect accuracy: buxom women exposed in all their naked glory, or draped tantalisingly in a cloud of gossamer silk, with perhaps a bosom coyly exposed; men, Charles Atlas types, showing . . . This vision faded abruptly, as Peeping Toms and the children glued to keyholes took over; police banging at the door; a national scandal with sordid headlines: 'Disgusting Orgies Claim Bournemouth Residents'; court scenes – my mother and Aunt Patience heavily veiled, fighting back their tears, fighting to save the family's good name. . . . Once a thing like that started one never knew where it would end – it would be as bad as letting brother Gerald loose. My sanctuary was heading straight for trouble, before I was even established.

'I am sorry, you cannot paint nudes all over the place.' I was desperately apologetic, feeling that I placed myself in the category of the mundane landlady.

'Not all over the place,' Edward Feather assured me soothingly, giving me a fleeting look of amusement from soft hazel eyes, a coaxing gentleness creeping in to battle my feeble defences. 'Only in one room.'

'But that is fifty times worse!' I cried. 'That would in itself cause suspicion – and what would my other lodgers say, if I get any? In fact . . .' I began to enlarge on the theme, 'there's an old girl down the road who sits up in her window with a pair of binoculars, and she misses nothing from what I hear!' We both laughed: the boys had recently passed on to me this little titbit of news, being more than absorbed in the binoculars, which they assured me could also see in the dark.

'It's a little disappointing to find you so adamant, I must say. I thought better of you.' He summed me up, half-serious, half-amused, but still persuasive.

'If it's a proper dwelling place you want I can probably help you,' I told him firmly, loathing to lose this man on mere technicalities and feeling that I had already lost considerable face. 'Are you married, or single?' I enquired tentatively, withdrawing a little to polite reserve, trying to decide quickly which bedsit I would show him and feeling suddenly slightly nervous at the first real venture into the domain of a landlady.

'I have an appendage.' He dismissed the fact carelessly and arose, showing off his needle-like hips. 'But let me view the mansion, dear soul,' he continued with a grandiose air, grossly exaggerating the situation. 'I will choose my flat – I feel like a change of atmosphere, and I have decided that I shall fit into this place admirably. Nice room you have here, too,' he remarked, looking round and, putting out a long hand with carefully manicured nails, he patted my knee in a paternal way at my disparaging dismissal of my room. 'A little woman without a man – perhaps I can paint you sometime,' he added thoughtfully. 'With your clothes on, of course!'

It was an entirely mischievous remark, but I knew he meant it. I replied with quiet and genteel horror suitable to my position, and rose hurriedly to lead the way, yet provoked to pleasant feelings by the obvious flattery. I hastily recalled the sagacious words of my aunt. There must be no familiarity between a landlady and her guests; she must always remain aloof, superior, rent must be paid in advance, and any lapse in payment of rent necessitates immediate action. Large plain notices must be placed in strategic positions: 'Leave the bath as you wish to find it'; 'Gentlemen will please lift the seat before using' (this heavily underlined); 'The use of newspaper is prohibited'; 'There will be no entertaining of the opposite sex after 10pm or before 11am'; 'There will be no loud laughter'; etc., etc. In fact she had had the notices specially printed in red, two of each and had sent them to me with a little note scrawled in her large generous writing: 'Margo dear, just place these where they will be seen – a most necessary precaution, I feel, if you are going to run your house properly. Your loving Auntie.'

'Come the lamb to the slaughter.' The laughing, good-natured voice broke my chain of racing thoughts and I turned, a little confused, to conduct my first tour.

I thought of the day I followed Mrs O'Grady

and I could not help thinking that in some ways the picture of eccentricity was almost the same as we swept through the house. My guest looked on with airy approval, dismissing the ablutions with light-hearted indifference, telling me between snatches of poetry and other pleasantries that he hardly ever took a bath owing to an unfortunate experience in the past, and as far as the lavatory went, it could be a Turkish one as far as he was concerned – which in some ways pleased me for I felt that here was a perfect tenant. Deciding at last to rent a big north room – 'ideal light for a painter' I was told – which lay in seclusion on the ground floor, with long windows and a large door, he sealed the discussion by placing two weeks' rent in my hand. I was lucky indeed: a lodger and two weeks' rent. I was jubilant as I watched the departing figure (who would catch one's glance in any place) with a mellowed look, broken by immediate remembrance of a point on which we had come to no decision.

'Mr Feather!' My voice seemed to fill the quiet road, which would certainly attract both Mrs Briggs and Miss Brady if they were about. He turned at my call. 'Remember, no nudes – at least not completely,' I compromised a little, after all one could not stop the fellow painting, and didn't two weeks' rent lie cosy in my hand?

The silver-topped cane flashed an indiscernible answer. I stayed a moment to watch with pride my first lodger, a streak of gay colour against Miss Brady's fence.

'The whole road will know our business if you yell like that,' a childish voice remarked cheekily.

'It appears . . .' I turned and looked at the owner of the voice accusingly, 'it appears that the whole road already knows our business.' And I wondered who the somebody was who had told somebody who had told somebody else.

Chapter Four

The shrill cry of a cockerel, one of Mrs Briggs' prize birds, heralded the dawn, and the slow realisation that this was *the* day when my advertisement would bring more lodgers thundering to my door plunged me into complete awareness. The town was already a network of hotels, boarding houses and bed and breakfast notices: was my advertisement going to be noticed amongst the rest, I asked myself fearfully, snuggling down lower in the warmth of my bed, loath to leave my cocoon too soon. I contemplated with envy the ostrich who could bury his head and live while presenting an impenetrable, unworried behind to the world.

There was a rattling of bolts: I listened indulgently for these were the early morning manoeuvres of my neighbour Mrs Briggs, about to appear at her back door to greet the world – a husky cough, a shuffling noise, a long drawn-out stretchy 'Aargh!' How quickly noises became familiar. On good days there would be a song. I waited for the song almost eagerly: there was a longer than usual pause, or could I be wrong about the song this morning? No – for now the strains of 'Under the Old Apple Tree' filled the alley between us. Throaty noises, but wholly human.

Mrs Briggs' recital came to a sharp close with the knowledge that 'a woman's work is never done', a state of affairs we agreed on daily with the appropriate signs that women reserve for these occasions. A chink of empty milk bottles and the sound of the door crashing told me she had disappeared – but not quite. There was a last faint bellow of sound as she cautioned her family to rise, followed by the prolonged silence of indifference born of habit. Should I follow her example or laze a little longer, listening to the early noises of suburbia? I lay on in easy comfort. Things had moved swiftly in the last few days. Edward and his wife had already moved in: he had come as arranged, and much to my surprise in a conventional way. I had expected a horse-drawn carriage or some other unpredictable method, and had felt a surge of disappointment to find an unspectacular taxi at the gates, jarring horribly with my preconceived vision of Edwardian splendour. He emerged, wrapped in a long duffle coat as if about to attempt a polar exploration. A young woman followed, with thick brown hair hanging to shoulder length. A long black jet necklace and scarlet coat immediately attracted me – I liked her.

Edward had come first, carrying with tender care a heavy cookery book, his easel, a square black paint-box and a pile of canvases tied together with rope, leaving his wife to attend to the other less important matters. I had curbed my enthusiastic desire to rush out to greet them, inspired by my Aunt Patience's warning, but a grin of welcome broke through in spite of my resolutions as I waited at the door with a rent book clutched in my hand. Banishing the rent book discreetly out of sight, suddenly embarrassed by it, I took the gleaming black box from Edward and with easy chatter I drew him into the house and made for the high-ceilinged north room which was to be his home.

Number one lodger was finally over the threshold and to confirm this, there had risen the first signs of strangers in the house, as an unfamiliar aroma of oil paint became noticeable, overpowered by exotic garlic smells as Edward, resplendent in a pale blue smock, had organised first the position of his easel and working materials and then, with vigorous interest, his built-in kitchen – for Edward loved to delight his palate and tantalise his fragile stomach with adventurous dishes. Although Aunt Patience would squirm at such extravagant feasts in the kitchen I felt sure that Mother and Edward would meet together in perfect harmony, once she had recovered from the initial shock of his rather unusual appearance.

Mother, Simon and Pavlo, were still holidaying happily in the company of Leslie and his future bride at the off-licence, half a mile away. This brought me to the sudden alarming thought that if brother Gerald found the family house across the road uncomfortable, he might just decide to descend on me. His antics would ruin any boarding house.

I had always been tolerant in my dealings with Gerald, but now things were different. He would have to realise that I was going to be a serious businesswoman and could no longer cope with his decidedly odd habits. It was obvious I should never keep a lodger if I allowed him to put one foot over the threshold of my new house with any species of animal – domestic or otherwise.

An upheaval through the house told me the children were roaming and were already engrossed in a lively conversation with our bearded lodger. Wondering what to wear I left my bed and wandered into the bathroom. My dress should be subdued to create a no-nonsense impression. Grey, perhaps?

Ready at last in red, with no resemblance to my prosperous aunt whatsoever, I went to restore my children to order and despatch them safely to school, away from what I hoped were going to be scenes of desperate money-making activities. I pottered about the house, doing things that didn't really need doing, and watched Edward's wife, heeding her husband's urgings, setting out to work, her dark hair blowing back from her face as she walked, the red of her coat glowing in the morning mist. She told me that she had been a model and, even now, sat for Edward. She went daily to work in a local store, confidently leaving her husband to run the home; in any case, she said, she preferred to work. And no wonder, I thought, for Edward could cook with a touch that equalled any woman's, and my own cooking appeared so lifeless by comparison that I was going to rush out at the first opportunity to buy his aromatic range of spices.

Mother was coming to have coffee with me. It was her first visit since the final completion of my plans. I was eager to show her that my house was at last ready and functioning, my first lodgers installed.

Eleven o'clock found me waiting anxiously in the bay window. Mr Beetle was deeply engrossed in conversation with Miss Brady, looking like some strange old bird with a frothy feather bow about her neck and a blue velvet coat and matching Robin Hood hat which accentuated her beaky feathers. She had stopped cleaning the pavement of leaves and, leaning on her broom, was listening to Mr Beetle with rapt attention. Mother was only ten minutes away, I calculated; where was she? If she didn't hurry she'd get involved with Mr Beetle. I wandered out to the gate impatiently and spotted Mother a few houses away, walking at a leisurely pace, a large basket over one arm. I could tell by the sudden panic on Mr Beetle's face that he had seen her too and was overcome at the vision, indecisive as to the next move. I laughed to myself, watching points with interest. Was the faithless man going to leave Miss Brady and sortie with younger prey? He was, for with a final hasty word he crossed the road at great speed, calling out: 'Nice to see you, Mrs Durrell.'

Mother's face fell into grim lines as he joined her, though I really couldn't see what she had against him, I reflected in exasperation, for surely those mythical rumours of millions made up for his fearsome dentures. I could hear him soliciting her in warm apologetic tones as he tenderly took the basket, provoking a shriek from Pavlo who was settled in its depths.

'I'm so glad to see you, dear Mrs Durrell. I hear

you are away for a long rest – I do hope it is doing you good?'

I had never told him Mother was away for a long rest and, as usual, I wondered who had. Miss Brady, though back to the job of sweeping leaves, kept an observant eye on them.

'Oh yes, thank you,' Mother answered primly. I could see that she was not enjoying the situation at all. Mr Beetle, sensing that he was not making good enough progress, slipped into a subject in which he knew Mother was greatly interested.

'I had a strange and mysterious discovery,' he said cunningly, letting Mother digest his words. 'I think there is a poltergeist in our midst. Strange goings-on, you know – pots and pans all over the place. My poor dutiful housekeeper is positively alarmed, though I haven't told her I suspect poltergeists.'

Mother's face lit up immediately and she stopped. 'A poltergeist? Now isn't that interesting. Has it manifested itself?'

'Mother,' I called hastily, trying to break up the liaison that was about to start, 'coffee's ready.' Poltergeist be blowed: if Mother was lured away with tales of spooks and other supernatural events I would never get her into the house. It was a subject that could completely engross her, and when once she had started reliving visions seen both by herself and her mother in India, and other strange goings-on, one never knew where it would end – in this case probably with Mr Beetle and the local vicar being invited in to exorcise my boarding house.

'I'm afraid I must go now,' Mother, hearing me call and sensing the urgency in my voice, told him reluctantly, taking back her basket, now loath to leave this most enthralling subject that had been raised. Mr Beetle watched her go with longing.

'Hello dear, sorry I'm late,' she kissed me. 'I've just heard a most interesting thing – a real poltergeist and so close too.'

'What rubbish,' I answered.

'Yes dear, it could be, but you never know in these old houses,' Mother said, not wanting to disbelieve Mr Beetle's story. 'Perhaps you'll be lucky enough to have one here.'

'God forbid,' I answered irreverently, condemning the idea.

We made our way indoors and I showed Mother the final tidying up of the old house. We met a blithe Edward in the hall carrying an empty milk bottle and I introduced them, watching Mother's face carefully. She could not fail to appreciate the splendour of tight trousers, a deep ochre shirt and Mexican sandals; a becoming picture, especially with the clinging aroma of garlic. He greeted my mother with interest, she replied in her usual quiet way, and I was satisfied that her face showed no signs of internal disturbance. But I was wrong, for a few minutes later when she settled down to a quiet cup of coffee in the seclusion of our own drawing room, I realised that her reactions, to Edward's trousers especially, were quite different from my own. They were summed up in a few words. 'Extremely vulgar, dear, he could be arrested going about like that. And I would not be surprised if he isn't involved in the white slave trade traffic. Where does he get his money from?'

I thought this was most unreasonable from

someone as tolerant as my mother and I rose quickly to defend him. 'But you'll love him, Mother, I know – he cooks divinely, curry and all that sort of thing, with masses of garlic: in fact, I wonder if he doesn't overdo it a bit sometimes,' I remarked, for I had noticed that since Edward's arrival the hall often smelt as if an army of Greek peasants had just left.

'Well, that's different.' Mother took off her hat, and brought out her knitting. 'Now I want to hear all about the children,' she went on. 'How are they doing at the new school?'

'Not very well,' I answered gloomily, remembering my children, my mother-love somewhat dimmed. 'Gerry caused an uproar yesterday and was sent home.'

'Indeed! I should have something to say about that,' Mother was indignant. 'Who is the monster who could treat a child like that? A child who's never done a wrong thing in his life, poor little soul.'

That was not strictly true but Mother always rushed blindly to the defence of her grandchildren; any children for that matter.

'Well, he didn't exactly do the right thing this time,' I added. 'He took that painting that Lawrence and Nancy left behind – you know, the one Nancy did an embroidery from whilst she was here and expecting?'

'That thing!' Mother snorted. 'I should have thought that Lawrence would have had more sense than to leave a thing like that lying about!'

'Yes,' I said. 'Adam and Eve leering at each other without even a fig leaf between them. He said he had done it especially for his mother's birthday, and hung it up in the classroom before they caught him.'

'It was a sweet thought, poor innocent child,' Mother looked pleased.

'I don't see anything sweet about causing trouble,' I retorted.

'But it had no business to be lying about, putting temptation in his way,' Mother was reproachful. 'And it was an extremely vulgar picture too, I thought, with that hideous serpent crawling about those bulging thighs. Nothing artistic about that, and I said so at the time,' she went on, thoroughly roused.

'I tried to get them to go to Sunday School,' I interrupted, my thoughts full of my children now. 'They went once and refused to go again – they say it's boring.' I got gloomier and gloomier.

'Well, boys will be boys,' Mother comforted, helping herself to some more coffee.

'I'm sure we weren't such awful children,' I went on broodingly.

'Oh yes you were, dear!' Mother said, with a reflective laugh. 'You and Leslie caused a lot of trouble between you, and you were more trouble than the others.' Mother's face took on a faraway look, the look reserved for Indian reminiscences of our happy childhood days – the glory days of the Raj when we were cherished and pampered by servants galore, and life was good. 'I well remember the time all you children went out to tea, and you returned home with your knickers full of their toys, and Leslie came home with a temperature of 104 – he always ran a temperature when trouble was brewing.'

I giggled. 'No, Mother! I don't believe you! I

remember Leslie and me trying to do our governess in, having successfully removed Big Granny with insults, and she deserved it.'

'Do not be irreverent about your father's dead mother, dear. And I am not exaggerating. Once when your father took you into a big store we found you had a box of soap under your coat, and you were only three. The episode caused us many sleepless nights.'

'Good God, a thief at three – what chance have my children?' I groaned.

The telephone buzzed beside me. 'It's Leslie,' I said aside to Mother, answering it. 'He's coming up to collect you on his way back from somewhere or other, in about five minutes. He says he's got a present for me,' I added as I put the receiver back. 'I hope it's not something idiotic.' I spoke from past experience.

Mr Beetle passed at this moment, on his way home. He scanned the window eagerly, spotted Mother, blushed and waved.

'Silly old fool,' Mother remarked and did not return the gesture. 'Oh yes, dear, I forgot to tell you and that reminds me. Simon died of natural causes, the vet said. I didn't let you know before as I thought you might worry.'

I was about to be solicitous, privately thinking that the cause was probably overeating, when we were interrupted by a belching noise.

'Leslie's car,' Mother said, looking in the direction of the noise.

There was one last shuddering sigh, like something dying and the black Morris stopped at the gate with Leslie at the wheel. There was a sudden 'yelp' of a dog, the car door flew open and a large black and white mongrel, a rope about his neck and looking like a warning advertisement against rickets, sprang out, dragging Leslie with him in a confusion of rope, dog and man.

'What the hell's Leslie doing?' I turned to Mother, puzzled.

'Goodness knows, dear,' Mother answered mildly.

I made for the door, but I was too late. Man and beast rushed past me into the front room.

'What the hell are you doing?' I roared. 'You'll ruin my house. Stop him! Stop him!' I cried, agonised, retracing my steps. I was just in time to see the dog lift his leg against my freshly-painted door.

'Too late,' said Leslie, 'he's done it.'

'What's happening?' Edward came out of his room. 'Anything I can do?' He was wearing his apron and waved a large wooden spoon and a paint brush.

'Oh no, thank you,' I said sweetly. 'Just my brother arriving.' I instinctively refrained from introductions, feeling it was not the right moment, and quickly shut the door.

'Who's that bloody pansy?' Leslie asked with intense awe and great interest, neglecting to lower his voice.

'Shut up,' I whispered back fiercely. 'He'll hear you. He's my first lodger, and a jolly nice one too,' I told him loyally. 'You ask Mother – isn't he Mother?' I turned to Mother to defend the character of my lodger.

'Well, he certainly looks it,' he said, laughing heartily and untangling himself from a yard of rope. Mother winced.

The animal crouched between Leslie's legs, gazing at us with mournful brown eyes, which sent a depressed Pavlo, who had refused to leave his basket through the entire coffee session, into paroxysms of twitters.

'What have you brought this dog for?' I demanded suspiciously. I still felt annoyed that Leslie had not appreciated my lodger.

'It's your present – it's all this morgue needs,' he smiled disarmingly. 'It's a long and sad story,' he went on hinting at tragedy, obviously trying to gain sympathy. 'He was going to be put to sleep, poor sod. The vet and I both thought it was a great shame.'

'That's all very well,' I remarked, unaffected by the sad story. 'Why should I be burdened with it? He's not even house-trained,' I moaned on examining my door.

'Leslie, please don't call Margo's house a morgue – it might bring bad luck.'

'Thank you, Mother,' I turned to Leslie indignantly. 'If you were so sorry for the animal why didn't you keep the wretched thing yourself? And that idiot vet, he wants his brains testing. The thing looks like something out of a Thurber dog book,' I said bitterly, examining the culprit. 'And wormy too, no doubt,' I ended lamely, weakening a little as the dog started to lick my hand.

'Stop arguing!' Mother pleaded, as she put on her hat, folded up her knitting and picked up the precious marmoset. 'I'm sure it's a sweet dog, Margo. You could have him on trial, couldn't you dear?' she suggested helpfully, wanting to appease all parties. 'But you had better lock him up for today, before all those people come this afternoon. He might not be used to noise. He needs a collar, too.'

'And, no doubt, a dog-licence,' I said sarcastically, giving Leslie a baleful look.

Leslie, producing a dog-licence, presented it as if he were giving me the crown jewels, and I knew I was lost: the dog was irrevocably mine. The children, of course, would be delighted.

Then I realised gloomily that there was one thing I had forgotten to ask Mother, watching the ramshackled car disappear: about the dentist's appointment, the date scrawled in red on the bathroom mirror in the now-closed house. That meant Gerald would be due back soon, and when he came where was he going to stay?

I turned and examined Leslie's present, which was sitting up and watching me with friendly interest. I christened him 'Johnny'. It soon became apparent why Leslie's gift had been a near victim of extinction: he possessed a nervous twitch when excited, which sent him cocking his leg in all directions. What a dog, I brooded, discovering the truth within a few minutes, and who knew what other inhibitions would come to light. This was typical of Leslie, to produce some stray and expect us all to mother it.

The subsequent ringing of the telephone killed all my other concerns as I remembered my prospective lodgers and rushed to answer the first call, speaking in a voice that was not my own.

'I believe you have a room to let,' was the enquiry. It was a woman's voice, soft and uncultured, and I found myself swinging into the role of a landlady a little breathlessly: the long-awaited moment was upon me, for Edward's entry into our lives did not, I felt, constitute that of a lodger – he was a 'gift'.

There was a resounding knock at the front door as I sat poised with a book in a purely artificial way, one ear cocked for the welcome sound of the first arrival answering the call of my advertisement. A small bedraggled woman apathetically awaited my attention. She was not very old, I guessed, but life had played havoc with her looks: thinness gave her the appearance of smallness, and dismal hair straggled lifelessly down from beneath a hat, its shape devised by wear and not by design. Radiating confidence by her side stood a well-fed monster of a boy of about twelve years old. His singing moon face was wreathed in smiles, his body bulged happily, and an unidentified school-cap topped the lot. A wide cheeky grin left me in no doubt as to which of them had knocked. A forlorn and battered suitcase stood between them.

This was not exactly what I had expected but I rose to a smile of welcome. The fat grin from what was obviously an incarnation of Satan was irresistible.

The plain face of the woman warmed immediately to my welcome. 'We're 'ere about a room, please Ma'am, for me an' lad 'ere. I'm Mrs Williams, and 'tis me son Nelson, called arter me 'usband's favourite character in 'istory, you know.' Pride stole into the timid voice.

I glanced from her to the historical monument, which returned my scrutiny with an unflinching challenge from small roguish eyes and consolidated my first opinion that the devil lurked about him albeit in a friendly way. Amused at the ill assorted pair, I ushered them in, reflecting pleasantly well-worn phrases concerning the weather to the diligent wiping of shabby shoes on the doormat.

'It's tiring walking up 'ill, I'm fair melted,' she confided in me, readjusting her coat and letting out a powerful whiff of body odour. Being allergic to this I winced a little, but all would have to be endured for the cause, I told myself.

'It's always yer bleeding sweat, Ma,' the boy complained bitterly.

'Quiet, Nelson, else you'll get a clip over ear'ole,' she threatened in an ineffectual voice, which told me quite plainly that she never lifted her hand to her bun-like child. She gave me a small apologetic smile.

A door opened, and a red beard appeared. 'Ah, I see you are busy,' Edward murmured. 'I thought I heard someone knocking,' and the door closed behind him again.

The woman, taken back, watched the closed door as if hypnotised.

'Cor!' There was a gasp of admiration from Nelson. 'Was it real?'

'Yes, of course,' I said truthfully. It was undoubtedly Edward's beard that had brought such praise, and I wondered if it had been a good idea to have his room so near the front door, and if Mrs Williams appreciated the colour effects of artists. 'He paints you know, lovely stuff.' I turned to Mrs Williams in some sort of hasty explanation.

She was still watching the door as if expecting the reappearance of the vision. 'Very interesting too, I must say, and 'e looks like a kindly sort of gentleman,' she remarked appreciatively, recovering her composure and tearing her eyes away from the door.

'Perhaps you would like to come upstairs now?' I suggested, glad that Edward's introduction had passed off well. 'If you feel quite rested?'

Nelson, evidently deciding it was high time he gave voice again, answered. 'Yes, come on Ma, get a bloody move on,' he bawled, giving her a playful push.

That 'get a bloody move on' sounded so like Leslie that I had to smile. It was obvious that Nelson's repertoire would be a good one, better than Leslie's no doubt.

I took Mrs Williams by the arm, and propelled her up the stairs kindly. Shrugging unconcernedly, Satan's incarnation followed, criticising soundly, thumping deliberately with his flat feet on every step – to test for rot, he said.

He stopped, awed before the stained glass windows on the first landing. 'Coo, Ma, look at that – it looks like a blooming church up 'ere, all them coloured bits of glass.'

'This is my musicians' gallery,' I told him sweetly.

'Now listen, Nelson, be'ave yerself, or the kind lady won't 'ave us 'ere, will yer?' She gave me an imploring look and her insipid blue eyes filled with alarm.

'That's all right,' I said quickly, reassuring her. 'Don't worry about Nelson, he's all right. I can always give you a clout, can't I Nelson?' I asked deliberately.

'Not bleeding likely,' he answered me, with a dark look.

'It's very nice, I'm sure,' Ma said, looking around the room we had reached, obviously having decided not to provoke Nelson to further cheek by reprimands. 'We'll 'ave it, won't we son?'

By this time 'son' was turning on all the gas taps and testing them then, satisfied that gas was pouring out freely from all corners, he ambled over to the bay window and, hanging out, examined the road.

'Wish I could ride in a wheelchair,' he reflected with envy, as he saw an invalid glide past.

'Come in Nelson, boy, yer'll break yer neck.' Mrs Williams' protective instincts were aroused by the dangerous posturings of her son. 'And go and get the case in,' she added. 'We'll stay if the kind lady will 'ave us,' and she timidly asked the rent.

Feeling that I had no business to ask this poor-looking woman for rent, I told her the amount apologetically, as Nelson, hefty as a baby elephant, stormed the stairs, whooping, delighted to do his mother's bidding. I felt sure it was the first time!

She told me nothing about her previous life, or where she had come from, and I asked no questions, taking it for granted that the first reference to her husband made him a corpse. The luggage, non-existent except for one cheap and breaking suitcase, did not spell a long stay – even to my inexperienced eye, the fact seemed plain. Could she be a widow? Suddenly I was not sure. In my experience widows were careful to explain this fact, as though pronouncing a status, demanding respect. I had often wished I was a widow in order to enjoy this privilege. Perhaps she had left her husband in a hurry: it must have been a hasty retreat judging by the sparse belongings. A major quarrel perhaps – probably that odious little rascal had been at the bottom of it all. My imagination, as usual roused, twisted intricately over Mrs Williams' problems. Nelson, having dutifully returned with the case, had gone back to the window where he was whistling shrilly after two girlish lumps in olive green school uniforms who were hurrying past. I watched him in consternation, hoping that he was not going to spend his days causing commotions out of the front window – that would give the house a bad name. Already a busybody, posing as an 'officer's wife', had tried to get up a petition because, as she put it, our garden was a disgrace to the road as it had not been touched since the day I moved in. Her child had brought the petition to my door by mistake and I had indignantly refused to sign it.

The telephone rang again and, leaving Nelson arguing with his mother as to which divan he was going to use, I ran down to answer it: someone else was on the way. I had scarcely put the phone down when it rang again: a honeymoon couple this time, imploring me for assistance. A blissful two weeks was being spoilt by the routine of hotel life. Although I really wanted permanent people, I couldn't refuse such pleadings. An artist, a model, a monstrous fat boy, a bedraggled specimen with an undefined background – so why not honeymooners? I told myself enthusiastically as I described a haven for two, warming merrily to my theme.

The children returned home from school: they were enchanted with the situation. A jolly fat boy upstairs, who had already greeted them with a volley from a catapult, a dog with habits guaranteed to cause trouble, a glorious world of oozing messy paints and tasty titbits – what could be better?

Waiting for the honeymoon couple I remembered with dismay that the room I had so gaily described housed only single divans. The spare double bed would just have to be moved, I decided, determined that no honeymoon couple should be deprived of a double bed on my account. My romantic spirits were aroused.

'I will go to any lengths to make my first honeymoon couple feel at home,' I told Edward who, drawn by the noise of a double bed on the move and unable to resist any sound that smelt of action, had poked an inquisitive face out. Equally touched by the tricky situation he agreed that something had to be done, falling into action beside me in the direction of what we now called our bridal suite.

Meanwhile, Nelson, from his new quarters, having decided his sleeping arrangements, was relating none too quietly tales of bravery to a small respectful audience, my children, who had been invited up for inspection with the lordly air of a reigning monarch.

'Rather a monster, eh – don't you think?' Edward summed up the fat boy. I was about to say that I was sure a heart of pure gold beat under the cavity of those enormous ribs, when a peevish call from the hall sent me scuttling downstairs to answer it. Things were certainly on the move.

'I've been ringing and ringing, and no one answered.' The angry complaint subdued me.

'I'm so sorry, the bell doesn't work,' I explained apologetically – it hadn't done since I had caught the boys examining it with a screwdriver on their first morning home.

The crusty feline eyes under a thin brown line of eyebrow pencil carefully applied in two long strokes, glared at me. 'I don't like being kept waiting, you know. However, what I want is a quiet room facing south, and no noise, you understand. I can't stand dogs barking, crying babies, or children.'

I watched crestfallen, as Nelson, a rolling jelly astride the bannisters, fell at our feet – 'Lummy,' he said in greeting, 'a witch!' – and as if by magic Edward appeared beside me, pensively murmuring that the bed was now ready, and what next – a few flowers perhaps? He was oblivious to the rigid figure beside me, or the cascading bulk of Nelson, so busy was he with the completion of plans for the bridal suite. His next words were caught up in a frozen look of disbelief from the stranger, and seconds saw her scuttling out of our lives as fast as her rickety legs would allow.

'That was a lucky miss, wasn't it?' I remarked, referring to what would obviously have been a difficult tenant, but Edward did not hear me. Still absorbed in the thought of picking a few flowers to add the final touch, he had disappeared behind the fleeing form towards the one and only bunch of blooms in the front garden. Here was the very best remedy for unwanted lodgers, I decided gleefully, as I watched him with a rising spirit of tenderness.

But there was no time for sentimentality, for my honeymooners had arrived; a middle-aged couple, whose predicament would undoubtedly bring a scathing comment from Mrs Briggs on sexual indulgences, and I swept them along behind Edward, carrying the posy, without ceremony but with pride to what was now indisputably the bridal suite.

I need not have worried, the town obviously had room for another landlady, I thought with relief that night, reviewing the day's events with satisfaction. My rooms were filling up fast – not perhaps in a way Aunt Patience would have approved of, but nevertheless filling up. The house was already melting to a new and living atmosphere, and unfamiliar noises blended with the familiar. I was just contemplating this last point, when out of the night came the sound of running water and Mrs Briggs' cry, laying down the law.

Sneaking a look, I picked out her wide solid proportions, a ghost-like reflection, in her best hat, a large flat motherly affair that sprouted an array of faded red roses; she was surrounded by her all-male family. She wore her black silk coat and I remembered that it was her birthday and that she had been going out to celebrate the occasion. The noise had suggested they were rather merry but apparently they were not. From above my head on our side of the fence a continuous stream of water beat against Mrs Briggs' back door.

'Blooming cheek, I call it, all over our door. Whatever next will be happening?' I heard. 'Been abroad too long, that's the trouble,' she grumbled indignantly. 'Hope she's not going to turn out barmy like the last one.'

A mutter of agreement followed her words. 'That's right Mother, you're quite right. Bohemian is the word you want.' Mr Briggs was airing his view now. He was short, robust, always wore a fireman's cap and he hardly ever voiced an opinion.

It was a change anyway, I thought cynically, as I sped up the stairs to see who was the cause of the current of water offending Mrs Briggs, with Nelson prominent in my mind. The bathroom door was closed; voices and a laugh came from within.

'Where's the flannel, dear?' a man's voice asked. I recognised it as that of my male honeymooner.

'Disappeared,' came the playful answer. 'Here catch this.' The sound of a scuffle ended in a resounding smack. Not exactly romantic, but very matey.

Edward, in peacock blue pyjamas, appeared at my side noiselessly; his feet, slim and long and white, repeated the delicacy of his hands. We were already conspirators.

'What's up? I thought I heard a rumpus?' he whispered, bending with his eye to the keyhole, reducing the scene to a comic replica of what the butler saw. 'Can't see a thing,' he murmured in disappointment, to my agitation that we would both be caught red-handed. 'Unfortunately, that airing cupboard is in the way.'

I realised now that Edward and I would irrevocably be together in every crisis, as I briefly mouthed the indignation of Mrs Briggs going on below. Lustful voices now filled the bathroom against the sound of running water, blissfully unaware of an audience. Feeling awkward, hearing the intimate noises of two people sharing the same bath, I drew Edward away to the top of the stairs. Olwen, his wife, was now also standing at her door, looking like a plump white angel in her lace nightdress, an enquiring look on her face.

'Trouble?' she called up.

I grimaced a non-committal answer. Edward ignored her.

'No good can come of this bath-taking,' he murmured to me seriously. 'I really should warn them of the risks they are running.'

'Not now,' I interrupted hastily, holding his arm tightly.

'I had a most unfortunate occurrence once – this brings it to mind,' he said, enjoying the feel of my hold and allowing himself to linger in it.

'Did you?' I whispered back, wondering if every unusual occurrence would mean a full gathering of the lodgers, as a shadow fell across us and Nelson loomed up like a balloon to join us; a splendid robust figure in red and green stripes, haunted by his ghost-like mother, a frightened huddle of pink flannel and iron curlers. He swung his catapult with intent.

'Summat goin' on?' he asked, his small eyes shining at the prospect.

'Shh! Keep your voice down,' I ordered.

'It happened like this,' Edward went on, giving Nelson a filthy look at his intrusion, and holding up his hand for complete silence, determined to tell his tale. 'I hadn't had a bath for months and decided eventually to do so – only, I might add, after constant and irritating nagging from my wife.' I looked to see if Olwen was still in the doorway. She was.

'Go to bed woman,' he commanded in a dictatorial, husbandly way, following my gaze. 'You've heard this story before and I don't want your interruptions!'

Olwen disappeared. Edward was certainly master in his own domain, I thought, with some surprise, a little embarrassed for Olwen, though she had seemed unperturbed by the bossy command.

'You know how it is,' he excused himself.

Nelson nodded vigorously as if he already knew the difficulties of dealing with a wife. 'Bah women,' he said. We both ignored him: for different reasons.

'So I filled the bathtub right to the top and climbed in, preparing to compromise and soak for a couple of hours while I contemplated my next painting. The nagging had mercifully stopped, and the silence of the bathroom was sheer heaven.'

'It's a woman's birthright, nagging,' said Nelson. 'Me Dad told me so.' I was quick to notice the mention of a father.

'Shut-up!' Edward said rudely. Nelson shut his mouth with difficulty, having been obviously prepared to give us a little more of what his Dad had said. I looked round for Mrs Williams: she had scuttled away like a frightened mouse at Edward's displeasure. I felt disappointed that the mysteries of Nelson's father had not been revealed to us.

'I must have been worn out,' Edward paused, still puzzled at the memory, and shuddered. 'I fell asleep, for hours it must have been. I chill visibly even now at the memory. When I woke the water was icy and up to my nose, the police were banging at the door because that idiotic woman downstairs had thought I'd committed suicide. Believe me, I thought I was a corpse. I tried to yell for help but my voice had gone. I struggled to rise but my body was so numb I sunk lower, paralysed. This is death, I thought, then the door fell in – the police had arrived. I never took another bath. . . .'

'Why didn't yer pull the plug out, mate?' Nelson suggested sensibly. 'That's what I'd 'ave done, pulled bleeding plug out with me big toe.'

'Yes, why didn't you?' I smiled.

Edward turned to Nelson a face of sheer pain, but the sound of the bathroom bolt being drawn stopped any further discussion and sent us fleeing guiltily in all directions. I raced downstairs, leapt the last four, and prepared to meet the belligerent Mrs Briggs. Sheepishly, I joined the party in the dark, the fence happily between us. I was glad that we were now in total blackness for the bathroom light was out.

'So sorry,' I apologised, 'something stuck. One of the new tenants. I think, honeymooners!'

'What! Your lodgers giving trouble already? You be careful or they'll get out of hand before you can say Jack Robinson.'

'Keep calm Mother,' Mr Briggs chipped in, trying to avoid a midnight female brawl in true male fashion. Mrs Briggs took no notice of her husband. 'It's not good to be too easy with your lodgers, let them know who's boss right from the start.'

'I know,' I hissed back. 'That's what I'm trying to do.'

'Well, it doesn't look like it to me. You'd better get things under control before it's too late.'

'Sorry, anyway,' I said contritely, in a desire to bury the hatchet. '*Au revoir.*' I smiled into the night at the black shadow, looking like a strange species of mushroom. There was a moment of complete ominous silence when our friendship hung in the balance then 'Awreevor,' she relented, and peace descended.

The first day was finally over.

Chapter Five

Any doubts that I had previously felt dissolved, as my advertisement and the consequent ringing of the telephone brought new people to my threshold, a collection of people who in no way corresponded to my aunt's previous suggestions. There were hectic moments when the enquiry for a room with a double bed when a single was all I had immediately called for a frantic manoeuvre of re-arrangement, which involved everybody in the house and at one point left me without a bed at all.

Edward, though frail in stature, was a pillar of laden gallantry tottering, on the verge of physical collapse, from room to room whenever necessary, advising me with touching sweetness after the third shift that I would really have to say double or single and then stick to it, adopting a take-it-or-leave-it attitude.

'But why do people always seem to want something different from what one has?' I moaned, panic-stricken that the new people's arrival would coincide with our manoeuvres. But this was minor, compared to the subsequent necessity for a discussion on rent, a problem from which I never failed to shrink and one which had to be faced with great strength of will.

Mrs Briggs' wrath had subsided to occasional squalls of remembrance when she would relive for a moment or two the indignity of our waste water polluting her premises. The culprits of her disdain, my honeymooners, their happy episode over, had left us satisfied and still very much in love, their bathroom episode remaining a secret – from them that is: to the rest of us in the house it was common gossip.

The Bridal Suite now harboured a very different pair of lovers, the Buddens, a sluttish woman and her mate, a coarse, squat bricklayer, not past his prime, who stormed the house as if he owned it, brawling for a double bed even before he had reached the first step of ascension to his quarters and from whom the more sensitive of us recoiled. I knew for a certainty that this was going to be my first mistake.

Meeting the bridegroom for the first time, I trembled for my precious room, but having agreed foolishly over the telephone, and at the time quite happily, to the persuasive and not unpleasant voice of the bride, I found it difficult to extricate myself from the delicate situation when I examined the pair before me with mounting alarm. The sight of the dog, the children, Nelson and the flamboyant Edward perturbed them not at all which, weighing up my losses, I decided was one thing in their favour.

Next door to the Buddens, another couple set up house. Aggressive chinned and Welsh, Barry had done well for himself in the R.A.F., but now he was out of a job, desperately frustrated with no outlet for all his energies. His wife, Paula, on the other hand, had found her niche. Never inactive for long, she now absorbed herself in daily employment as a beauty consultant: clothes, make-up and impeccable grooming were an inseparable part of her life. Her hair was tinted from brown to a red fox colour, while the unusual slanting green eyes shone like a watching cat. Barry, whose only real trouble was that he was too healthy, was driven to a state of hypochondria by his frustrations. Though all he needed was a good sedative, he carried an inexhaustible supply of pills for every ailment. A previous short employment behind a chemist's counter had allowed him to acquire a certain amount of medical jargon which he now used with leisurely pleasure. He was always ready, if needed, to help a fellow man in times of physical stress to a healthier way of life and, in consequence, he was a popular figure with any member of the household who was suffering.

In another room, competing with Barry for idiosyncrasies, was a thin, pleasant-looking, but mournful bachelor. Pale-faced and penniless, Gordon clung with the tenacity of a cat with a mouse to a large moustache and a yellow self-built sports car, which he tended like a mother with her first child, and he nursed his own bodily ailments with a well-stocked medicine chest from the National Health. Unlike Barry's, his worries were merely surface agitations. Each week brought him some fresh complaint: a boil in the nose, a painful pile, or just the slightest telltale doubt of a bald patch. He watched the opposite sex with dog-like brown eyes, raised with surreptitious care as he tinkered with his car and lovingly polished the battered paintwork. After pottering with his casual chores to a certain scruffy standard of living, he would scrape together his paltry earnings as a radio mechanic. Barry, in close sympathy with his new neighbour, supplemented any defects in his National Health supplies.

The arrival of Blanche and Judy, two very glamorous nurses, one as dark as the other was fair, threw the entire male section into excited disorder. Temperatures ran high and all the barriers of reserve were down. Alone Nelson's mother, non-committal and still a supreme introvert, went silently about her secret business, only stopping to reprimand Nelson in her timid ineffectual voice, as he wallowed in sentimental literature and craned dangerously from all angles to catch a better view of swirling femininity. Edward broke his pledge, and took a bath: alerting us to stand by to assist in case, as he put it, 'anything unforeseen happens – you never know, dear soul.'

Meanwhile an army of competitive male callers began to stamp past his door, much to his annoyance, and up the stairs to compete for both youth and beauty. There were young men with dashing new sports cars, which brought Gordon out in a fresh crop of boils as he struggled to keep both prestige and his ageing baby on the road; middle-aged men of experience, smooth, with a keen eye to seduction. A roué paved his way with luxury for what he lacked in sex appeal he made up for in hard cash, fluttering like a tattered moth to a lighted inviting window, while the girls, unashamedly confident, played man against man and enjoying life, endeared themselves to me with good humour and explained that after exploring numerous lodging houses they felt that they had now come home!

Then, as if fate had intended to keep things evenly balanced, my next advert produced, another amateur nurse, retired by way of a nervous disposition. A skinny, parsimonious plain Jane, flat-chested and efficient, wearing horn-rimmed spectacles, she spent her forced retirement in dreamy hospital reminiscences, relating in a sterile clinical voice the more harrowing details of gory operations she had witnessed, taking charge of any situation that presented itself – 'keeping my hand in,' she called it. Dressing Gordon's boils, in cap and apron, adding cotton wool, lint and surgical spirit to his already bulging medicine chest, the smells brought back to me memories of my brother Gerald's activities as he poured over an entomological corpse he hoped to save for posterity. In both their eyes gleamed the identical light of a calling.

Tucked away in a quiet corner another two male lodgers had sent us women into a vulnerable state of acute romanticism. Roger and Andy, musicians and artistic characters, were sharing together in complete masculine harmony their material assets. Unaware of their disturbing influence on the female population about they settled in with casual good-humoured friendliness. Roger, attending art school, spend much of his day absorbed in artistic endeavour with the concentrated agony of a hen about to lay an extra large egg. He ruffled oil paints as thick as treacle across smooth canvas with a passionate concern to feel the touch of the Master. The complete antithesis of Edward who, with the same artistic desires, gave life to a still canvas with complete composure. For Roger there were always the moments of utter disillusion when he would abandon his painting, turning to his trumpet, his other love and drowning himself in jazz, a turbulent peace that had been born out of squalor and loneliness, eagerly fumbling out a new riff on the gleaming metal. Thumping out, a sombre picture in thick dark woollens and a pair of heavy boots (a relic of his army days), his precious trumpet carefully wrapped in an old cloth, he went to blow his heart out in some nocturnal dive. Single, he had flown from yet another landlady who had considered him undesirable. 'No respectable man,' she had told him severely, 'comes in at all hours of the day or night, not only with suspicious looking bundles under his arm but with *women*. He should go to work at 9am and come home at 6pm' – and she had given him a week's notice. His consequent wanderings for new lodgings had brought him to my door.

Having left a trail of women behind him, he was at the moment of entry into our house being kept in check by a dark, broad-hipped Maltese girl, with pensive black eyes and big masculine hands. Magda was constantly by his side so a frequent visitor, coming from a small sparse lodging in the heart of town.

Standing head and shoulders over him, his companion, a shy north countryman with soft eyes and humorous mouth, appreciated the tantalising qualities of productive art and shared his love of jazz. He carried a mundane job lightly. Playing all hours with equal intensity and with equal reverence, he handled his trombone with firm square hands that sent an uneasy longing through me. I watched him secretly, disturbed, against my will; standing a little aloof whilst Jane and Paula openly discussed his finer points. Olwen, producing her words carefully as if deciphering an obscure prescription, remarked that she had never seen a finer pair of shoulders, while the nursing glamour girls openly threw him their inviting flirtatious glances: who would not be inclined to succumb, I asked myself, reflecting dismally on the competition about me. Even Mrs Budden, absorbed between new wedlock and the migraine attacks which incapacitated her, took note, and with Mr Budden safely out of the way murmured: 'but isn't he handsome!' Mrs Williams succumbed too, in her small way, and darned a frayed patch to oblige, as I curbed with difficulty the desire to rush forward and seize the frayed article saying 'I'll do that.'

The house, I felt, was now well and truly launched and seemed to be weathering the consequent upheavals. In moments when I spared my aunt a fleeting thought, brought on by some trifling incident, I sincerely prayed that Pussy's confinement would be a long one – there was not a paragon of Auntie's ideals in sight and the melodies and hectic discussions on all planes of life, not to mention the dogmatic left-wing opinions of Mr Budden, would have outraged her narrow concepts.

Now that Mother could see that I was not being organised by the white slavers, raped or murdered, she began to regard my venture with a slightly calmer heart, even suggesting that she came up and stayed for a few weeks to reorganise my larder, which she said seemed sadly lacking in taste. Edward had now become a great favourite with her, and subsequently with Leslie who, with the appearance of Edward's wife, was now convinced he was no pansy. His discovery, he said, now allowed a carefree friendship to flourish. Both he and Mother quickly grew to tolerate and even like Edward's bizarre appearance. United in strong approval of the delicious odours that invariably filled their visits (for Leslie was also an epicure), they would hail him merrily when he appeared from his bedsit at the sound of their voices, having been busy with all the genius he could muster, supervising his cooking while he painted fluid lines of vision in glowing blending colours and attended to other trivialities: the washing he refused to do. With the distraction of visitors he would immediately organise himself a leisurely hour to gossip, discussing the advantages of an Indian curry against a Malayan one, a subject on which no one could excel, and Mother would repeat to me aside, with the look of sheer satisfaction, 'what wife wouldn't go out to work if her husband cooked like that.' Then, discovering by chance, with great joy, that Edward was as interested in ghosts, spirits and supernatural manifestations as she was, this subject became a common haunting-ground for them. Now there were spells of ghost-spotting; moments of apprehensive hush, when they waited for a sign of manifestation which so far had not materialised. Disappointed, they swore that the nervous giggle from the pent-up member of a curious audience had destroyed the final moment of truth or, alternatively, they condemned the house as neither ancient nor hallowed enough.

Nelson measured up the household carefully to see just how far he could go with each one and played his cards accordingly. In certain quarters where his charm fell on stony ground he retaliated with an invisible hand; scoring a bull's eye he would disappear quickly, shaking with silent laughter. To my mother he presented a face of sheer innocence and she rewarded him with money and sweets. My children were enchanted with this Jesse James and Robin Hood rolled into one: with him they did all the things they longed to do but dared not, and his range of blasphemous words and confident, constant use of them was an added rapture. They paid homage willingly; even his most paltry turns such as spitting and hitting any object at ten feet were applauded without restraint. I was Mother no longer – 'Ma' became my official title. When I remarked, after a particularly exasperating day, that I should have to get rid of that fat boy, there were loud cries of dismay: 'Oh Ma no, he's such fun – let's have him here forever.'

'Fun!' I had shouted, 'what fun?' having come in and received a smacking blow from a large and ancient volume of Shakespeare which had been carefully balanced on the front door and intended for the returning bricklayers (Nelson's greatest enemy), as a reprisal for a small dispute concerning noise.

Nelson's enemies never knew from where or when he would strike: unfortunately sometimes the innocent were forced to suffer with the guilty party and Nelson's popularity would deteriorate to sordid depths. In spite of all this he grew on me; his grin and rolling figure invariably brought a laugh to my lips, even if sometimes the sound was one of hollow mirth, for he was a cheery soul. 'Surely this is a good sign,' I argued with Edward, whose reference to him as 'that odious fat boy' had brought a protest to my lips – for Nelson had just treated me with one of his special smiles and a soggy chocolate, and I was completely won over for the moment. The matter was left open for further discussion.

My rooms full, and satisfied that my worries were at least temporarily over and my lodgers settled in comfortably, I decided to forget the house for one day and spend a morning browsing around the shops in town, to acquire some of the ingredients for improving my cooking.

On my way out, I fell into the clutches of a moaning, uncombed Mrs Budden, in a rose pink kimono with a flourishing green dragon embroidered across the back. She was holding her head and on the hunt for aspirins. Soothing her chronic migraine with a cocoon-shaped pill that Barry had passed over to me as the only remedy worth mentioning for migraine and other womanly ills, I tried to escape, with pointed references to the lateness of the hour and my shopping list a foot long, but Mrs Budden, happy to have found a reasonably sympathetic ear, kept a hand on my arm asking my advice on all sorts of major issues: reorganisation of her straight bobbed hair growing untidily long, which she had overheard Paula saying was a mess; an appetising supper dish for mister; angry warnings of varicose veins . . . I felt

I was fast involving myself with the least desirable of my lodgers.

Why did everyone tell me everything, I wondered. I was in a no-man's-land, hearing all, discreetly quiet, or repetitive according to my mood, completely neutral on most issues. Jane, shamelessly eavesdropping, heard me suggest cold compresses for Mrs Budden's varicose veins and cold baths for her husband's odour, and couldn't resist the temptation to join us, sweeping down the stairs with an important air.

'I think,' she said, 'I am the one to deal with this: don't you agree?' And she hustled the pink bundle upstairs to her quarters. The sufferer, satisfied to have a new prey who showed such interest, and having no choice anyway, left me without regret and I heard the voices silenced by the firm and business-like closing of Jane's door.

Preparing to make a second exit, I was forestalled by yet another obstacle: Edward, with a most disquieting look of urgency on his face. It was not unusual for Edward to appear for with the sudden need of a change of occupation he would join me casually at any time and anywhere I might be – and I would do the same when fraught by similar feelings. However, today I could see that things were different; it was neither glad tidings nor a whim that had brought him to my door. Normally I welcomed the intrusive whim that brightened my day but now, anxious for my larder, I felt he would have to wait for my return.

Edward, sensing my eagerness to be gone, looked disappointed. 'This is a matter of grave seriousness,' he said, looking somewhat like an undertaker on holiday in an all black outfit with a red scarf at his neck.

Seeing Edward blocking my way I wondered what the new crisis could be. A mixture of hilarious female titters and a wailing blues number on a trumpet floated down from upstairs, and I pondered, worrying a little if this noise wasn't prolonging Mrs Budden's migraine: but I should no doubt soon know in the form of a complaint.

'Trouble!' Edward's voice was hollow, through a smell of stale garlic, dropping to ominous tones to match the sombre black of his garb.

'What's happened?' I asked quickly, feeling a hasty little jerk somewhere deep inside that the expectation of bad news brings: had one of my children been run over? Was Andy ill? Perhaps Nelson had fallen out of the upstairs window? Poor Nelson – tears sprang to my eyes.

'I overheard something,' he hesitated.

'What?' I said quickly. 'Don't keep me in suspense. For heaven's sake, what?' If it was bereavement then let me face it bravely, I prayed.

'You know that sour-faced neighbour, Lady something or other,' he pointed behind him toward Lady Booth's residence. 'She says that you are running a brothel and that the police should be informed.' He put a hand out to catch me comfortingly, no doubt expecting a total collapse of my resources.

I digested this bit of news in silence for a moment, stunned: then, relieved that it was not a matter of life and death, I was overcome with mirth, disputing the authority of Edward's statement with honest disbelief.

'But it's true, dear soul,' Edward impressed on

me gently. 'She was talking to that woman in the velvet coat – and a nice bit of velvet it was too,' he remarked, side-tracking. 'It would make an admirable waistcoat . . .'

'Go on,' I said, 'explain . . . the sordid details, and never mind about the waistcoat.'

'You know the one I mean, across the road, that seems to spend all her time intent on the destruction of the most vulnerable parts of our four-legged friends' anatomies.'

'The bitch!' said I, hurt that Miss Brady was also intent on my destruction. 'I wish I was, though,' I added emphatically, reflecting thoughtfully, astonished how such a rumour could start. 'I'd make a quick fortune and no mistake – we'd have all the material we need, I should think.'

'Don't joke,' Edward implored, interrupting. 'I think it's quite scandalous.'

'But for goodness sake, don't tell Mother,' I went on, remembering that she wouldn't take the gossip as a joke. 'She would only start to worry again, just as she's taking things more calmly too.' I thought of Aunt Patience: such a thing must be kept from her as well.

'I think it's quite preposterous,' Edward said hotly. 'We might be subjected to a police raid.'

'So do I,' came in agreement above. It was Jane, hanging over the bannisters in amazement; her eyes like saucers peered down at us from behind their thick lenses. 'Absolutely awful. I heard every word,' she added with satisfaction, a light yellow sweater accentuating her breasts to a mere apology. Jane, who never could resist the call of Edward's voice, had obviously left the delicate subject of her patient's health and returned stealthily to discover what the object of her admiration had to say.

'I feel like giving her the toe end of my boot,' Edward added, not over pleased at Jane's appearance.

'What boot?' I asked innocently, looking at his slim foot in open sandals.

'How can you laugh? I think it is most serious.'

I shrugged, still laughing. 'Well what else do you expect from suburbia? They thrive on gossip.'

'Isn't it dreadful,' Jane darted a look at Edward with her big eyes, and her tone of voice, though shocked, suggested that she really was enjoying this delicious piece of news.

'Yes it is,' Edward said. 'Gossip is the most dangerous thing on earth.'

'And something we indulge in frequently,' I retorted with a sly grin, remembering our hectic suppositions on every member in the house.

'Yes, but our gossiping is not malicious.'

'I suppose not,' I said. 'But it's not surprising really, is it?' I summarised the situation slowly, 'if you have an imagination like those of our neighbours.' I was reflecting over recent events, and the clientele that could possibly have led to such false suppositions. Blanche's Nordic good looks, and her room-mate Judy, whose short black curly hair and doe-like eyes were as seductive as Blanche's fairness, were a fair target: for they were on night duty at the local hospital and consequently spent most of the day wrapped modestly in dressing gowns, taking refreshment from room to room when supposed to be making up for lost sleep, or holding court in their own. Then of course, apart from our resident males, there were the 'extras', the throng of male admirers clattering in and out. You could hear the girls now, filling the hall with their female chatter, even from behind closed doors. As far as I could guess Gordon was the lucky man, for there was only his car parked outside today. It was unusual.

'Of course *they* are suspects,' Jane remarked spitefully of the nurses, aware of the critical thoughts and glad for a chance to torpedo her rivals.

'And Gordon is obviously contaminating himself at this very moment,' Edward sounded jealous.

'I quite agree,' said Jane.

I thought of Gordon. He was now neglecting both his work and his car as he struggled with his rising passion and the everlasting threat of thieving competition. Morally upset, he could not acclimatise himself to the sight of female bodies in fragile bed-wear floating so close past his door. He was frantic for the love of Blanche. There were no pills to mask his frustration suspended on the verge of his own private breakdown as she tantalised with a soft mouth, pointed breasts and cold mocking eyes. He longed for the young body wrapped casually in a revealing white robe, turning more and more to the medicine chest and Jane's cool hands, comforted by Barry's faithful 'steady on, old boy' as he passed him another tranquilliser, with shaking hands.

'Gordon is obviously open to grave criticism,' Edward insisted, noting with some dismay that I did not agree.

'What about the other two, I say,' said Jane waspishly.

I looked at Jane, our sterile flag of hygiene, whom we had all looked up to as the strength of our womanhood in those first days. Jane was in no position to point a finger of criticism I decided severely. Envying the sex appeal of the others, which she had never possessed, she succumbed quickly to influence, slipped from the tracks of convention on a swift treacherous move: launched on a shopping spree and abandoned herself overnight, not only to glamorous intentions but to what she called 'Bohemia', preferring now to lounge in off-beat poses, open to suspicion assuming décolleté negligees that left us women breathless and the men still without desire. She hung about the hall in shadowy corners, waiting intently for an audience.

'Personally, if I were the landlady . . .' began Jane.

'We're all equally to blame,' I said, firmly ignoring the injured looks of Jane now thrown in my direction, 'even Olwen,' I went on determined. Olwen's seductive figure and flowing hair, which sent the imagination soaring, would undoubtedly cause comments in suburbia, especially if caught in a modelling pose by a keyhole viewer.

'What about Paula, then?' Edward was a little crest-fallen that contaminating evidence was spreading into his camp.

'I shall move,' Jane announced grandly.

I thought of Paula. Paula had not helped matters either; she had changed the red of her hair twice since her arrival and it now matched the red of Edward's beard.

'There is only Nelson's mother,' I announced with startling truth, 'who doesn't really give cause for comment.' Mrs Williams, that down-trodden figure of respectability with the air of widowhood, her past even now shrouded in mystery which the wagging tongue of Nelson had yet to reveal. But Nelson was not blameless, embroidering, with an innocent air, the trivialities of life to delightful and impossible proportions, and no doubt was himself the instigator of many a rumour.

'Have we to conform to a colourless pattern in order to plead innocence?' Edward's question was full of disdain.

Jane blamed Paula's hair dye – 'The colour is outrageous.' I was silent, thinking of myself. Even I, not to be outdone by my female lodgers, ignoring my Aunt Patience's warnings, was not blameless: I was aware of Andy's presence about me with deepening unrest, while dabbling with the affections of a blond giant who, judging by the size of his girth I suspected was going to run to fat, and mighty quickly too. Edward was painting him: a thoroughly respectable picture, in warm pinky browns and yellows, reclining on the divan in the attitude of a debauched Roman Emperor, a loin-cloth attempting to disguise his obvious rolls of fat.

A howl from Mrs Budden for Jane changed my self-analysis. 'And what with her,' I said to Edward, 'relaxing late into the morning in that pink kimono, meeting the baker at the gate looking like a fallen geisha girl, does not help to raise the tone of our establishment.' There was quick agreement from all sides.

'What with the watchful eyes of neighbours,' I

went on, 'the chatter of the milkman, not to mention the baker . . .'

'And the possible chance word from the children,' Edward emphasised.

'No wonder rumour has made you a madam,' Jane finished Edward's sentence calmly and with evident delight.

I saw myself for a second in an entirely new career. Sitting in the hall at my brass table, heavy in shiny satin and dangling diamond earrings, enormous rings flashing searchlights on my small hands, eyes hooded in heavy make-up, and the merry tinkle of the till clattering in the money as I sang out, 'Time, gentlemen, please.'

But aloud I murmured, 'Cheek, what an absolute cheek!' as I stormed out, leaving a crestfallen pair behind me, eager to discuss the threatening rumour. I hoped that I was going to meet Lady Booth or Miss Brady and give them a verbal rocket but I met no one as I stalked the road looking for trouble.

Chapter Six

While my house was suffering the post-natal pangs of readjustment, the town had become an impossible blockage of humanity as holiday-makers poured in for the summer season: I found this to my cost as I struggled into the city centre bent on my shopping expedition.

Hours later, or so it seemed, I returned home, glad to leave the bustling town and the excruciating agonies of people determined to enjoy their holiday. I was glad to be back, gossip or not, in the quiet of our road. In my basket nestled spices and an assortment of things from the extensive list that Edward and Mother had compiled together, and which they considered most necessary to my larder.

It was a warm day; the heat scorched the road to a glistening blackness and walking was a hardship. On the hill two ladies in straw hats idled on the bench; they stopped their chatter and eyed me openly. Were they carriers of this ridiculous rumour, I asked myself, glaring at them as I passed. Gordon, tearing himself away from his temptation, sped by in the roar of an unsilenced engine, making tracks for work I supposed, cheered that he was at last showing strength of character and facing his responsibilities, if a little late – he was three weeks behind with the rent too, I calculated doubtfully, watching him vanish in a haze of speed.

My smile disappeared at the distant sight of Nelson hanging out of his window on the first floor, his rear cheerfully in the air, an active portion of dog beside it. His mischievous plump hands, clutching a sheath knife, were busy digging at the bumpy surface of my pebble-dashed wall, probably collecting ammunition for his catapult. I scowled angrily up at the happy, busy shape, quickening my step as a small crocodile of lime green, pink-faced schoolgirls fled past me. They came from the sedate girls' school around the corner overlooking the park, and the mark of Nelson was upon them. My first instinct was to beat the fat boy firmly over the head, but I restrained my sadistic desires with a transient thought: I'd try a little psychology first and see what a few words of love could achieve.

'Nelson, dear,' my voice rose on a cooing note. 'Don't do that, you'll spoil the wall, and the position you are in is most dangerous. And bring Johnny down, dear, he might jump out and hurt himself.' There was no response to my new methods. 'If you fall out you will surely break your neck' – by now I secretly hoped he would: my voice was still sugary, though the sugar had grown less honeyed with the veiled warning.

Nelson, as if sensing my uncharitable thoughts, lifted his face and gave me a reproachful look from clear round eyes, followed by a seductive smile entirely manufactured for the occasion. 'Oh, you there,' he remarked in a friendly fashion. ''Ere's a sweet, I saved it for yer special like,' and straightening awkwardly for a moment he fished in his pocket and threw me a bull's eye, sticky and covered in dog's hair.

Johnny, on hearing my voice, had left Nelson at the window and was now endeavouring to scratch the door down. Nelson's kindness filled me with a moment of quiet remorse: how could I wish the boy dead? Nelson was unique, a clown of circumstance, and allowances must be made, I thought, gazing up at him with grudging affection, in his ill-fitting clothes and cap perched like a pimple on the back of his head – it never dislodged between sunrise and sunset, however hazardous the adventure. He appeared to have no school, and I expected the education authorities to storm down on us at any moment.

Mrs Briggs' face rose above the fences: 'And just what's going on now? More trouble, I suppose?' From behind the stone wall the heavy breathing of a disapproving titled lady told me that there was another hostile viewer.

Feeling that Nelson was about to drag me into another situation, I used the only weapon I had, hitting him below the belt, for he loved his tummy even more than stunning his fellow man with guided missiles; he was ever ready for a taste of a sugary dish, which probably accounted for his large proportions. 'Very well then, if you don't listen you just will not be able to have tea with us again.' I kept my voice cold and meaningful: it was no empty threat, for Nelson frequently attended our tea table.

'That's right, give it to him,' came Mrs Briggs' inevitable sally. I pretended not to see her, and to my relief saw Nelson right his rear at my news and disappear into the gaping window without a sound – victory was mine. As I turned to go I could not help thinking it was a miracle I had not received a stinging blow from one of my own pebbles.

'You're learning,' came Mrs Briggs' parting shot. The dignified silence from the other side told us exactly what Lady Booth thought.

Nelson and I met in the hall, our differences forgotten. Johnny, who was by his side, lifted his leg, saw my face, and hurriedly dropped it, fleeing past me into the garden.

'Did yer see them dames a few moments ago?' Nelson was chuckling all over at the pleasant memory.

'What dames?' I asked – I had seen no dames.

'Them bits of stuff in green. I fancied last bird, one with fat legs.'

'Nelson!' I said reprovingly, 'I hope you are not going to upset one of the most respectable schools in Bournemouth.'

He did not answer, but pulling a chewed lump of gum from behind his ear, returned it for further mastication and followed Johnny into the garden; with the children at school Nelson roamed the place aimlessly, a lone tubby figure.

Having lodgers, or at least Nelson, was not exactly a peaceful occupation, I decided, as I picked up a long pink envelope from the hall table and noticed the handwriting of my Aunt Patience. I tore open the letter quickly: a single sheet of scented paper floated to the ground. Picking it up I read the clear writing:

My Dear Child,

After weeks of careful attention, Pussy is now well on the way to recovery, and we shall no doubt be able to face the journey down to Bournemouth in the near future; so expect us when you see us.

You are no doubt by now conducting your house in the proper manner, befitting to your education and upbringing, but we shall see.

Fond love,
Auntie

I groaned aloud: 'Expect us when you see us.' What a threat to have hanging over us! I tottered to the vicinity of my kitchen.

As if sensing my return Edward appeared at the back door, a look of tender concern on his face: 'I thought you were back. Look, I have finished it.' Enthusiastically he held up a large canvas and was obviously trying to make up for the disturbing rumours of earlier.

'Have you?' I replied without interest, frowning at the reclining giant. The rumour no longer worried me; I had dismissed it.

He placed the picture up on the window ledge.

'The colours are lovely,' I had to admit grudgingly, as I closed one eye with a professional air deciding to give the picture the benefit of a longer look even if my dwindling regard of this male species had left me without interest.

There was a crunch of breaking glass and heavy steps in flying retreat: the steps of Nelson escaping retribution, syncopated with an arrangement of 'Nobody loves you when you're down and out'.

Edward groaned: 'Those musicians will drive

me mad. I can feel one of Mrs Budden's headaches coming on.'

'Then Jane can put her cool hand upon you,' I revelled in the tender picture, maliciously provoking.

'Over my dead body: the woman's utterly sexless. But you're different.'

'Me?' I was astonished, feeling rather pleased that I had been placed in such a high and interesting category.

Then Edward saw with pleasure my loaded shopping basket and, his attention diverted, went into ecstasies of pleasure on a different plane. Then he slipped away murmuring something about 'competitive sounds' and that he would be back in a moment for further conversation, suggesting that I made coffee.

The blue eyes of my diminishing love leered at me. I picked it up and carried it to the bathroom and propped it against the bath for prolonged inspection while I threw off my town clothes and slipped easily into blue jeans. I always changed in the bathroom for the last rearrangement of divans had temporarily left me without a place of rest – I was a nomad in my own house. My feelings were definitely dead I decided with one eye on the canvas: for the watching eyes caused me no tremor. It was a relief. Belting my jeans, I lifted the canvas and carried it to the drawing room and draped it casually in the window.

Nelson's face appeared framed in the open window: 'Cor, wot a monster!' he blurted out, guffawing. 'Wot some women see in some men.'

My dangerous look made him disappear hastily, surprisingly agile for the bulk he carried. I smiled tolerantly. Nelson was Nelson, and we must all suffer I thought, not without a certain tenderness, as I went to make coffee.

Mrs Budden's curtains, rattling open to let in the light of day, suggested that her migraine had been conquered by the combined efforts of Jane and Barry. Barry would be well on his way to yet another interview, I remembered, in a sudden rush of sympathy. If only one good job would turn up to rebuild his confidence in life. It was lucky, I reflected, that both Paula and Olwen were capable of holding down good jobs, for both their menfolk were far removed from security. I was glad that I was my own mistress.

Nelson passed the window again and held his head in an attitude of proud aloofness, intending to provoke me to a mood of regretful generosity. I whistled after him, jeering, 'Hi, handsome!' with intended insult, but there was no response. I remembered for the hundredth time that I must ask Mrs Williams why he did not go to school.

Edward reappeared treading gaily now, his good humour restored. He carried a few records under his arm and a big brown envelope, and was humming genially. 'This is music, much better stuff than that hideous broken noise from upstairs that sears my eardrums. I shall have to wear ear-plugs if it goes on,' he told me quite seriously, throwing me the brown envelope and preparing the gramophone for action. I sat down and opened the brown flap, blushing as a most comprehensive collection of pornographic postcards showered into my lap. I gathered them up hurriedly with what I hoped was a good imitation of one of my mother's reproving looks when one of us had gone too far.

'Edward really! Have you been drinking?'

'Leslie did call whilst you were out and we had one or two tots – rather weak, they were, as we were both a little broke. I felt the need for something substantial after that shocking news this morning.'

'You can be had up for this sort of thing, you know,' I told him seriously, indicating to the cards.

'I had a little bet on,' he said suddenly, standing in Nelson's way.

'And did you win your bet?' I asked with heavy sarcasm.

'Yes,' he said calmly. 'You are the best landlady I have ever met. Nothing seems to shock you, it is most unusual in a landlady . . .' He sounded a little puzzled.

'But, of course,' I answered calmly. 'Is that so bad, then?'

'No, it's Barry and Gordon who would be perturbed by those things, not I,' I said, with every good reason, giggling. 'They leave me cold.'

'Pity,' he said ambiguously. 'Talking of Gordon,' he went on, 'he has just rushed off to a funeral. A relative, I think.'

'Oh. For one blissful moment I thought he had decided to drag himself back to work. How disappointing.'

'Work!' Edward scoffed. 'He'll do no work with so many women about. Come to think of it, I find it rather difficult myself,' he added truthfully, putting on a record. The gramophone was old – antique, in fact.

His next remark was drowned by the wail of a

'belly dance' vibrating through the room, making more noise than anything that came from upstairs. 'Turn it down!' I implored. 'Remember Mrs Budden's migraine.'

But Edward was away, throwing himself into a frenzy of movement as he started to dance. His arms flayed the air, his shirt was off, the slight body, bending, twisting. His stomach drawn tight as if in agony, caved in under his chest grotesquely. The skeleton-like body had captured new life, sweat clung to the pale skin in dewy softness. I wondered if his brain had snapped and if I should call Jane: but would she react in the proper manner? Her reactions to things were debatable now in the new mood, but surely at a time like this she would forget her feminine role and remember the glorious call of nursing? I was indecisive and absorbed as I watched the moving figure: suddenly I was engulfed into the spirit of the thing. Here was an outlet for inhibitions in which anyone could join. I stood up enthusiastically and was about to fling off my restricting garments and join him when a collision stopped the gramophone, as Johnny, attracted by the weird noises, leapt through the open window and followed the dancing figure in a mad whirl of barking hysteria. Caught up between the spindly legs, dog and man collapsed in a heap. Fortunately, for Mrs Briggs had just called by to give me a bunch of rhubarb, and her incredulous face, with Nelson's beside it, was glued to the open window.

'Just having a few dancing lessons,' I explained innocently, not looking at Nelson.

'Sure, sure,' she remarked, with disbelief,

giving me and the draped canvas of rolling rosy fat, still in the window, a strange look. Dropping the rhubarb over the sill she backed away quickly, as if I were contagious. 'Dancing lessons!' she said. 'Hum, some dancing lessons!'

I looked at Nelson. A devilish grin had spread across his face: 'Na good will come of them dancing, I know,' he said, candidly. 'More like a sex horgy,' and he vanished. The bundle of rhubarb missed him by inches.

There was a thunderous knocking at the door. Mrs Budden, hair still uncombed, swayed in the door, but she had exchanged the pink kimono for a check skirt and the usual shapeless floral smock. Her feet were thrust into comfy pink slippers: she was a picture of sloppy domesticity. Edward, raising himself from the middle of the floor, fell into a chair, a trembling slim form, with an admiring animal crouched at his feet.

'I must ask you to make less noise.' The voice at the door was plaintive. 'My head is throbbing again dreadfully.' The pink-rimmed brown eyes brimmed with tears. 'And the other music's been blaring all morning too. I feel quite exhausted. Haven't they got any work to do? These musicians and artists are an idle lot – says my hubby. He says they need a bit of the old whip!'

'That is their work, they live between painting and music.' And I tried to explain away the intricacies of the artistic soul to a completely uncomprehending Mrs Budden, who did not intend to be appeased by explanations.

'What an apparition,' remarked a voice from the depths of the armchair – I could tell he resented the reference to idling painters and intended to get his own back in an ungentlemanly way.

Apologising fervently for the row, drowning the reiterated criticism, I closed the door hurriedly in the astonished face of my caller: she had never been treated like that before.

'Must you?' I asked accusingly.

'No business to come here, interfering, with her ignorant insinuations,' Edward was peeved. 'And what's more the woman looks pregnant.'

'Shut up!' I hissed. 'She'll hear you.'

'Well, doesn't she?'

'Yes, I suppose she does,' I said slowly, mentally examining Mrs Budden's unbecoming figure for the first time.

'And do you allow pregnant women here? Most landladies don't.'

'I don't know – I've never thought about it,' I reflected slowly. 'She certainly hasn't told me, though she tells me practically everything else,' I ended, with a sudden laugh.

'Well, Roger, Barry and Nelson all think she is, and I haven't discussed it with the others yet. I suppose we'll have sleepless nights soon with a bald-headed brat braying like a horse. And . . .'

'A horse doesn't bray – and what does Nelson know about pregnancy?' I enquired scathingly, my illusions that men did not gossip shattered.

'More than you think,' he replied knowingly. 'He is a bundle of accurate and inaccurate knowledge.'

'Well, I'll ask Mrs Briggs,' I said laughingly after the fleeing form of Edward. 'She is naturally clairvoyant.'

But I didn't have to ask, for on my next trip to

the back garden I heard a 'hiss', and there was Mrs Briggs, the incident of the dance forgotten in the more important light of a new discovery.

'One of your women is expecting, I see. Did yer know?' Her eyes were dancing.

'No,' I answered truthfully, not wishing to discuss my lodger's intimate details with outsiders.

'Mark my words, she'll have one before you can say Jack Robinson,' she warned. 'I had a good look at her today: surely you noticed that smock – it's obvious. She is married, I suppose?' she demanded, after a long pause.

'Yes, but lots of women do their housework in smocks,' I reasoned.

'Yep, lots of birds do 'ousework in them smocks – our Ma does an' she ain't h'expecting.' Nelson was hanging out of the bathroom window engrossed by our discussion. Normally Mrs Briggs would have reprimanded Nelson, but not this time. 'Twenty-fourth of the fifth,' Nelson offered dates, disappearing in an uproar in what seemed to be a dispute with Jane over the bathroom.

'Ho, ho, you'll be in for it now,' Mrs Briggs remarked delightedly, ignoring the small tidy male figure with the middle parting, who had appeared at her kitchen door. 'Nappies and babies crying, that's what you'll have. You should never have had her – she's too old for babies anyway. She ought to be ashamed of herself: women ought to keep their skirts down, I say.' And Mrs Briggs, who had given birth to four children, put a masterful arm out and propelled her man indoors.

We were done for. Edward was right, and Mrs Briggs was the oracle.

Chapter Seven

Mother and I were taking tea in the bay window: she was in the usual position, hidden by the curtains, that she adopted now when sitting in such a prominent place, to hide her from what she called the hounding curiosity of neighbours. The chink of knitting needles accompanied our conversation as a shapeless object rolled out from Mother's busy hands and lay across her knees – small coloured squares, intensely involved, which lengthened visibly as we talked.

Across the road, sheltered from the sun by the boughs of the horse chestnut which spread like an umbrella above them, Mrs Briggs, her cheeks glowing with natural colour, in apron and washed-out striped dress, discussed animatedly an unidentified subject with Miss Brady. Looking as though she were about to take a facial, her head carefully wrapped in mauve chiffon tied in a large bow, which, standing up like rabbits ears, bobbed merrily, Miss Brady answered Mrs Briggs word for word. In the alley between our two houses, the usual haunt of Mrs Briggs when she wished to attract my attention, rose persistent accumulation of sound, the hollow thudding of a hammer splitting wood: a disturbance which, so far, although I had found it irritating, I had been too lazy to investigate as I related to Mother the latest gossip – missing out Edward's savoury piece about the brothel – of how Mrs Budden had exploded in our midst a bouncing boy weighing nine-and-a-half pounds, thereby consolidating Mrs Briggs' position amongst us as a soothsayer, gleefully remarking 'the truth will come out', which had sent Mother into a fit of righteous indignation against scandal-mongering neighbours.

Edward called for attention and we responded. His room was in perfect order: before the window a table carried brushes and paints stacked tidily and a pile of books lying together neatly in a pyramid. The door to the garden was wide open and reminded me that something must be done about that wilderness. The kitchen was a combination of warm smells and neatness. Inspection of the strange-looking fluid with greenery on the top gave us no immediate solution to the problem, however: it looked like something brother Gerald preserved dead animals in, and I made a hasty resolution that if Edward offered me any of this brew my answer would be an emphatic '*no*'. Mother, tantalised by the inexplicable subject, stirred the contents of the solid stone jar, poring over it with deep concentration.

'This stuff looks rather like chickweed to me – I should be very careful,' she warned, reflecting on the growth of thriving coverage, and they both dived into the wine-making manual for the third time.

But Mother was defeated. 'It's no good, Edward,' she announced at length. 'You must have got your recipes mixed somehow. You will just have to leave it to the full maturing time, and then give it another examination. 'Patience,' and she straightened, sniffing a clove of garlic appreciatively while her gentle, very blue eyes examined Edward's latest painting, a galaxy of yellows. 'Now isn't that pretty, Edward dear.' Mother walked towards it, passing over, with a slightly embarrassed start, a large painting hanging over the double divan which held a vision of Olwen (painted before our time) stark naked, resting on a bed of cushions. She clutched hurriedly at a small canvas of wild flowers, examining it with great intent. 'Such beautiful flowers, you can almost smell them.' She placed it back, and stepped towards the next canvas, her back firmly towards the pink body on the wall.

'Look at this,' I exclaimed quickly, thinking that Edward's room was fast becoming a hazard, and I led her speedily past my blonde has-been and his fatty waist-line, which Edward had returned to his easel for further titillation after Nelson's and my criticism. I pointed out a still life: a wicker basket caressed a gin bottle and two green glasses winked patiently beside a bottle opener, a cohesion of subtle greens.

'Charming!' Mother acclaimed the picture wholly. 'You really are clever, Edward. I am sure you will be famous one day.'

Mother's uncensored genuine applause would hearten any struggling artist and make him feel that life was yet worthwhile. I liked it too, and said so, but I was interrupted by the bouncing shape of Nelson carrying a large placard, a hammer and a tin of nails, and followed by his usual crowd of admirers. He was very happy, for the children had started a holiday.

Nelson was ever on the alert, nosing his way ferret-like to enjoy any situation at someone else's expense, so naturally he stopped by the open door to gaze at us.

'Wotcha, Grandma!' he yelled airily to my mother, making this sound endearing, giving the room a nosy searching look, and taking in the whole picture at a glance.

Edward slammed the door. 'Evil little boy,' he said, but not unkindly, then changed the subject for he knew that Mother would never agree to any infamous suggestions concerning her favourite fat boy.

After prolonged minutes of varied and earnest discussion, we left the cosy room to return to our own more spacious quarters. In the hall Jane was lurking; she hugged a first aid kit, and a slight smell of ether hung about her. She was a nurse now, no longer the *femme fatale*. I could not make up my mind which was the most comical: who, I wondered, was getting first aid. It couldn't be Gordon, who was still away, or Mrs Budden who had been carried off groaning and weeping to the hospital; the nursing glamour girls were completely silent (for a change) and were obviously reviving themselves in sleep for their arduous night duties – it was unusual. In any case it was doubtful if plain Jane would administer her aid to her secret rivals, however needy. Could it be Barry, returning home early from job-hunting with a blister? Maybe Roger was suffering, or Andy needed help? I stopped, dismayed at the very thought of my absence at such a moment.

'Everything all right?' I asked, faking disinterest but demanding an answer.

'Roger's cut himself. His cut-throat slipped,' was the calm reply.

'Good God, not suicide? I knew he would injure himself with that thing.' Edward poked his head out of his door for a final remark.

'Oh, poor boy,' Mother bustled anxiously. 'Those cut-throat razors ought to be banned, dreadful things.'

'It's all right now. I soon cleaned up the gory mess.'

'Good.' I was relieved that it wasn't Andy.

'Is Edward well?' Jane enquired tenderly, forgetting Roger's lacerations in the more important light of the welfare of her favourite neighbour: the hastily slamming door had already told her that he was in.

'Yes, quite,' I answered lightly, fearing for Edward's morals, feeling that with such persistence she would get him in the end.

Roger's Maltese girlfriend swept in and passed us up the stairs. I noticed a bristle of dark hair showing beneath her arm-pits; perspiration touched her top lip. We heard the heavy steps across the landing, a sharp knock, the opening and closing of a door, and then there was silence.

'I wouldn't like to trust her with a septic wound,' Jane remarked scathingly.

Taking a firm hold of Mother (for Mother too had trained as a nurse) I manoeuvred her away from the conversation and determinedly marched her towards our own part of the house.

A large notice displayed brilliantly on our gate told my neighbours that we were about to open a pet shop.

'Really Mother, that Nelson goes too far,' I

complained heatedly, having made a quick trip to the gate to investigate. Digesting Nelson's illiterate hand I returned to impart the news.

'I don't suppose the dear children are doing any harm,' Mother consoled, 'but I shouldn't be surprised if you have a few complaints at the noise,' as the never-ending sound of violent hammering had now brought Mrs Briggs back to her side of the road to investigate.

'Now, now, what's going on?' she called.

From the corner of my eye I saw the white of Mr Beetle's panama and a beige object settled on our lawn. 'The enemy,' I warned, and Mother and I ducked as Mr Beetle strolled by at a dithering pace. I caught a quick glimpse of his shining countenance scanning the windows hopefully. 'We're flanked by the enemy on two sides,' I said in a stifled voice. 'And I wish he'd control that damn dog of his,' I muttered, in sympathy with my withering front lawn.

'Mind my knitting, you are trampling all over it,' Mother said in agitation.

'Look out, he'll see you!' I warned, as Mother came dangerously out of hiding.

'Silly old fool!' came the expected comment. 'He wants his brains testing, hanging about ogling women like some teenager. I am inclined to agree with Mrs Briggs' views on him, I must say.'

I felt this rather unfair criticism of Mother's suitor, and said so. 'You seem to like him if he wants to discuss spooks,' I remarked, popping up to view the situation and removing Mother's knitting from under my foot.

'That's different,' Mother said coldly, rising cautiously. Mr Beetle had disappeared with Miss

Brady, and with Mrs Briggs' protests subsiding into angry mutterings, with her back door shivering on its hinges, we knew she had disappeared too.

'You don't seem to get much trouble from Lady Booth,' Mother reflected in a relieved tone. 'That's one less to worry about,' and she settled herself back comfortably, picking up her knitting again and examining it carefully for signs of damage.

'No . . .' My answer was slow and uncertain, thinking of Edward's rumour. Which was worse, subterranean gossip and watching eyes behind a lace curtain, or Mrs Briggs' open attacks? For Lady Booth, finally discovering that I was possibly going to out-do even Mrs O'Grady, now languished in reserved volcanic grumbling, only occasionally breaking forth to bleat a protest as a deft kick from Nelson sent a football bounding against her wall, or the noise of Gordon's engine revived every nerve in her body.

The hammering started again. I bounded up exasperated, in full sympathy with Mrs Briggs and made hasty tracks towards the noise.

'What are you doing? The noise is driving us mad!' I demanded aggressively, rounding the corner in the vicinity of the back door and reaching the source of the trouble. My voice trailed off as I found myself looking at the upturned face of Andy squatting beside a tea-chest. The actual culprit of the din, hammer aloft, gave me an innocent smile of welcome.

'It's a truly paying proposition,' Nelson explained away the noise grandly. 'We need every blooming box we can get.'

'Yes, Ma, mice are going to breed like flies!'

Gerry announced, as though he were the world's expert on breeding.

'We're going to make some dough, aren't we?' Nicholas, hugging Johnny, turned a face of trust towards Nelson. 'Nelson says the back lavatory is just the place.'

Andy gave me a grin and bent his head, concentrating on the hinge he was attaching to the piece of wood. 'Eh, lass,' he said shyly, 'just giving the kids a hand. Didn't think you'd mind.'

'You are one of us,' Nelson said proudly, giving Andy's shoulder a hefty squeeze.

I noticed Andy's strong neck; his brown hair needed cutting, curling down thickly against tanned skin. I felt a sudden urge to touch the bent head, darn the aging rollneck sweater and threadbare trousers. He looked very handsome, I thought with certain reserve, not wanting to admit that which was already common gossip in our female community and dragging my straying inclinations back to Nelson's activities. Nelson gave me one of his special knowing looks, missing nothing and, sensing that with the presence of Andy I was immediately undermined, spoke to me man-to-man: 'It's like this,' he explained confidently with a flourish of his plump hand. 'We're going to make some dough from this 'ere mice,' and pulling out two white mice he let them scamper up his arm.

'These mice,' I corrected.

'These 'ere mice,' Nelson went on. He stood hands on hips, in the attitude of Mrs Briggs, legs splayed; a mouse-dealer and man of finance. His short pants splitting at the seams spoilt the picture.

I smiled unwillingly, alarmed at the prospect of fornicating mice in our back lavatory.

'All our pocket money is going into the business; I reckon we'll make a mint of dough,' Nelson said, hoping to reassure me.

'Eh, lad, you will.' There was kind amusement in Andy's deep voice.

'But I thought you were going to housetrain Johnny for me – that's a full-time job I would have thought,' I reminded Nelson of his promise. 'Oh, all right,' I capitulated finally, unconvinced but not wanting to spoil the glow on three childish faces, and unwilling to belittle myself foolishly in Andy's presence – for Nelson could make you look very foolish if he tried. I left it at that, turning to go.

'I've some new records, luv. Bessie Smith blues. Would you care to hear them sometime?' Andy glanced up briefly and smiled with his eyes.

'Yes!' I breathed, quickly turning to meet his look. I didn't care what records they were, the invitation was enough to send my spirits soaring. I killed with difficulty the urge to prolong the happy moment with trivial gossip and forced myself to return to Mother, in a state of mixed emotions.

'They're breeding mice in the back lavatory, isn't it awful?' I moaned, with my mind still wandering helplessly back to that bent head.

'The nursing home down the road seems to be doing good business, that's the second ambulance I have seen today.' Mother was oblivious to my state of mind. I repeated my statement more loudly.

'Breeding mice!' she gasped, as though at last

comprehending, and behaving as though I had told her that an epidemic of smallpox raged through the avenue. 'It's a most unhygienic occupation, and they do smell dreadfully dear. It might start an epidemic.' Mother put down her work, a faraway haunted look in her eyes. 'I well remember the occasion when I very stupidly allowed your brother Gerald, as a little boy, to keep mice. I regretted it bitterly – had to put my foot down in the end. Perhaps you remember the incident?'

'Yes!' I said decidedly, 'but I do try and forget the more sordid memories.'

The picture of Mother putting her foot down amused me: I had no doubt at all that Gerald had bred mice to the bitter end.

Our reminiscences were interrupted by a dejected Magda walking down the path in a blundering way. Her head was down and she was crying.

'Oh dear, more trouble,' Mother murmured sympathetically, her eyes on the distressed figure in the mauve dress.

'Perhaps she has had a row with Roger,' I reasoned, a little bewildered. I didn't know Magda well, but she had always seemed wholly confident; a tempestuous, full-blooded girl, spoiling Roger willingly. 'Perhaps Jane's come between them,' I added, not believing it for a moment.

'What she sees in that scruffy-looking individual, I can't imagine,' said Mother grimly, but a braking taxi and subsequent uproar at the gate distracted our attention.

Into our midst, well before schedule, came my brother Gerald, and his arrival eclipsed all else for the next twenty-four hours. Mother's face, unlike mine, cheered delightedly at the sight of her youngest son. I groaned aloud as the familiar boyish face, very like my own, grinned at the mob racing to the gate to greet him.

'It's our uncle!' Gerry shouted joyfully at Nelson, who was frantic to be first, followed closely by Nicholas and Johnny.

He stepped from the car; tall, fair and debonair and typically English, holding a sack carefully in one hand as if carrying a rare gift, but I knew better than that. Greeting his nephews jovially, he shook hands with the enormous Nelson, eyes twinkling. There was an involved gesticulated discussion which seemed to involve both the house, the garage and the large wooden cage that was resting on the boot of the taxi: he appeared to regard the place as his own, for in a matter of a few minutes an unusual entourage made its way to the empty garage. I knew the meaning of the sack and the wooden box. I glanced slyly at Mother – a look of dismay had now crossed her face too, as no doubt she remembered other times when the presence of a sack or box had meant eventual trouble.

'If he puts one foot over my threshold,' I said in a voice of doom, 'I'm done for.'

'Too late, dear,' said Mother in a queer voice, as many hands lifted the crate and it cleared the gate tipped at a crazy angle: the party, under the loud instruction of Nelson's directions, crossed my boundaries. Followed by Mother, I went to face the inevitable. I wished I hadn't been so hard on Aunt Patience. Her visit would have been nothing compared to this.

'Just a few monkeys,' Gerald called out airily, seeing Mother and me for the first time and throwing a saucy eye heavenwards towards an upstairs window, where two half-clad female bodies, disturbed from their slumbers, watched him. The small inquisitive face of plain Jane appeared like a ghost at the hall window.

'I hope there is nothing dangerous in that sack, dear?' Mother enquired, kissing her youngest tenderly.

'It's a six-foot python, but harmless,' Gerald replied carelessly.

'My God! We can't have it in this house, Gerald!' Mother said, in her attempted firm voice that meant that he could. 'You'll have to keep it hidden from your lodgers,' she whispered aside to me, sweetly compromising, trying to pacify my obvious scowling displeasure. It was unusual for Mother to take the Lord's name in vain.

'Too true, I'll keep it hidden,' I replied with considerable feeling, and wondering if I couldn't off-load Gerald onto Leslie's girlfriend. After all, if she could take one Durrell, why not another? I put the idea to Mother tentatively, as Gerald turned to organise his affairs.

'No dear,' Mother was kind but firm. 'There's no room. I'm afraid you'll just have to be patient, dear, and hope for the best.'

'Well, can't he go and sit in the house across the road?' I asked unfeelingly.

'Oh no, dear,' Mother replied. 'The poor boy would be lonely. Besides, Leslie has practically sold the house to some solicitor or other, and we couldn't have Gerald making a mess in there if that's the case, could we?'

'No, I suppose not,' I agreed, my hopes diminishing as the noise of reorganisation amidst the excited and delighted chatter of Nelson and the children told me that all was lost.

Paula, returning from a day spent like an alabaster castaway behind a softly lit shop-counter, coaxing customers to spend money, advising her own sex on beauty and helping rich *passé* women to camouflage their drooping eyelids, stopped as she saw the general confusion in the drive. She noted the female interest glued to the window and turned her attention back to the centre of attraction. He looked like a happier proposition than the one that awaited her, coming home tired from work to cope with her precarious married life. If she had to do the breadwinner's job, surely Barry could cultivate a few feminine virtues as Edward did?

Olwen, also having made tracks for home after a tiring day of hectic persuasion in the footwear department and hungry for the comforting aromas manufactured by Edward, joined Paula in the garden.

Gerald, though he appeared absorbed in the safe housing of his animals, had in no way missed either the faces at the window or the entrance through the gate of the two most attractive women. Through a blaze of clamour he noted with an appreciative eye, strangely akin to Mr Beetle, the Rubens proportions of Olwen, which even the business-like black and grey outfit failed to disguise, and the slim girl with legs from the first row of the chorus, hair like the brush of a fox and strange eyes crinkling up at the corners in a welcome smile.

'It's some of the women, the ones that go out to work,' Nelson informed him. 'The place is full of women.'

Gerald beamed. 'Any good?' he asked, treating Nelson as an equal. It was a strange thing, we often did with Nelson.

'Some,' was the reply, and he shrugged composedly as though unwilling to give away any secrets. In fact, though enthralled by the nurses' glamour, he treated the rest of us women, with the exception of my mother, with a healthy boyish scorn. We were an army of hags in our twenties and he preferred to save his ditties for the ranks of the lime-green crocodiles that passed, feeling no doubt that his humour was better appreciated in that quarter.

Then Barry returned from his fifth day of job-hunting, and Paula had to postpone the interest that Gerald had aroused in her.

Mr Budden's entrance, cocky (for he behaved as if he had been responsible for the birth of a Messiah) in a pair of grimy overalls, carrying a dejected paper carrier bag which had housed his lunch, made a down-to-earth picture and sent the watching Jane to her room for safety; if anyone struck terror to her heart it was the coarse, gangling bricklayer, who cursed his wife when displeased and dabbled at unconventional hours with groaning copulation, appearing blatantly with bloodshot eyes and swollen face and the satisfied look of a mated bull, which left us all with the limp feeling that we had been witness to a crime and that he should be given notice.

I greeted each of my lodgers in a different way, camouflaging the rough sack, my hand uncomfortable against what felt like a thick coil of rope, conscious that it was actually a python.

Barry turned to tell me, without great joy, that he had taken a temporary job down on the beach, starting immediately. He followed Paula indoors with the usual look of disdain at the working man entering the gate, not stopping to indulge in their usual squalls on political policy.

Edward's sarcastic inquiry if his wife intended to linger in the garden all evening, made from the vantage point of the nurses' window, where they were sustaining their curiosity with cups of hastily brewed tea, sent an alarmed Olwen scurrying indoors to protect her mate.

The way now clear, I pulled the sack out from beneath its protective covering, laying it to rest behind the garage door, and there, I thought, it was going to stay if I had anything to do with it. Mother had disappeared. I heard her on the telephone, spreading the good news of Gerald's arrival to Doris and Leslie, delighted at the prospect of another family gathering; she had a short memory.

Darkness found Leslie speeding up to join us, laden with drink and good humour and by his side, the big-hearted, big-voiced, laughing Doris. The drawing-room, fully alive for the first time, vibrated with laughter, discussion and reminiscences. Soft lights cast grotesque shadows across the high walls; outside the moon hung in the sky like a white lantern; in the distance of Miss Brady's garden the stray cat moaned softly, for he was in love again.... And because no family reunion, however small, was complete without argument, eventually there was a heated discussion, as I urged Mother in a determined whisper to speak to Gerald about causing trouble. Mother, taking Dutch courage from a double gin, spoke.

'Now Gerald,' Mother's voice rose firmly above the general noise: we all turned to look at her. 'I do hope you are not going to cause Margo a lot of trouble with your animals. We've had one or two nasty little experiences you know, and we don't really feel up to coping with any more.'

I urged Mother on silently, glad that she had at last broached the subject.

'Was that the time the dangerous rattlesnake escaped, or the baboon?' Doris asked tactlessly, having heard the story from Leslie.

'And neighbourly goodwill was severed for life,' Leslie added with pleasure. Doris, framed in empty bottles, gave her good-natured bubbling laugh. I laughed too, in spite of my hidden fears of losing all of my tenants with one of Gerry's visits.

'I don't know anything about a baboon, but the snake was as harmless as a newborn babe – a gorgeous specimen.' Gerald's blue eyes gleamed fondly, in the way Mother's did when she looked at her grandchildren.

I enlarged on our displeasure at having once been saddled with a baboon, while Mother looked grieved at her own memories: she had been in the midst of an over-forty ladies' tea party with a few remnants of her past, when Gerald, with the deftness of a conjurer, had produced from out of a small bag a three-foot snake – no one knew the snake was harmless. Screams had brought the tea party to a close and the snake, taking fright, had slithered in a fluid movement to the floor and made a cunning escape to the next door shrubbery, Miss Brady's, while a party of well-bred Bournemouth ladies, gathering up their belongings, had swept down the drive.

'Shows you don't know anything about newborn babies,' Leslie joined the debate heatedly, after a moment's thought on babies and snakes. 'The bloody thing was definitely poisonous. I saw a fang about six foot long hanging out of his mouth – if I could have reached for my gun I'd have put a bullet between his eyes.'

'Leslie, you really must be more tolerant; the fangs couldn't have been six feet long,' Doris complained, in a tone of voice that suggested she knew Leslie very well indeed.

'Yes, let's stick to facts,' Gerald said icily. 'No snake has fangs of six foot, however extraordinary.'

'Don't exaggerate, Leslie dear. It's not fair to your brother to make it sound worse than it really was.' Mother usually ended by turning to defend the one who was attacked, even if they were in the wrong.

'Gerald is either saying "gorgeous" to some animal or to some female: I'm sick of him. Leslie's quite right, a bullet would take care of either,' I said wickedly, feeling daringly voluble, now sustained by liquor.

Mother interrupted me nervously. 'Don't encourage Leslie to murder please: shooting someone between the eyes is not a matter for joking. You'd better pour me another gin: how I've managed to live so long with you children is a miracle. Your dear father would turn in his grave if he could see you arguing and fighting without an atom of sense.'

'Well, Gerald shouldn't say gorgeous to everything. Last time he called something tangible gorgeous, it was that droopy blonde who sat about with her hair flowing in a silvery cascade of abandon down her neck, while we were left to do the housework. Do you remember, Mother?'

But Mother refused to take sides.

'She was a natural blonde, however dumb – that was one thing in her favour,' Leslie said reflectively.

Ignoring Mother's pleas and encouraged by Leslie's ribald remarks, I resumed the topic cheerfully: 'Mother and I had endless councils of war behind closed kitchen doors as to the best method of saving you from a fate worse than death.' I chuckled heartily. 'Didn't we, Mother?' Mother didn't answer.

'Yes a lucky escape, my dear boy,' Leslie agreed, with a broad smile and a wink at me.

Gerald, a small smile hovering at the corners of his mouth remained thoughtful, twirling the glass gently in his hand, his eyes watching the brown liquid intently. It was inevitable that we should attack one another with sarcastic verbal comment; not physically as we had done as children belabouring the enemy with the nearest object able to cause harm.

'Then there was that policeman's daughter from Whipsnade . . .'

'A dozy wench, I remember her. A female Friar Tuck with bosoms like a battleship,' Leslie ended the description that I was about to start. 'I well remember her!'

Gerald, his smile turning to a grin which lit up his eyes, gave a slow, teasing look. 'Ah, but what about your boyfriends,' he interrupted. 'In your time you've had some swooning around you, God knows why. You've practically killed off one husband, who is recuperating in a monastery, Larry wrote to say.'

'Well, Larry's a liar,' I retorted quickly.

'No, no, Gerald, that's not true,' Mother insisted hastily, hovering to see fair play.

'Not to mention,' Gerald went on, determined to finish, 'that bull-necked English Lord Something-or-other with a permanently constipated look, a detestable bore; a rag and bone merchant. And Leslie says she's had a blonde beast in tow whose face resembles a street accident.' He turned to Mother. 'I'm surprised you haven't put your foot down.'

'Gerald, dear, you are going too far. Margo's friends are really very nice.'

'That's not what you said before, Mother. You were moaning on about how foul they were.'

'Mother!' I said accusingly. 'Whose side are you on?'

'And now,' Gerald went on mercilessly, 'I hear from the delectable Nelson that there seems to be jostling for first place in your affections, some fool with a trombone, who is either dashing in or out, or lurking in the shadows, constantly blowing flat notes from a fungus-infected instrument – a sort of street musician as far as I can gather.'

I looked around indignantly. How dare the family discuss my private life? How dare my lodgers gossip? I thought furiously. I would strangle Nelson in the morning.

And we drifted into another argument.

The moon, streaking down in a narrow glimmer, brought an exclamation of the late hour to Mother's lips, and the family prepared to go. Gerald, of course, stayed. The hall, wrapped in the atmosphere of night, like a jungle was full of light noises: the creaking agony of an unoiled spring; heavy nasal snoring, followed by a groan; the wafting scent of bath salts, mixed with Nelson's fish and chips. I urged the family to tiptoe as we crept to the outside door.

'It strikes me,' Gerald remarked, whispering loudly and looking around the shadowy hall with interest, 'that there might be a spook or two in this place.'

'Now that's very interesting.' Mother was immediately on the alert before I could add a bitter comment. 'And the same thought has passed through my mind more than once, especially out here in the dark. Edward and I have already tried to communicate with them with the glass method – you know, dear – with no result yet, unfortunately. I must say it's heartening to have a second opinion.'

Leslie's voice rose up behind us: 'The only spooks you'll get around here are wolves disguised in sheep's clothing, intent on rape – I should think.'

I pulled the door open to bundle the grinning face out and bumped into Roger, a thoughtful tired-eyed figure, blundering in; remarkably quiet in spite of his heavy boots, cradling his precious instrument beneath his arm. He was followed by a tall figure muffled to the eyes, a trombone swinging lightly. My heart stirred oddly as we exchanged silent greetings.

'Really, dear, I don't think you should have men creeping in like this, it might give the house a bad name,' Mother remarked almost silently, alarmed at the passage of dim male figures.

'It's too late,' I murmured instantly, thinking of the rumour and smiling to myself in the dark.

The rumour of men creeping in to despoil our wares was nothing to the worry of Gerald's presence: crates of monkeys, possibly dehydrated specimens; white mice breeding in the back lavatory, like Communist China, creating a stench that would grow steadily worse no doubt, widening a rift between Mrs Briggs and myself to insurmountable proportions. Unconcerned by suburbia, Gerald would most probably sink into a peaceful slumber while I spent a night of restless thought. In the kitchen, and against my moaning complaints, a six-foot python, having gorged on white mice, browsed contented and tested his sack for escape: Nelson's pockets already jangled at his first sale to Gerald, however gruesome, for he said 'nature fed on nature', so his Pa had told him. He had fought for the honour of a night with the python, but the collapse of his mother at the thought decided the question. Which was the far greater menace? Nelson or Gerald? It was a debatable point indeed!

Gerald's arrival went down better than I had expected. He stayed a few days, charming the household into submission and acceptance of his eccentricities; attended his dentist; organised the children on zoological expeditions. Alarmed at the possible mutilation of that evil-smelling amphibian on the bathroom cupboard across the road, he retrieved it and presented it to Nelson as a memento. Hearing the tappings that Mother had referred to, he diagnosed them as the death-watch beetle attacking the foundations, panicking the household into journeys of inspection with Rentokil.

Succumbing in typical male fashion to the charm of the local 'glamour', he tried a little light seduction on Blanche during Gordon's absence, competing with bald heads and money and winning easily. He teased Jane mildly with the ancient Chinese proverb, 'if rape is inevitable, lie down and enjoy it', leaving her a figure of anticipating emotion, her love for Edward on the turn, convinced that she had now reached the peak of true womanhood by her brief encounter with one of even greater experience than Edward.

He exchanged recipes with Edward, dabbled a brush with Roger, drank with Andy, flirted outrageously with all the married matrons, festering the germs of discontent, listened to Barry's symptoms, quarrelled with Mr Budden who stubbornly refused to yield to his charm and admit his superior intellect, and who objected strongly to the python, which he referred to as 'venomous' and whose exercising period coincided with his trips to the dustbin – a job normally performed by his patient wife.

Disorganising the entire household, Gerald collected up his python with a showy tenderness and, putting me in unwilling protesting charge of the monkeys in the garage, he left me with the unhappy thought that he would be back soon, the only consolation being that so far none of my lodgers had given notice.

Chapter Eight

The weekends so far had brought their own atmosphere to the house; a complete unit of its mixed population as the throng of regular workers who, in the week, disappeared so smartly, stayed at home to enjoy the leisure of time to spare. A feeling of luxury prevailed as bodies lingered late into the morning reluctant to leave the cosy warmth of a slept-in bed, or rising to potter with deliberate aimlessness, flaunting time with careless intent.

Suddenly circumstances spoilt the pattern with Gordon off to attend his funeral and Mrs Budden departing for medical aid and returning home, missing my brother Gerald by minutes, still large but carrying a brawling bundle of child, and a new pram – a chariot – filled the hall. The master bricklayer, rejoicing in his offspring's homecoming, was determined to enjoy every waking moment on show with his son and heir. He stalked the house triumphant, awaiting applause, a superior gleam in his eye which made us all tremble afresh for his martyred wife.

Barry, too, was to forfeit his lazy weekends: in his new job with the local council he now found himself in hectic seven-day employment, organising the hiring of floats to the milling motley holiday-makers. Hectic because the work, which in theory represented an easy beachcomber's life, idling away the summer hours as bathing belles frolicked tantalisingly in the surf, was, in reality, a monstrous regularity of tickets and the pushing and pulling of wooden floats, heavy with sea water, while snotty-nosed boys gazed in envy, pleading their inevitable question: 'Mister, can I help?' The first daydreams of seducing luscious brown maidens evaporated and became a myth – there was simply no time – and Barry, unaccustomed to long hours and facing the elements clad only in bathing trunks, withered before the unusually hot sun. The first few days were spent in the tortured tensions of sunburn, forcing him to work in Wellington boots and covered like a veiled woman. He would return eagerly to the shady house at nightfall, as if it was a balm. We sympathised with consolatory hints, Jane especially, delighted with a case of what she kept referring to officiously as 'first degree burns' as she readied herself for action, while Paula, with her professional knowledge of skincare, thought he must have been a fool to get sunburnt. But after the first harrowing days, with the agony of sunburn over, Barry emerged from his cocoon. The salmon-pink skin turned to a mellow earthy colour, his sex appeal increased and, with a hopeful Neapolitan song escaping from between his pure white teeth, he threw himself back into his job with gusto and enjoyed it.

Jane, conspicuously bound up in household affairs, especially gloried in the weekend, and the added cast with which to play. She had a general air of idleness that allowed her to wander freely without fear of disturbing a masterpiece in progress, a musical problem, or just a tired breadwinner. Her submission to Bohemia, her thirst for appeal, and subsequent wanderings into entirely new fields which had thrown her into that intangible mix-up of theatrical emotions, sorted itself out – at least temporarily – by the exciting presence of Gerald and his flirtatious, attentive remarks, which she felt placed her undoubtedly on the attractive planes of the other women. She no longer felt undesirable or unwanted; she no longer had to pretend – that was the important psychological issue – and having bordered on neurotic extremes in all directions to attract attention, she fell now into a contented middle path of liberalism and accepted graciously the fact that had been hidden for so long – that she was a queen among women!

Gerald had certainly left his mark, I mused, watching Jane; gloriously happy now in the illusion of herself as the combination of Salome and a nightingale, dropping her seven veils calmly as she danced with blithe heart through the week to the crowning two days, her first in this new role – a kindred spirit of pride to that of Mr Budden. She was naturally drawn to the parts of the house which, in her opinion, needed her most. She would have liked it to be Edward's den, but his place was impeccable and Olwen and I were already on the alert to solve any little problems that might crop up there. Barry had escaped, a bounding figure of physical good health. Getting over her first horror of Mr Budden, Jane confided to me that she felt there was *need* there but that the man resented help with a coarse indifference.

So it was Roger who carried the can of hygienic reform, as he sat back contented and unashamed in his own sort of mess and awaited, with male impatience, the salubrious attentions of his Maltese maiden in her free time. It was very apparent that Magda was losing the gaiety that springs from a contented love, souring at the persistent necessity to keep a watchful eye on his possible infidelity. She sensed a new indifference, the first signs of boredom, and was unable to find a remedy to thwart it. I awoke fully to the realisation that the buxom creature was a delicate mechanism of dangerous sensitivity, and what I had shortsightedly accepted for strength in the mould of a strong body, was quite illusionary. Temper lay dormant, for a woman in love is a vulnerable thing, I reminded myself in sudden fright.

Like Jane, I too was drawn to this vibrant setting, as usual for different reasons, especially liking the weekends, feeling the relaxing quality of normally busy men sitting back to enjoy trivialities. But, unlike the perfect Jane, whose major part of life had been spent as a symbol of princely cleanliness walking austere hospital wards, the unmade beds and singular, identifiable, heavy smell of male bodies was as undisturbing to me as a light breeze. I listened for the first time to pure Negro jazz, longing to assimilate the sounds, which, to my unaccustomed and inexperienced ear, were a hotchpotch of discords; a feat which would draw me inevitably closer to our musicians' world which occupied most of my mind, one way or another.

So it was that I now found myself, this weekend, also with the added displeasure of a cage of chattering monkeys in the garage which fought and flourished in disharmony. A dispirited female face had appeared over the wall more than once, at a spot nearest the offence, to whine a complaint, while on the other side Mrs Briggs stalked, handkerchief already to her nose in an exaggerated way, threatening loudly to call in the health authorities and the police. I turned a stubborn back, for I was getting a little hardened: the mice were there to stay, for the moment anyway, until I could persuade Nelson, without an exaggerated fuss, towards a healthier appreciation of life. However, I did decide to remove the monkeys away from the pained eyes of Lady Booth to the sanctuary of the summerhouse, a dome-shaped structure in the seclusion of the back garden, where the wall rose to an insurmountable six feet and divided us firmly.

Faced with all these problems at sunrise on Saturday morning, I naturally went in early search of Edward. I often leaned on him in times of indecision, for his constant good humour was an invaluable asset in these hectic days. He was my Father confessor; his time never too precious to waste, his advice freely given and seldom taken. In fact, as I grew to know him, I blessed his lack of artistic temperament and loved, without passion, his easy laugh and fertile imagination which turned most situations into absurd comedy.

Knocking without reserve, I joined my friends, for the smell of breakfast cooking told me that at least Edward was up. He was, as usual, hovering over a large frying pan, while Olwen languished, determined to spin out every moment in the large divan. Garlic, coffee, beans, bacon, clung fragrantly about the room and turned my stomach to a niggling void.

'Driven to this by an early hunger,' Edward greeted me cheerfully, pointing to a trail of blue smoke.

I apologised for my intrusion and explained briefly about the wails of my neighbour, who was this morning not only complaining about the strange noises in the garage, but also about 'cruelty to animals, pining in a cage for want of fresh air and freedom.'

Edward, undishevelled even at this early hour, appeared not to have understood the dire significance of my tale, as he waved a fat-laden fork towards the mantelpiece. 'Look at the drawing your firstborn did of me – it's good, you know. Look at the hands. My teaching must be excellent,' he pronounced, without vanity. Pleasure lifted his narrow face to exalted heights.

I examined the sketch. It was a lively image in rough pencil, and the likeness was remarkable: even the hands were Edward's, delicate and tapering, and I found myself suffused with pure motherly pride. I had given birth to a genius! What a comforting thought amidst my other worries. But this was not the best moment to dwell on the cleverness of my offspring; with neighbourly war so close I left the subject unwillingly, and turned back to Edward to repeat my suggestion, if necessary with embellishments, for depositing the monkeys in the summerhouse.

I saw with relief that, after all, Edward was now pondering the question in his own way: in a curious huddled posture, a life-like emulation of a ruffled parrot. He emerged a few moments later into the respectful silence awaiting him, in complete agreement that something must be done to quell the riot brewing, and the summerhouse seemed the only tangible answer.

Satisfied at my first recruit (Olwen lay in non-committal silence), I departed to enlist Nelson, my children and anyone else who might like to spend an energetic few hours. By mid-morning the house was, as usual, divided into two parties: those that were otherwise occupied or disinclined for exercise, and the rest who welcomed the venture, treating it as an unusual sort of social occasion.

Roger, a still-healing scar across his jowl, firmly entrenched in freshly-laundered orange pyjamas (delivered by the hand of Jane with a lecture), refused to budge on the grounds, he said, of not being able to 'leave the strange and comforting feel of fresh laundry'. There must be something in what Jane preached after all! I hoped fervently that Magda would not, on her arrival, sense the active presence of another woman's hand, and attack the irritation in a female brawl, to weep on my shoulder later and distract me from my work.

Blanche and Judy, returning home languid and heavy-eyed, yet trim in starched blue and white, after a night of silent watchful attendance on the sick, involved themselves readily, following Nelson closely down the path with merry teasings. This, I could see, immediately threw him into a dither of indecision as to which role he should play – the gay philanderer, strong man, or comic. Deciding on the role of strong man, he proceeded to show off. He organised and reorganised the small throng that gathered, until his mother, crocheting a square white object, left her seat in the bay window directly above ours and, appearing round the side of the house, threatened to 'give 'im one in the lug 'ole', a threat which had already been preceded by one from Mr Budden, who had realised in the cold hours of his first sleepless night that the once gloried-in arrival of a new baby now threatened his whole way of life, and he was in an unhealthy temper, refusing to co-operate in any way. He had spent a night of unaccustomed torture, he moaned, to receive a sympathetic look from Jane, disturbed by kittenish whimperings which not even the dairy quality of his wife's bosom could silence. His Saturday morning was disorganised, too, for lack of attention, and the swish of never-ending nappies being washed had forced his nerves to the vibrating pitch of stretched elastic.

Mr Budden's lack of charm was compensated for by Olwen, having second thoughts and leaping from the elegance of green sheets to join us. The sound of the other women's hilarious giggles, obviously enjoying the upheaval of one of Mr Budden's tantrums, had been too much for her and she was now determined to miss nothing.

Jane had arrived for the same reason – to miss nothing – though refusing to be contaminated by something that might be infectious. She stayed at a safe distance to weather the spectacle, while explaining to us in the voice of a professional guide the first, second and third degree monkey bite. The cure was an injection the size of a garden syringe, which made even Nelson turn green and provoked the teasing scorn of the older male members, with a hail of unusual comment from Andy, who was watching from the upstairs window with the orange-clad figure. Andy seldom passed a dogmatic opinion unless it was jazz, which sometimes provided an uneasy thought on what did stir behind the shy front. Now I wondered critically why he wasn't helping, but Nelson jeered back good-humouredly, for he loved Andy like a brother.

But strangely enough it was Paula, loathing monkeys and postponing her journey to the beach, who won the real laurels for self-sacrifice. Now, bravely determined to do her share, attractive in black silk jeans and corded turquoise blouse, baubles dangling from her slim wrists, her bright hair held back with a gold band, she stood shoulder to shoulder with Edward, their red heads matching in the strong sunlight for a brief moment. Brief, because Nelson's foot landed heavily on a dainty gold sandal while a fat hand crushed a delicate one, and she went limping, with a ladylike curse, to a safer place between the nurses.

I found myself quickly shuffled between Nelson and Edward. The odour of monkeys, garlic and peppermint bull's eyes swept me into a feat of breath-holding. The possibility of Nelson's twelve stone landing on my foot was not a pleasant one as I told him to 'bloody well watch himself', while Edward wandered irrelevantly into a plan no one understood and explained how monkeys were related to man in a series of curious bone structures, and man to God, until he was silenced by a deliberately insulting insinuation on the trumpet by Roger. We stumbled on our long march across the lawn to the summerhouse. No one thought of blaming Gerald!

An independent figure, Andy joined us at this late moment, and sent the females jostling like jockeys for position. Again I was stuck, firm between Nelson's girth and Edward's wiry appeal: there was nothing I could do to compete with the rest for the honour of placing my hands against those of the most fascinating member of the household. Meanwhile the inmates of our burden rivalled the noise of the trumpet and disturbed Johnny, turning his attention away from the back lavatory where, since the arrival of the first mouse, he had sat drooling. He now followed us in a hysterical state of friendly suspicion. Mrs Briggs, hearing the commotion, was again with her nose to the ground. Having established the worst, we heard her terrified but triumphant shout: 'Lord have mercy on us! Mister, come quick, wild beasts in our midst! It's them bo'emes again, something's got to be done about it.'

'Just a few tame little animals, aren't they, Edward?' I remarked in a loud voice, feeling some sort of retaliation was necessary from our side. Edward, winded with a blow from my elbow, grim-faced made no answer, but there was a chorus of different opinions that had not been called for . . .

Though I agreed with Mrs Briggs in some ways – the smells from the back lavatory, for instance – I could not agree with her attitude towards 'bo'emes', or monkeys, and all my devotion to my brother and my instincts as an animal lover and my love of the unconventional, came rushing to the surface to defend the liberty of free-thinking people and of (as they appeared to me now) innocent, sweet-smelling, creatures, against the barrage of bigoted, narrow-minded, neighbour's criticism.

Unheeding, I carried out my plan to the bitter end and the last gasping, sweaty, lodger went in for refreshment, leaving Nelson, Johnny and me together.

Nelson, I suspected by his expression, had reached a moment of decision and was about to turn over a new leaf. I had heard this morning the first breath of discontent, a whisper to a female ear, that breeding mice was not, unfortunately, just a question of filling his and the children's pockets with spare cash, and he was now getting a little bored with the work involved; the feeding and cleaning were taking up more and more of his precious time. In this weak moment, while still heady with perfume and the close presence of its wearers, he had given a vague promise, open to a change of heart. I prayed silently beside him that he might bring the smelly saga to a close and call a truce with Mrs Briggs – if it was not too late.

Sitting now on his large behind, long after the others had gone, in a forlorn gesture of energies spent, Nelson examined the monkeys with puckered interest that could border on the criminal side, I knew, if left to ferment. Announcing at last, a little pathetically, conscious of my Gestapo vigilance, that a change would do him good, he subsided into a broody silence.

'What change?' I was quick to ask, ever suspicious, tying wire netting firmly across the summerhouse with a final knot. But Nelson was not in the mood to discuss his innermost thoughts today. Getting up and leaving a large portion of flattened grass behind him, he whistled for his mates, climbing the pear tree, and whooped off noisily to meet Gordon, who was roaring to a standstill with a series of loud revs – sounding remarkably cheerful for one who had just attended a funeral. I followed Nelson past the new baby, snoring, red as a poisonous toadstool and the image of its father, the pram shining with newness on its great wheels, collecting dust. Mrs Williams, polishing her windows with a gentle rotary movement, was now more interested in the noisy arrival. Ready to commiserate at the loss of a dear one, her face was composed in the abject lines of mourning.

Gordon emerged from the floor of his car, disguised as a racy type in checked cap and twirly striped scarf of abnormal length. I expressed our regret at the death of his father and the depression he must be suffering, in which I was joined by Mrs Williams in the monotonous tones of condolence. He shook off his sorrows manfully, unwinding his long scarf and letting it droop like a giant moustache as he confided, not without a certain show of good spirits I noticed, that he was now a man of means, having been left a considerable amount of money, and that loathingly he would have to drag himself away from his dream girl and my happy house to organise his new-found estate – it was extraordinary what a taste of money could do!

I felt a momentary pang: so I was to lose my first lodger, just when things were getting settled – it was an ill wind. But I covered my feelings and flew into a flutter of excitement at Gordon's lucky break. In our house good news spread as quickly as bad, and Nelson, master of repetition, added a bit here and there to give himself more scope, ending finally with a death by a rival band and had Gordon being left the Taj Mahal (he had lately been introduced to the Far East by the pages of his latest comic). Gordon had returned with a bag of diamonds and in his opinion he would have better luck with women in future, as he was now second to none. This yarn was seconded only by Nicholas, for by the time he heard and delivered the story Nelson's father was also dead and Nelson was also the proud owner of a fabulous jewel, so it was best to keep in with him.

Mr Budden, nerves somewhat restored by a couple of pints of beer, deigned to listen to Nelson's fabrications, with a condescending sneer marking his face, but when the true significance of the yarn came to light – a legacy for Gordon – he could bear it no longer. His political instincts rose to a fury. Illuminating his feeling with good old English stock phrases, and jealously disapproving of what he considered to be a typical conservative move by the moneyed classes, he sullenly retired, refusing to be drawn any further into the general happy excitement at Gordon's good fortune. He silenced his wife's congratulations with a look, especially reserved to destroy pleasure, as, in temporary relief from migraine and nappy washing, she sipped a cup of tea with

Margo Durrell

Gerald Durrell

Leslie, Mrs Durrell and Gerald

Leslie Durrell and
his wife, Doris

The front of Number 51

Margo in the garden of Number 51

Margo, Nicholas, Gerry, and Gerald in front of Number 51 with some of her lodgers

Nicholas and Gerry with Johnny on the beach at Bournemouth

Margo with Johnny

Margo and the nurses

The jazz
musicians

Margo, Nicholas, Gerry and
the musicians

Chumley, one of Gerald's escaping monkeys

Chumley

Margo partying with two of her lodgers

Gerald, his wife Jacqui and his secretary Sophie in the top flat of Number 51

Gerald and Jacqui in the garden of Number 51

Margo with her sons, Nicholas and Gerry

smacking relish and showed pleasure at such a bit of luck. For she had a kind heart.

Persistent thoughts of the small back room reminded me that Roger and Andy were again engrossed in their own business and had probably not heard Gordon's return or the glad news. The relaxed voices, discussing devotedly the attributes of a lately deceased jazz musician, deadened my quiet knock and I wondered if I should hint disparagingly about the musical sounds that rocked the place on many occasions. Once again I sadly felt that it was too late: Aunt Patience's notices, the coward's way out, lay untouched. It was increasingly obvious that I was never going to be the indifferent, dominating landlady, a hidden threat, but one of them – even to my cost!

The family were right: a landlady is born, not made. My dream of wealth accumulating in the bank was forgotten as I came face to face with reality, opening the door and stepping inside, between unwashed coffee mugs and forgotten crockery. I smiled across a small room where two pairs of eyes met mine inquiringly and voices drifted to a standstill, to echo the dejected air of the abandoned easel, its canvas incomplete at its feet. Roger was in his cold period; reflective blues sighed at me depressingly from all his latest paintings, while their master, in orange pyjamas, sat cross-legged, cleaning his nails with a toothpick. I turned from the coldness, remembering Edward's warm hues: my yellow and pink giant; the gin bottle twinkling in the living shadow of red roses. No wonder Roger behaved as though he was permanently in labour. I turned to examine the face, smouldering even in repose: a black growth struggled to thrive on his smooth skin. He lived a full life on a small grant, and it was remarkable that he managed to scrape his share of the rent together and pay me regularly, I thought with some compassion, at the same time blurting out that Gordon had returned with some marvellous news. Conscious of Andy's eyes upon me, I was oddly stirred to a nervous movement of stacking up the crockery that littered the floor. Magda's absence was always felt, for much to Roger's surprise she had failed to make her customary visit to attend to his wants, backing up Edward's conviction that the affair was well and truly rockbound.

'He's lost his virginity to a rich widow and married her!'

'Indulged in a new car!'

There were a series of derisive suggestions.

'No, he's been left a lot of money,' I said joyfully, as if I were the lucky one. I left out the colourful garnishings of Nelson.

'Just his luck,' Roger grimaced without rancour. 'It's always those sort of weedy-looking fellows that get the money. Why the hell doesn't someone die and leave me some?' he moaned, counting up his relatives in this noble category, and forgetting that he was a self-confessed communist.

'Don't be so callous,' I retorted, having already wished that Aunt Patience's death might mean my ultimate happiness, while Andy informed us that, die who might, his chances of a legacy were remote.

'No slave today?' I asked, deliberately innocent, knowing full well the answer and unable to resist the chance to goad Roger into a feeling that he was losing his grip. Roger feigned collapse with touching male helplessness – to those who knew no better.

'Well, you'll have to get off those pyjamas and get down to a spot of housework, won't you then?' I was one of those who knew better!

'There's always Jane,' Andy remarked indulgently, helping Roger out of a spot, aware of a certain amount of truthful sarcasm behind my remark.

'I don't intend to leave my pyjamas until tonight!' Roger revived to announce emphatically. 'I rather enjoy the cosiness created by my private Advance Laundry.'

'I'm sure Jane would be flattered to be likened to a laundry – has she seen you glowing in clear colours?'

'Of course! And we have her approval, haven't we?' and he winked at Andy, sharing a private thought in his entirely mournful way. 'But let's get back to Gordon. How much is it exactly – borrowable proportions?'

'I've no idea, I haven't liked to probe the exact amount – and I shouldn't go on what Nelson says, it multiplies every time he mentions it! And his intentions are criminal, I'm sure.'

'Without a doubt – his reactions are much the same as those of the rest of us.'

'He's a bugger that boy – why doesn't he go to school?'

'I wonder if it will make a new man of him? They say money does.' Roger stretched, feeling his body with loving indulgence.

'It's worked miracles already. There is a new

feeling of abandonment about him, and given time, who knows?' I answered.

'I need something to make a new man of me.' Roger was suddenly gloomy.

'A new woman, perhaps?' I suggested, exchanging a quick look with Andy, my nervousness melting to a mood of comforting composure.

Roger did not deign to discuss this question, preferring to linger on Gordon's welfare. 'He's never managed to pull that blonde in room one, and I've left the field wide open for him too – in pure brotherly love, of course.'

'Of course!'

'Perhaps the money behind him will give him the necessary confidence,' Andy was hopeful.

'If only he'd stop worrying about his piles and get on with it,' Roger spoke as if in the throes of acute melancholia and Gordon's failing affected him personally.

'It's not a question of money, or . . .' I stammered, bursting out laughing – though why someone else's piles should throw us into hilarious mirth it was hard to say, for the whole house had watched Gordon's wooing with friendly and sympathetic interest. 'Nelson says he will now,' I added, when the other two had stopped laughing, still grinning.

I could see that in spite of Andy's spontaneous laughter, he was slightly embarrassed at Roger's reference to a subject that was not normally discussed with such abandoned hilarity, and was struggling with silent mirth, mixed with a good righteous north country disapproval.

'You're a hopeless lot,' he growled, flushed, his eyes down and a grin breaking forth. 'Leave the lad's ailments to Jane and the Almighty. Is there nothing left to the imagination in this house?'

I took my punishment lightly. 'Almost nothing!' I flashed him a cheeky look, now thoroughly at home. Little did he know how he was discussed!

'I only mentioned the obnoxious,' Roger complained, 'because they are a constant stumbling block to the boy – the root of all evil so to speak – and should be remedied. And with so many nurses about us it's difficult not to talk like a doctor, anyway.'

'Your excuse for vulgarity is quite flimsy,' I said firmly, my mirth under control and naturally going over to Andy's side.

'I wonder if the lad's as dim as you all imagine. A lot of unnecessary din floats out of his room at times that's not all tea-making.'

Roger guffawed loudly. 'Bet you my last ten bob he's bloody Tory virgin, there you are! I've been robbed!' he wailed, fishing in his breast pocket and not finding his bet. 'If that thieving Nelson . . .'.

'It's up there, lad,' Andy indicated patiently to a nail embedded over the mantelshelf on which hung a scruffy note.

Roger looked relieved. 'Ten to one, he's a virgin. Is the bet on or isn't it?' he demanded roughly, all out for a bit of gambling, seeing Andy's awkward hesitation and scarlet face.

'It's not a fair bet,' Andy said stiffly. 'Must we crucify the boy with our intentions?'

Could Andy be a virgin? I thought guiltily, acutely conscious of his discomfort. Men usually boasted of their conquests, Andy never did. A new depth crept into my feelings. It somehow seemed an incredible thought and I wished we were on another subject – this one was suddenly too near and too acute.

'Enough,' I said hastily, 'the next religious maniac that comes to the front door I shall direct straight up here to aid you to a higher level of thought.'

'Oh, all right, if you two don't want the chance to do a little betting, it's off, I suppose.' Roger was disappointed. 'And I should welcome the chance of a religious discussion with an outsider,' he said, foxing my plans. 'It will be a change from Jane bleating of my reform. Do we get many coming to the door – you sound as if we do?'

'Jehovahs are constantly knocking to be let in; last Sunday I sent a battered-looking Mrs Williams to answer the call, to say "Madam is out". The women must have thought I ill-treated my servant as Mrs Williams looked as though the dog had played with her all night.'

'Was it a she, then?'

'Yes, young and beautiful.'

'In that case I am prepared to accept the challenge at the first opportunity.' Roger lay back.

'Edward says the last time he was in town a woman in a complete tennis outfit, a ball bag over her head, followed him shouting religious slogans. He said he was quite embarrassed by the exaggerated behaviour and it took some minutes to lose her in the crowds.' We all laughed again, this time at Edward's expense.

'Really, the place is getting full of cranks,' Roger remarked.

'It's hardly safe to leave the house. There's a slow revolution taking place in this town, you know. It's something in the manner of the French Revolution.'

'And there's an invasion from the North . . .' I looked at Andy.

'The nouveau riche, ugh!' Roger shuddered.

'Well, it's better this way,' I stated categorically. 'The other atmosphere of suburban refinement is slow strangulation. Can't think why my mother ever bought a house here.'

'Why did she?'

'Somebody told her the sun shone here more than anywhere else in England, and as we always seem to chase the sun. . . .' I shrugged.

'But why did you get this house?'

'On the advice of my Aunt Patience – an investment or something like that.'

'Well, let's drink to our mistake, and Gordon's millions,' Roger suggested heartily, producing a bottle from under his bed. 'And to what might possibly affect us all in the way of generous loans.'

Andy willingly produced some well-thumbed glasses, and we drank solemnly to Gordon, to his millions, to loans galore and the fine qualities of those who gave generously on death. Warmed to a glowing unconcern, I pointedly reminded Roger that, after all, he was a communist, which forced us all to swallow a round to Stalin. A plug for Attlee was Andy's choice and I, of course, drank to Churchill, to the scowling darkness of the opposition. Roger complained about the new baby's bawls, of Mrs Budden's untidy habit of littering the bathroom with nappies and of Fred Budden's domination.

'Marriage is death,' Roger announced with deep feeling. 'Men are martyred from the moment that small gold band goes into play. I should watch it, Andy; never get on that hook. And can you tell me,' he turned to me in an attitude of perplexity, 'just as a matter of interest, why women fall in love with you one way, and then immediately want to change you to a complete antithesis?'

'Human nature,' Andy reflected.

'Edward says you should look at a woman's mother before you marry her,' I quoted our bearded philosopher with confidence.

'He's right, the lack of that "look" certainly cost me a lot,' Roger threw himself easily into a gesture of despair.

'Aye, how we men have to suffer for a moment's folly,' Andy summed up the situation easily.

'Well, it doesn't seem to have burdened you, spiritually or otherwise,' I retorted bluntly, attacking Roger, irritated that Andy had not risen to my defence. Loyalty to my sex surged up, as I thought of Magda, and of the others left washed-up on the beach before the saga had been played here.

'I am just getting over it,' Roger confessed heavily, and untruthfully.

Men invariably pretended they were suffering acutely at women's hands, I thought with scorn, looking at Roger lying there, and Edward, too, could wear a crown of thorns at a moment's notice, though his seductive wife was the envy of most, and the slightest trace of neglect would send Fred Budden scowling for attention. It seemed in a man's world of suffering and self-sacrifice it was a physical necessity to magnify to vast proportions a simple mental or physical ache, to consolidate sympathy, and in our house, if it wasn't for the enduring likes of Jane, ready with a swab of sterilised lint and a cool hand, they would not survive – the poor dears! I turned the matter over sardonically. Andy's amused eyes had never left my face, as he listened to Roger's banter. He was healthy, considering the all-night jazz sessions and excessive drinking. The yellow and black shirt clung casually across his broad shoulders and was open to the waist and I noticed a pale shadow of hair across his chest. An invisible tide of friendship flowed between us, but I felt disappointed in him now.

'The men are right,' he murmured at last, weighing up the consequences, in his heavy Yorkshire voice that sent a flutter through me every time he spoke. He turned to me: 'Anyway, what do you know about life, born well-to-do, public school . . .' he spoke the words with a deep and bitter scorn. 'A useless southern butterfly, a capitalist!' he mocked seriously. I knew he meant it.

The knowledge sent me floundering. What did I know about life indeed, wasn't I struggling with it now? And how I hated the phrase 'well-to-do'. But I was no 'southern butterfly', no social glitterbird. I was of Irish descent, born in India, schooled in England, a traveller – I had even fulfilled myself as a woman. Who was he to try and judge me, an ignorant council school boy, brought up in a row of terraced houses in a grimy northern town, son of a struggling chemist? I attacked him, tearing my dream as if it was waste-paper. What had he done for redemption? Nothing! Trifling in several conventional careers, drawn back inevitably to his goddamn jazz, haunted by it; his background and childhood environment, dominated by Labour tendencies, threw him automatically into the bigoted political boat of Mr Budden and had been, as yet, an unseen barrier between us. Now it was seeping out like a canker. And how they hated my public school education, even in the merriest moment! It was an attitude I could do nothing about – we were born into different worlds, it was as simple, or as complicated, as that.

I turned away to Roger with inner frustration and despair, getting back to Gordon's fortune. 'You should have heard Mr Budden carrying on, all his Labour ballyhoo is roused.' I had a sudden desire to tantalise Andy into political argument and hurt him. 'I can't stand that class of bigoted, ignorant, uneducated, Labourising fool!' I did not know if there was such a word as 'Labourising', but I used it with confidence just the same. 'If he was left some money it would be a different story, I bet!' I ended a little bitterly, subsiding to prickly silence, knowing I was going too far.

Roger looked at me blankly, astonished, sensing that something else lurked behind my uncalled-for outburst. A slow flush had deepened the contours of Andy's rugged face. My anger melted at his vulnerable look to a surge of churning regret. 'I didn't really mean all that,' I said awkwardly, speaking directly to Andy, desperately trying to recapture the warming tide of a moment earlier. There was no reply.

His thoughtful condemnation pricked me to a sudden resentment. I was his landlady, however tattered, and no one was going to place me in the position of Magda. I turned away to the window, viewing the garden with an unusually critical eye.

'Where's Magda? Why hasn't she come?' I changed the subject with a casual enquiry, watching Nelson, who was explaining the finer points of the summerhouse as a zoological garden to Gordon, who held his nose and looked rather faint. The comic combination of the two figures forced me to smile and I thought callously that if Gordon fainted Nelson would probably rifle his pockets.

'All that boy needs is a tail and a pair of horns,' Roger criticised, as if reading my thoughts, leaving his bed and joining me at the window. Then he began to hum a little halfheartedly; he sensed that something had gone wrong between Andy and me but was not sure what.

'I wonder why she isn't coming?' I kept stubbornly puzzling on the question of Magda's absence (we all knew she never worked at weekends), feeling a comradeship with Roger now, and comforted by the fact that there was maybe another in the same boat of disapproval as myself. My eyes still followed Nelson, but thinking of Andy's dull refusal to accept my apology, I felt suddenly frighteningly empty.

'Me thinks the woman doth play with my affections,' Roger answered, seemingly unperturbed.

Silently I thought of Magda's tears and I dimmed still further at the memory of the argument and tried to concentrate on gardening. The still unpruned pear tree, twisting weirdly, reminded me of one of Edward's pirouettes, but it was the lawn, strongly resembling the shrublands of Africa, that seemed the immediate problem – perhaps Nelson could be bribed? The rubbish dump at the far end did not increase the beauty of the picture, and the children's old pram, lying squat and frog-like on the top, gave the whole thing a derelict air.

'Look at the sheer blueness of that mound,' Roger breathed, forgetting the problem with Magda quickly. I saw no blue, except the sky, and feeling a little annoyed over the question of his callous attitude towards the Maltese girl I refused to be drawn into an artistic appreciation of anything.

'I think I'll paint it this afternoon,' he went on, not waiting for my comment. 'If I may?'

I gave my consent readily, not knowing whether he was serious and not in the mood to find out.

'You paint the rubbish dump, and I'll join the lass downstairs,' Andy was suddenly behind me. 'I promised the girl I would mend her wireless.'

Although I was older, I suddenly felt young and defenceless. He took my shoulder and turned me gently towards him – I was forgiven.

'If you like,' I said airily, shaking myself free, regaining confidence on my reinstatement and I marched out, quaking inwardly but outwardly five feet of feigned nonchalance – my aunt would have been proud of me.

Chapter Nine

Into this inglorious battlefield of human conflicts came the crusaders, my aunts. The scene was set, not by the soft waftings of chamber music to a garden's reply of tender rose blooms, but by a disgruntled Mr Budden, sauntering his way to the dustbins with a bucket of garbage and empty milk bottles, while an air of bustling merriment filled the place. For Edward's suggestions of a farewell party as a tribute to Gordon had brought cries of approval and put the womenfolk into a pantomime of preening as new dresses became the talk of the day.

I was doing just this, posed before the only long mirror in my part of the house and examining myself for indolent bulges. Swathed in a hectic combination of candy stripes – a petticoat of patriotic colours, the skirt a mass of tucks and lace – pirouetted as my fancy took me to see the effect it would create under a dress, while giving a running commentary on my progress to Andy. He was squatting earthily in the middle of the drawing-room floor, busy disembowelling the wireless set while listening to me with divided attention, for Nelson was also calling to be noticed. He was established, king-like, in the bay window in Mother's usual position, even to the curtain, discreetly pulled in places to allow light and observation but not the unwanted attention of a passer-by. He was instructing the children in a game of crap. I was unprepared for the knock, the door opening and – posed in the attitude of a Giles cartoon – the visitors.

Being quick of action in a crisis, I threw myself out of the already open door and into their midst. My first thought was to stop an entry into the den of vice where dice were being thrown with the obvious hand of experience and an unforgivable northerner, cross-legged and completely at home, would be the immediate target for criticism. I remembered, too, that Nelson's mother, crochet completed, was doing her weekly wash and over-large garments were beginning to fill two lines – untidily – while, unperturbed, a slippered and pyjamaed figure, beside a fertile mound of suggestive relics, filled in his lonely hours, daubing blue paint across a canvas with a lazy eye, swigging at a beer bottle and delivering an occasional threatening grunt towards the summerhouse noises.

'Darling child, there you are,' my aunt Patience sang out, complete with Pussy dangling from under her arm. I found myself enfolded in cat, perfume and bags as I welcomed her with inward panic.

Extracting myself, I turned expectantly to receive the usual kisses, but I was clipped to a silent surprise by a glare of rapt attention and an expression of bristling disapproval, as Great Aunt Sarah's eyes followed my bare shoulders (now tattooed by goose pimples), traipsed across a red, white and blue bosom – which Edward had remarked was 'in its prime' but I had wished the reflection had come from Andy – down to a mass of seductive frills and waving lace about my knees, ending with a dangerous pair of red Turkish slippers encased in sequins, giving me the tinge of a fourth-rate Carmen Miranda.

There was no time to fumble for modesty if I was to save the situation and I threw myself across the open door on my right as if holding back a football crowd. Nelson, lifting his eyes from the table, was chanting loudly for a double six: he noted my agonised posture, sensed a crisis and, being a tactful soul at times – if it was to his advantage – scraped up the pool in a fat, hot hand and propelled himself sideways through the window, leaving his two compatriots screaming for their share.

'I thought I saw a strange-looking fat boy,' said my aunt Patience puzzled, as she pushed past me into the room.

There was no time to answer, because Pussy, so far dangling blissfully relaxed, spotted Johnny reclining in the best chair and suddenly became rigid, her claws streaking out wickedly in a jealous urge to fight, while I was only conscious that Great Aunt Sarah, inattentive to any other drama that might be going on, had kept her beady eye on my slip in a long unblinking stare.

'A most scandalous dress! Whatever is the child thinking about?' came her comment at last, as movement was restored amidst the hissing and snarling and the soothing cries of animal-lovers trying to restore order to their pets. 'Where are my spectacles?' she demanded, trying to disentangle her leashes and looking hopefully down at the bulging string bag.

Aunt Patience took no notice of her mother, as she pacified the furious bundle in her arms and commented on her entry, 'the gardener showed me in, dear. A common sort of man, and improperly clad too – red-faced, looks as though he drinks,' she added disapprovingly. 'He was rummaging about the dustbins, looting no doubt, and judging by the state of the front garden, he is no good at his job. Give him notice,' she advised imperiously, 'you cannot afford to be slack with the working classes.'

I thought of the back garden and my heart sank. I thought of the gardener, the blustering, blundering Mr Budden, and I feared now the consequences of my letting. Great Aunt Sarah, mesmerised, kept to her own point impatiently. 'Margo's going about in scantily clad dress, almost naked in fact; tempting fate, I say. Patience darling, find me my spectacles,' she ordered, 'I must take a better look.'

'It's not a dress,' I said weakly, attempting to justify myself. 'It's a slip. I was just – um – ' How could I explain the petticoat – or the manly figure as yet unnoticed, practically at my feet.

But my elderly relative, firm in her belief that I was caught in the act of flaunting myself in a regalia of sin, would not let the matter rest. Tossing aside my plaintive pleas she attacked me. 'There is nothing worse than to see immodesty in a young woman! May God guide this child before the police get her,' she added piously.

'Shut up, mummy, do. Margo will get out of that ridiculous apparel in a minute.' Aunt Patience, who was always unpredictable, seemed for the moment to be unperturbed by my state of dress. She was busy examining the scene about her with a critical but not unfriendly eye. Finally her gaze fell on Andy, who, with the intrusion, was discreetly collecting up, in his typical slow movement, the debris that was once my wireless.

'Ah, I see you are having a wireless fixed. A good firm of electricians, I trust, dear?' She gave him one of her small patronising smiles, especially reserved for tradespeople.

A piercing whistle, obviously intended to attract, made us all look outside.

'Men whistling at her, too. It's outrageous . . .' Great Aunt grumbled distractedly, setting herself down in lines of unfriendly stiffness. I ignored the Nelson call in a flustered moment of indecisive panic. Aunt Patience's remarks challenged my loyalty to Andy and at this moment I was unable to cope with the delicate situation. My aunt, I knew, would abhor him – it was a dismal and foregone conclusion. Watching him with pleading eyes, and feeling foolish in the gaudy petticoat and degenerate slippers, I mumbled something about the best firm in town and dismissed him callously, turning to the children who were waiting impatiently for justice to be served on Nelson. I called them forward for inspection with the usual glare of silent warning. I never saw Andy go. . . .

They came with reluctance, sensing that discipline was not far off, now anxious to heed the strident call of Nelson's signal: Johnny had also heard the call. Glad to leave the chair where he was sitting in nervy misery, he tore past us and leapt through the window to freedom, while the visiting Bedlingtons, the victory theirs, sprang to fill the vacancy.

The room, a mixture of gay colours and tempting divans, contrasted crudely with the respectable aura of Kensington. Great Aunt Sarah, portrayed as a misfit by a red divan and clustered cushions that spoke of Roman orgies, was rummaging frantically in the string bag: at last she lifted her head triumphantly and held up a pair of steel-rimmed spectacles. 'Ah, there they are,' she said with pleasure. 'I knew I had them,' and placing them above her aristocratic nostrils she reviewed the situation again fiercely, to another silencing remark from her daughter, now busy wooing my offsprings.

'Dear little souls,' Aunt Patience beamed, throwing out a pair of scented arms towards them as they sidled past to attempted freedom.

'Yes, aren't they?' I agreed hastily, with another threatening look in their direction, while I felt with disquiet the mesmerised eyes behind the steel glued to me.

The boys, forced to stop, greeted the visitors with pure hypocritical shyness and childish sweetness.

'Being good boys, and helping your mother?' Aunt Patience suggested lovingly. They nodded together shyly, ignoring the open sweet-scented arms waiting to engulf them. 'And doing well at school?' she asked brightly, dropping her outstretched arms. Two heads nodded again. Aunt Patience, working on the assumption that children can be bought, took two dim pennies out of her giant handbag and gave them one each.

'There, darling boys, buy yourselves something nice – but not dangerous, mind,' she added, playful as a young kitten.

There was a curious glint in both eyes as they took the small offering; I noticed it with increasing alarm.

'Ma's got a pansy in the house – so Uncle Leslie said,' Gerry remarked suddenly, softening towards his aunt, examining the penny carefully for fraud.

'A pansy, how lovely, my favourite flower,' Aunt Patience beamed. 'That's one thing I must say in Leslie's favour, he's got green fingers.'

'And a foreign woman, too,' Nicholas, encouraged by his brother's confidences, added, testing his penny in a similar way in a completely brotherly reaction. 'It's all right, Gerry,' he remarked, removing the coin from between his teeth, 'it's a good one,' and he proceeded to paint a further picture of my residents with chirpy confidence. 'There's a painter, and there's a mucky woman with frizzy hair. Nelson says Roger's the most unfaithful man next door to his Pa that he knows.'

'What's that darling boy saying?' Great Aunt Sarah asked, leaving the subject of my dress and bending forward to hear better. She was almost stone deaf.

'And Ma was telling lies – you know, that man was no wireless-mender.'

Aunt Patience gave me a quick searching look. So far she had listened to the children with frank disbelief. I looked back blankly.

'. . . and Nelson says he's fallen for Ma, he

reckons something is going on, or will be soon.' (Murder will be done, I thought angrily.)

'What's that? Speak up!' Great Aunt Sarah cried. 'I can't hear a word. Is there no elocution taught in the schools of today?'

Fortunately Pussy, leaping away from the soft bosom to scratch herself, decided to be sick over the carpet with a throttling noise that caused a much-needed distracting element.

'The poor darling creature's been sick,' Aunt Patience wailed, forgetting the subject under discussion.

'I'm not surprised in a dress like that,' Great Aunt thundered. 'Probably pneumonia,' she added, callously determined on my fate as, blessing Pussy's unhealthy stomach, I tore off to get a cloth, calling for the children to follow from between clenched teeth.

'Go down the garden and stay there, and take Nelson, and don't start the monkeys chattering,' I hissed, shutting the back door firmly behind them. I turned and rushed to the bathroom, tore off my petticoat and threw it to the ground. I'll never wear that thing again, I thought, kicking it aside and struggling into a sober black dress hanging on the door. Not only had I presented myself as a bawdy Jezebel and probably lost any money that might have been left to me in the event of death, but I had lost Andy too. I moaned silently, distressed at having proved myself to be a person without loyalty – and so soon after we had buried our differences.

Collecting up a large cloth, a bowl of water and a bottle of disinfectant, I returned to the scene of chaos to redeem the situation if possible.

Aunt Patience was petting Pussy gingerly: the cat gazed suspiciously about her with narrow, sick eyes.

'Dear, dear, Pussy,' I said sweetly.

'Do you think she needs a hot-water bottle?' her guardian asked, anxiously protective.

'A decent dress is what she needs,' Great Aunt Sarah said firmly, back to a mood of destructive criticism.

'I shouldn't think so,' I answered the first question, as I bent over the steaming mass without a tremor; the rearing of babies, and being schooled by a zoological brother had robbed me of a sensitive stomach. My only hope lay in keeping my aunt talking briskly about Pussy's health but aunt, satisfied that Pussy was not running a temperature or ready for the little plot at the bottom of her walled garden, turned her attention back to me. 'What were the children saying?' she asked, a little confused now, stroking the animal's head and reorganising it on her lap.

'They love to tell stories,' I said innocently. 'You know, *Arabian Nights* stuff.' I dismissed them with a merry little laugh.

'Really, dear?' Aunt was immediately bright with interest. 'Perhaps they will be writers, and a credit to the whole family.'

'Yes, perhaps,' I agreed thoughtfully, and sprinkled Dettol about the carpet. 'Are you staying long?' I asked desperately.

'Only for the weekend, dear. We thought it would be such a nice surprise for you.'

'It is,' I said feebly.

'And now dear, take all that unmentionable stuff away, then come back and sit down; I want to know all about everything. Are the notices up? and who are your paying guests? and are you making money?'

'In a dress like that,' Great Aunt Sarah reminded us, 'she'll get no guests. Only . . .'

'Do be quiet, Mummy, business first and other things after.'

'But you must tell her, Patience dear' – she insisted as though my whole future depended on this one item.

'Tell her what?' her daughter asked impatiently, anxious to get to the more important subject of my finances.

'About the dress, the other dress. Margo must *not* be allowed to go about like a Nell Gwynne.'

'I really think the old lady is going off her rocker,' Aunt Patience remarked to me aside, ignoring her mother and seemingly unperturbed by this possible mental condition, showing all the signs of going into a remarkably good mood.

It was a purely Nelson-like reflection, and the unexpected struck me as funny. My floundering spirits rose a little against the still nagging doubts of Andy's disgust. I patted her hand fondly, with sincere promises of future modesty, inquiring tentatively where they were going to stay.

'An hotel. A good family hotel, with good solid plain food,' she went on. 'We motored down quite pleasantly with only one incident. An ill-bred monster backed into my front mudguard. I've taken his name and address and will sue him.'

I smiled tolerantly. 'Good for you,' I said, and wondered what news I could possibly tell her.

Great Aunt Sarah, reassured by my contrite promises, sank back, quiet at last; her age was telling on her, I realised with sudden pity, for she was indulging more and more in refreshing snoozes, yet the ageless skin belied my thoughts, as I inspected the recumbent figure, while my mind completed a mental list of my lodgers, wondering who I could exhibit at this precise moment.

Roger perhaps, with his cultured voice; he was after all reputed to be the illegitimate child of a Lord and a Cochrane girl, and I felt that the title outweighed the facts – there was no need for my aunt to know every detail. His appearance was against him though; she would never appreciate the unwashed look, and those pyjamas would have to be changed. Nelson and his mother were out of the question; so was Edward. He would undoubtedly be dismissed as 'one of those'. Paula and Barry, officer class, with their perfect diction would pass – but they were still at the beach. Jane's standing as a nurse would hold her in good stead, they could talk about kidneys: Aunt loved to talk about her kidneys, only one of which worked as far as I could gather. Gordon too, walking with a new dignity now that he had gained considerable prestige with his inheritance, would certainly impress my aunt if only in a purely business field; she would no doubt be delighted to advise him on how to invest his money. I could present him as 'the fertile seeds of virtue', of an aging C. of E. parson, or a Canon perhaps, or we might rise to Bishop. But he, like Roger, would have to go through a soap and water process first. Judy and Blanche, though ladylike, were too openly glamorous and would probably be suspected harlots at once. They were most likely in a state of in-between dress anyway, which would, without doubt, send Great Aunt Sarah into another storm.

'There's that fat boy,' Aunt Patience interrupted, pointing towards the garden.

'Really?' I said, as if the sight of a fat boy was something unusual. 'I wonder who he is?' I remarked, going to the window. 'Go away and stay away,' I hissed softly, 'and take that "sale" notice down too, quickly, before it is noticed.'

Nelson dropped back heavily and left without argument. He knew I meant it. I pulled *The Times* and *Good Housekeeping* into view, thankful that Edward's porn photos were safely locked in his bottom drawer – he had refused me permission to destroy them. Having organised a cup of tea, and with my aunts busy refreshing themselves, I slunk away for a few moments to bring my rent books up-to-date and place the notices Aunt had supplied in strategic positions, just in case they wandered. Feeling that I now had everything in hand, I sped through the house looking for Gordon, Jane, those that could show themselves, and warn with tactful kindness those who were forced to remain obscure.

Edward was temporarily and safely occupied, I thought thankfully, my ear to the door. 'As I was saying,' came his drawling voice, unusually loud, 'the general theory is that if you mix that blue you're swilling up with yellow ochre, you'll get that bilious stalemate you have produced; so I can't possibly agree about the degree of blues felt by vision – stand still do – no the other arm a little higher . . .' 'Mind the pins,' – that was Olwen. 'Do you want me to fit you or don't you, imbecile woman?'

It was obvious that Olwen suffered for a perfect fit, and that he and Roger were discussing art separated by the length of the garden. I tiptoed away and mounted the stairs. I'd never counted them before but I did so now with malice aforethought, hoping my relatives would balk at such a feat after a day of steaming car travel. I passed my hand over a thin trail of dust and wiped it clean, and bumped into Mrs Williams looking as though she had just been rescued from drowning.

'That Nelson,' she said, ''e's a mucky one,' and I watched her depart to the garden, a trail of water in her wake. The usual scathing tones of Mr Budden contradicting his wife on some trivial point came from behind his closed door. 'Odious man,' I said aloud, passing on by Barry and Paula's silent room. The girls, tired but unwilling to go to bed, were twittering together, still enjoying the news of Gordon's fortune and discussing the best ways to spend it and which dresses heightened their sex appeal. I gave them a quick summary and warning, and we giggled together like schoolgirls.

Gordon was nowhere in sight, where was he? Perhaps in with Andy? I began to worry as I made for the next door, and knocked timidly; the door of the smallest room where so many world problems were thrashed to a conclusion at all hours of the day or night. Andy was lying back on the wide divan, the covers ruffled beneath him, blowing pensive smoke rings. The shell of a wireless waited attention beside him and there was an unusual air of subdued inaction about the place. From outside floated in the voice of Edward,

Roger and the tired subservient pipings of Mrs Williams.

'My, that's ever so nice, Mr Rogers, you've really got that exact like – even to the wheels being damaged – 'asn't 'e, Mr Edward,' she called. 'Isn't 'e clever!'

And Edward saying: 'But you should just see my wine, it's coming on nicely now, I do believe. Try some. I must ring Mrs Durrell and tell her' – sounding like Mr Beetle.

Then Olwen's, 'Yes that's better shorter there – it droops a little.'

And Mr Briggs being called in from his garden to a cup of tea. Thank God the monkeys seemed less noisy.

I felt my intrusion keenly: who was I to plead for mercy, I asked myself anxiously, searching the dejected face. Was he irrevocably lost by my easy lie, with a disloyalty that was unforgivable. I felt a moment of pain at the bare expression before me, a sense of loss; the next instant I was on my knees pleading shamelessly for forgiveness, and we were clinging together kissing for the first time.

'I'm sorry,' I moaned helplessly. 'I wouldn't hurt you for anything, not really,' I ended lamely. 'It's just that. . . .' How could anyone explain their aunts?

'It's all right lass, don't fret. I understand,' the voice was husky with emotion.

'How can you be so generous?' I asked wonderingly; the soft touch of his forgiveness obliterated everything else.

I heard Nelson's voice telling the entire back garden that I had visitors of no real value. I rose quickly. Was I mad? With Aunt Patience so near, a breathing menace down my neck. 'I must go,' I said feverishly, but wishing desperately to prolong these precious moments, hastily stepping to the door.

'My,' came Mrs Williams' voice again, 'as green as green it looks, Mr Edward, proper strong.'

I turned. 'By the way, if Edward offers you some of his brew from under the kitchen table, don't take it. Mother thinks it's poison.' We both laughed at my warning in wobbling relief.

A wail of disgust from Olwen, and a sudden tirade from Edward on the deficiencies of the average woman's appreciation made me hesitate again in my flight. Then I closed the door and hurried away happily to the top of the house, convinced that I was capsizing fast and strangely, and frighteningly satisfied to do so.

I found Jane in an immaculate overall (her instrument of work) poring over both the renovation of a tattered net dress, embedded with the odd sequin, and a diet for Nelson who, she said, would die of a fatty heart before he was twenty if he didn't do something about it. She had come to this conclusion after hearing him breathe while helping to carry the monkeys. On the bed, splayed out in tired slumber, a compress on his head, lay Gordon.

'Rise!' I woke him unsympathetically. 'Rise, I need you. My rich aunts and party have arrived, and if you all don't want me to be out of their favour and consequently you lot turned out onto the streets like refugees,' I said, desperately exaggerating the picture, 'you had better titivate yourself, and come and be presented as the offspring of a celebrated clergyman.'

Gordon rose, grumbling at the disturbance, reminding me of his lucky windfall and that, in future, landladies presented no problem to him. But seeing that the situation was a delicate one, and feeling flattered that I had chosen him as one of my allies, he consented to co-operate; he treated himself to a hurried wash and followed Jane and me down to meet my visitors. Jane, as excited as a child, a picture of studied efficiency, said that she hoped I wasn't going to be so foolish as to produce the uncouth Mr Budden. I reassured her that he was already in the category of head gardener.

The next two hours were spent in a show of subterfuge and camouflage to a dogged pair of sightseers, who far from being too tired were determined to see everything. I murmured a series of untruths and half-truths as I steered them rapidly past the windows to the garden with a tell-tale view; past the door to the men's room discreetly closed ('the Guards, you know; related to the Duchess of Leeds, I believe. Just a trifle eccentric perhaps, but with such good breeding . . .'). And the vision of Andy smudged itself into a pose of a gentleman worthy of my aunts. Roger's background, grossly distorted, moved into an aroma of blue blood. 'Father's a peer, you know,' I murmured discreetly forgetting the Cochrane girl in a skirt of pink feathers.

'Yes, by Jove!' Gordon helped me on. A clean face glistening, oil-free hands and grey worsted suit gave him the true air of ecclesiastical heritage; then we would go back again to the subject of my Aunt Patience's perforated kidney – for it was not, as I had previously thought, a sole organ deprived of its mate and struggling to perform its duties, but something that by the time my aunt and Jane had examined it, had the appearance of a tin can heavily peppered with lead – until Great Aunt Sarah shouted: 'Stop, stop, Patience dear; you'll never sleep tonight,' and Aunt Patience, now thoroughly alarmed at her condition, despatched me for a jug of warm barley water.

Then, feeling that perhaps she had overtaxed her strength in the investigation of both my affairs and her organs, she decided to return early to the family hotel and rest; while inviting me to come later and join her for dinner, just managing to crawl to the telephone and check both dinner and price with the head waiter before she departed, followed by a disgruntled Great Aunt Sarah who was enjoying a nice little chat with Gordon about potted plants.

'Good old Jane,' I decided, waving a temporary farewell from the front gate, 'she really knew how to handle the situation, and the white overall over Roger's pyjamas was a very good and impressive move.'

'See you had visitors,' Mrs Briggs shouted, forgetting we were at war.

I answered coldly and went indoors to telephone Leslie and Mother to tell them that Aunt Patience was in the vicinity, to fill the boiler, feed the monkeys, coax the children to an early bed, and wait for nightfall, satisfied that the day's events had been no worse.

Then, as dusk blurred the image of our road

and storm clouds hung heavy in the sky to crown a brilliant day, I closed the door behind me and left the house to join my aunts in the dingy vaults of their hotel.

I had dressed to please my great aunt in a modest garment with no frills. A full black skirt scattered with Persian figures, topped by a severe black blouse – I was trying, if possible, to eradicate the picture of a fallen woman that my previous apparel had created. But an urgent sound made me turn hastily to acknowledge the call. Nelson's familiar bulk was in his darkened window and he was making frantic signs for me to return.

'What's cooking, Nelson?' I called up softly, retracing my steps a trifle, working on the assumption that it was better to find out now rather than later at a possible cost.

''Ere, I want to show yer something,' he whispered down.

'I haven't really time, Nelson, I'm going out to dinner at a posh hotel with my wealthy aunt – I'm late already,' I said, hoping to impress him with the importance of the occasion. He was supposed to be guarding the family fortunes in my absence; I imagined he took his duties very lightly.

'Ain't yer comin' up, this is *reely* important – it's a matter of life an' death. Yer'll be sorry if yer don't.'

'Oh, all right, but you'll have to be quick,' I heeded the warning and capitulated weakly (I always did with Nelson). I turned indoors to join him. Nelson met me at his door; the room behind was unlit. He blew a low expert whistle of approval from between his teeth.

'Cor, yer looking smashing,' he praised.

'Behave Nelson, do; have you forgotten your girl with the chubby legs?'

'Oh, 'er,' Nelson shrugged disparagingly. 'I'm trying a pair of thin legs this time,' and he guffawed.

'Where's your mother?'

'Wallowing in the bath like one of them sea creatures – but never mind 'er, this is more drastic. Follow me,' and tiptoeing across the room, he beckoned me to follow. 'Shush, don't yer make a sound,' he murmured as I hit my shin against a hard object.

'I am not!' I replied, prepared to argue.

'Keep yourself down,' he ordered. I followed his gaze down the shadowy road. 'It's just coming up to time,' he whispered, sounding like Mother and Edward waiting for a manifestation.

I began to feel creepy. 'What's going on, Nelson?' I demanded, reduced to a frightened whisper.

'Coffins coming and going after dark – I know 'cause I watch, see. 'Tain't half exciting, like a Dracula film I saw at the Roxy.'

I peered anxiously down the road past Miss Brady's, past Mrs Briggs', towards the nursing home. 'What coffins? I've never seen a coffin,' I remarked. 'Where?' I felt as if a spook was already sitting on my shoulder.

'You never watch, do yer?' He brought out a small torch, and checked his notebook and with a clock sitting on the mantelpiece. 'I'd like to know what goes on here. I reckon we ought to call the cops in. Police inspection is what we want.'

Just then the arrival of a hearse, like a dark stranger, shocked me to mute rigidity.

'Bang on,' Nelson remarked delightedly, checking the time. 'It's a good view from this window,' he turned, satisfied that fate had not let us down. I peered uneasily through the gloom.

'My God, Nelson, don't watch; it will give you nightmares,' I pleaded, as a long black box and two dark figures disappeared through the far gate.

'I reckon they're bumping off two a week,' he surmised in a matter of fact voice, 'and collecting the insurance. Must do, people don't die like flies in this 'ere bleeding place – that's what Pa used to say. I reckon I'd do the cops a good turn if I just tipped them the wink.'

'You can't call the police for every little suspicion you have,' I said. 'And I must go now. You have ruined my evening, I shall have to call a taxi.'

'Ain't yer going to watch it out?'

'No I'm not, it gives me the creeps,' I said defiantly, full of sympathy for Miss Brady's complaints about the comings and goings at her very door.

'Pity,' he remarked, and glued himself back to the window.

Feeling as though I had just attended my best friend's funeral, I telephoned a taxi and managed at length to reach the hotel where my aunts, thoroughly refreshed, were waiting impatiently in the foyer.

When, hours later, I returned home, I found that Nelson's room was a blaze of light and for one awful moment I thought he must still be up coffin-watching; but the figure wasn't Nelson's and the noise was not a Nelson noise, it was a thin sound. Then I saw it was Nelson's mother, a pathetic shapeless figure of distress.

'I never should have clocked him one,' she cried piteously, 'it doesn't do no good to clock our Nelson, it brings out his Pa in him.'

'What's happened?' I called, astonished. Nelson's mother clocking him one was unbelievable.

'I gave 'im one in the lug'ole; me 'and slipped.'

'And about time, too,' I couldn't help adding.

''E's locked me in, and buried the key; just when me bowels are on the turn,' she confessed with innocent frankness – household candour was catching. She broke into fresh cries: 'I think 'e might be dead, 'e threatened suicide, hanging somewhere perhaps.'

'Nelson committing suicide? Never!' I answered with complete sureness. 'The one thing he would never do is harm himself.' I thought of Nelson dead, it was an impossible image.

'If 'e's not dead, 'e's run off somewhere, perhaps out of me life forever.'

'He'll soon come back when he's hungry,' I consoled confidently. I knew our Nelson.

The children's window opened, their faces white in the blackness. 'Where's Nelson?' came the demand. 'Has he committed suicide, throttled by a rope?' There was interest in the voice at the possibility. 'He was practising hanging himself yesterday, seeing how far he could go before it was too late.'

'That fat boy will never hang,' I declared, deciding the question. 'Hop back to bed while I rescue his mother.'

I trotted indoors, telling Mrs Williams that I would be back in a minute; I had already handed over my last key to Nelson, with the determination to make him pay for the other one which he couldn't produce, adamant that no door was going to be pushed in on his account. The house seemed deserted; only a tell-tale light glowed from beneath Jane's door. Climbing the narrow stairs to the dwelling at the top of the house, I demanded entrance. An answer pitched low and seductive from our woman of experience made me enter. Jane was reclining beneath her sloped ceiling in a low-cut black negligee. Her tiny, child-like breasts were lost amidst the softly flowing garment and an artificial rose sprouted up gaily in the valley: where there was no support a discreet safety pin did the necessary. The hair, loosened from its normal bun, rippled like Medusa's and without her glasses she peered at me as a baby owl would in strong sunlight.

'Oh, it's you,' her voice went flat, disappointed that I was no one better, letting her voice go back to her normal matter-of-fact squeak and replacing her glasses.

I noticed she was browsing through the *Nursing Mirror*: an intricate diagram of a gaping wound with all accessories made me close my eyes. 'Look at this,' she indicated – the magazine, her nursing voice taking over. 'A kidney operation, most interestingly displayed. I thought your aunt might be interested too.'

'Please,' I begged, 'not now. Not after my six course dinner! Can you help me? Nelson's locked his mother in and disappeared, and the poor woman is having hysterics. I thought perhaps we could borrow a ladder from down the road, from that house that is being decorated.' I had noticed yesterday, among the assortment of equipment, a long ladder.

'Where are the men of the house?' Jane inquired, rising and stretching in her transparent coverage.

'You know what it's like on Saturday nights, they are either boozing, wenching, jazzing . . .' I shrugged.

Jane gave a 'Bah!' of disapproval.

'You'd better put something more practical on,' I said, watching the flat body floating ghost-like inside the voluminous folds. 'Remember it's a ladder we've got to carry.'

Jane reluctantly threw aside her finery and, taking her nurse's blue mackintosh from behind the door, she slid into it, remarking it was high time somebody did something to Nelson.

'But that's just it, somebody did, and this is the result,' I told her, as we sallied forth to the rescue through the first drops of rain, calling out consolingly to the desolate wilting figure. We located the house and the ladder. The ladder was much heavier than we had expected and we had difficulty in clearing the house and the gate. We had just managed to reach the pavement, our muscles tingling to breaking point, when a man sauntered towards us out of the night. He was indistinguishable in the dark but it was obvious he had been drinking.

'Heave ho, me hearties!' he bawled, sensing our predicament with the inner vision of a drunk; giving Jane a playful little dig, his hands wandering happily, which made Jane, with a loud piercing exclamation, drop her end of the ladder. This was the cue for our drunken Don Quixote to take over. Seizing the fallen end, he barked encouragement: 'Come on, me hearties, I'll give you a hand. The Navy to the rescue.'

His legs wobbled as the effects of liquor were struggling with his strength, and hiccups took charge. I wondered in which house in the avenue he resided; he was obviously one of the disreputable newcomers but we couldn't dispute the fact that we needed help. Jane was by this time incapable, struggling with nervous laughter, terrified that he might pinch her again and terrified that he might not, thereby depriving her of a fresh experience. I, too, was seized with an irrepressible urge to laugh and only the pathetic face of Mrs Williams made me hang on firmly with some sort of composure to my end of the ladder.

'Which way, me hearties?'

'This way, my hearty, this way,' I retaliated, getting into the spirit of the thing, and with Jane close beside me we marched forward to the rescue, giggling openly now as the situation threatened to incapacitate us, as every third step brought a hiccup and a 'pardon', and we wafted along behind a trail of liquor fumes. Our rescuer, his perception still keen, estimated the situation at a glance as we stood huddled in the patch of light. Somewhere in the darkness I heard the exclamation of a watchful neighbour.

'Up she goes,' he yelled, as the ladder hit the right spot, more by luck than good judgment, where Nelson's mother still waited, now promising death by strangulation to Nelson if he was still alive and leaving no doubt as to who needed rescuing. The threat was out of character.

'Ladies first!'

Our hands met in a secret squeeze. 'Don't turn your back on him,' Jane implored from between tight lips, and she went off into a fit of delighted laughter.

'She's got to come down,' I explained, pointing to the victim, who was now noiselessly and pensively disturbed. Could this be a fate worse than death? Yes, undoubtedly! Mrs Williams burst into fresh cries.

'Do not fear, madam, I will bring you down to safety,' our friend told her, agitated by her renewed distress. I put out my hand and stopped him.

'I shouldn't go up the ladder if I were you,' I said hesitatingly. 'I'll go. You're a little merry you know, not quite capable, perhaps. . . . It was only a suggestion . . .' I realised immediately that I had said the wrong thing. The man threw back his head with a proud gesture, and straightened his body carefully.

'Never let it be said that James Smart isn't a perfect gentleman, in charge of his faculties at all times,' he said and, seizing the ladder with both hands, he jumped on the first rung. Steadying himself briefly, he disappeared rapidly towards the light.

We watched breathlessly – would he make it? He did, and surfaced up face to face with Mrs Williams. There was a faint scream as Mrs Williams no doubt smelt the tainted breath and decided that this was worse than being starved to death in a blocked room with a thwarted bowel movement. There was a feeble cry, soothing reassurances, and slowly and timorously Mrs Williams climbed onto the top of the ladder, under the personal direction of Mr Smart and was rescued. We heard his refrain long after his footsteps had died into the night.

We thought it best to leave the disposal of the ladder to the others, as we settled down to await Nelson and justice, for our searching had proved that our fat boy was truly missing.

Chapter Ten

Sunday started with a disaster, and as so often my first moments of the day were heralded with involuntary action, so it was today. Persistent filterings of ominous sound, probing, roused me from a heavy sleep. Somebody was crying. Nelson was dead, poor Nelson. I felt a moment of great personal loss. We would spend pounds on a large wreath worthy of him: the coffin would have to be extra wide, a foot perhaps.

Something touched my face: I shot up to find Gerry standing by the bed crying. Nelson, like a nightmare of over-indulgence, was by his side.

'Come and see, the mice are dying,' Gerry sobbed.

'I thought *you* were dead,' I told Nelson bluntly as I focused, feeling that I had wasted my sympathies now that he wasn't and remembering last night and poor Mrs Williams' dilemma. Sheer tiredness had forced me to bed in the end, leaving her dozing fitfully on the drawing-room sofa, her anger turned to anxiety and forgiveness, as she hoped and prayed for her offspring's safe return.

'Not on your Nellie,' he remarked casually. 'It's these 'ere mice breeding like flies, causing over-work, and women's nagging that is driving me to near suicide – and now this financial disaster.' He held two fat hands up in a gesture of despair.

Nicholas appeared around the door: he looked small and anxious and moaned of death and destruction.

'Wot a burial we are going to have,' Nelson surmised, plunged into further gloom – hypocritically, I knew, for I could see by his eyes that he was suddenly cheered at the prospect of a funeral session, which might possibly be turned to financial gain. He was quick to seize any advantage to better his own financial position at the expense of a good cause, in what might be loosely called 'press gang sweeps', guaranteed to force the last coin from his victim.

Throwing a dressing-gown on, I staggered out still heavy with sleep, food and wine. 'Where the hell have you been, anyway?' I demanded sourly over my shoulder of Nelson, who was following me meekly, a robust convict in striped pyjamas. 'The last time I saw you, you were counting coffins with all the diligence of the local cops.'

'I was around,' he murmured, evading my question with the face of an overweight angel, and he endeavoured to change the line of thought by a completely irrelevant remark, one of his favourite manoeuvres.

The scene of upheaval, at the place that caused Mrs Briggs so much heartbreak, was the obvious hand of a stealthy marauder. 'Who did this? Mrs Briggs?' I suggested unfairly, with the irritation that too much rich living and little sleep produces.

'It's that perishing cat,' Nelson stated. 'I 'eard the crashings and raised the alarm, but I'll get 'im with me catapult, see if I don't – the stinking ol' bleeder.'

I was so used to Nelson's constant and varied reflections on the word blood that I scarcely ever rebuked him now. It was like his grammatical errors; they were as much a part of him as the chaotic roundness of flesh and bone.

'Where's Pinky?' I demanded, still grumbling, examining the debris.

Pinky was a favourite, a plump little feline who showed a disquieting lack of self-restraint, giving birth in unnecessary profusion, with total segregation as the only answer if keeping of mice and harmony with the Briggs family was ever to be indulged in. Nelson righted a box and raised the corpse with the gentle hand of a sorrowing mother, and placed it in my own. Observing the gentle touch, showing all the facets of maternal tenderness, I softened inwardly towards my youngest tenant – but one outward step to the brink of softness and Nelson would be playing me on his line again, I warned myself, frowning.

'Well, this is the end of this,' I snarled with mixed feelings, picking up yet another white body and examining it carefully for signs of life.

'And about time too, I must say,' came the clear chant of Mrs Briggs from the bedroom window next door. 'It will be the health authorities you'll have to reckon with next time, my girl.'

I ignored her, too vulnerable in my weakened state to enter into battle, and a flicker of movement from a solitary body had already sent Nelson moving excitedly.

'Look!' he yelped. 'Life!'

'Bring it inside, and the others,' I ordered, my

instincts to preserve life aroused against my better judgment. I sped indoors to light the fire and heat some milk, endeavouring to remember what my zoologically-minded brother would have done in similar circumstances. Amazingly, with the warmth and sips of milk laced with brandy, some of the mice responded feebly, stretched their grotesque little bodies, and felt for new life.

'I have quite decided,' I told Nelson in my plainest tone of voice, 'you have got to do something about these mice. Today, not tomorrow or the next day, but today. You promised, remember.'

'Yep,' the answer was given grudgingly. It went against Nelson's nature to respond with promises, however false. Seeing the situation was now under control, he quickly dropped his mourning and became his usual nonchalant self. 'Come lads,' he caroled gaily. 'We can leave everything in safety now. You're a good ol' bird,' he praised affably, turning and giving me the kind of affectionate pat usually reserved for Andy, 'and quite a little nurse too, ain't yer?' and he cantered off.

I was going to take him to task, not only about last night but about the key to his room, but the bit of unexpected genuine praise left me silent. The 'old', so often used as an added insult, was now thrown in as an endearment; this was a moment that could not be spoilt by female haggling. I let him go without reproach. There were, of course, hails of subdued criticism from Edward, roused, he said, out of the best dream he had had for years. I felt we all shared the same yoke of suffering, as I remembered the heavy day ahead. Monkeys to be fed, the boiler to stoke, the promise of a picnic and the reunion with my aunts, who were no doubt still peacefully slumbering on deep comfy beds, in the silence of vault-like rooms. No time even to linger over the memory of Andy's yearning touch, or how Mrs Williams fared. She would undoubtedly be overjoyed at Nelson's safe return: he would never get another clout, that was a certainty.

A commotion that sounded like Mr Budden having one of his political arguments – normally brought on by the *Daily Mirror* headlines – now seemed to be the most dominating sound around the house. Surely my male lodgers weren't indulging in the argumentative field of politics at this early hour? They were of such a variety that a peaceful conclusion was an impossibility, I decided, listening for the fatal heckling which would deteriorate to a common brawl and involve us all in irrelevant insults.

But it was not the first festerings of an all party rumpus, as I had suspected. Mr Budden, while wandering about his ablutions, had been headed by a heavy weighted object dropped from the next floor. By the time he had revived, the incriminating object had mysteriously disappeared in the uproar.

Nelson had been the first suspect as usual but as he stood by innocently watching the scene of revival with marked sympathy, no one could prove anything. 'Really, you will have to give that boy notice,' Edward remarked unconvincingly, knowing perfectly well that I would never give that boy notice, even if I had been a landlady of one hundred years' standing.

The telephone ringing ended our personal

dispute and alerted me to a new chain that was about to start.

My introduction to Lord Booth was brief: the unsavoury prattling of an irate neighbour with justice on his side. 'There is an animal in my bedroom that has knocked over the light, and is eating my tobacco!'

'Really?' I replied, wondering what it had to do with me. This was the first time my neighbour and I had communicated. I hoped it was going to be the last. There was a nasty pause and a threatening sound of heavy breathing: I waited for further disclosures.

'The thing has now escaped by the window. I am going to make my complaint to the right authorities.'

A click, then silence, told me I had been deliberately cut off. Thoroughly alarmed, I turned to investigate whether the accusation had anything to do with me, and came face to face with Nelson. 'The monkeys are out,' he announced. 'Every blinking one! Blimey, look!' he pointed over my shoulder with some excitement. 'A cop car!' and he took up an immediate vantage point in the window with a grand show of bravado.

A police car had in fact stopped at the gate. Throwing on some clothes and passing a quick hand across my hair, conscious that I was in no way looking my best, I went out, halfheartedly, to meet them. My tone was respectful, blandly innocent, following my unfailing rule that one must always be nice to a policeman and exercise charm to soften the blow of any reprimand that might be forthcoming. Driving a car had taught me this valuable asset.

Two faces of good British stock watched my approach with a pleasant interest and, being male, their expressions were now not entirely professional.

'Good morning,' the driver touched his cap. 'Are you missing anything – some monkeys, perhaps?' Bad news travels fast. There was just the slightest tinge of mocking friendly humour in the voice.

I replied tentatively as a criminal might, reluctant to identify myself with my brother's monkeys and feeling slightly uncomfortable under the keen scrutiny of the law. Paula floated out of the house, sexy in beach wear, showing off her colt-like legs to advantage, making mine feel inadequately short. She stopped, surprised, obviously impressed by the uniformed mates at the gate but puzzled at their presence, having not heard the news of the monkeys' escape.

'Good morning, officer,' she called out, smiling a big welcome smile from scarlet lips, (she knew the tactics, too). The crisp atmosphere surrounding the law crumbled and we exchanged friendly smiles. She managed one of her mercurial remarks at my expense.

'How many are missing?' the driver asked without formality but with a remnant of professional regret as he accepted an evil-smelling French cigarette from Paula.

'About a dozen,' I calculated uncertainly, not having the slightest idea. I wished that I had something to offer them as impressive as a French cigarette, thinking that the whole wretched, degrading situation could no doubt be softened to still more cosy and intimate advantage by the presence of more foreign tobacco.

'What's going on, then?' the policeman asked interested. 'Are you starting a menagerie, or something?'

'No, it's just my boarding house,' I explained a trifle foolishly. I omitted to say that I had inherited a mad brother. They both laughed again at my expense, joined by Paula – of course.

'Three have been sighted anyway,' he told us, rattling off a series of addresses. 'We have called in the RSPCA and no doubt you will be hearing from us again,' he ended kindly, as if he enjoyed the thought.

'No doubt!' Paula encouraged – she too enjoyed the moment. I could hear the telephone again, but I let it ring revengefully. I breathed a relieved mixture of thanks and admiration: I could have kissed the solid handsome face for purely professional reasons. With a backward glance of farewell, they left, pulling away noiselessly from the kerb, leaving us with a new and dizzy respect.

'Of course, the RSPCA. Why didn't I think of them sooner?' I said to Paula regretfully. 'They could have taken over the whole lot in the first place.'

'That was a hunk of attractive male,' Paula remarked with relish, her eyes following the black car. 'Pity it was business and not pleasure.'

'If that brother of mine puts one foot over the gate again, there'll be trouble. I'll call in the police force to turn him out,' I decided threateningly, realising for the first time that the police force were going to have other advantages.

'He's marvellous, and devastatingly attractive,' Paula was brimming with open praise.

'Who is – that bobby with the tender blue eyes?' I was more than willing to agree.

'No, Gerald of course.'

'He's a bloody menace, that's what he is.' Words failed me.

Paula smirked at my disloyalty. 'When is he coming back?' she asked with carefully applied nonchalance, which I saw through immediately. Those green eyes softened for the second time that morning.

'We can expect that two-legged troublemaker to return any minute,' I told her frigidly.

Paula stood thoughtfully. 'I was going to go down to the beach,' she remarked, 'but there is so much going on here that might prove interesting, I think I will hang around; although I must say I can't really stand monkeys, or their smells.' She wrinkled her slender aristocratic nose disdainfully. 'And if it wasn't for the charm of their owner. . . .'

But I wasn't listening any more, as I counted my misfortunes, full of regrets. If only I'd never moved them in. Heaven knew where they all were by this time. 'Why am I the one to be plagued by an animal-minded maniac, and a boarding house full of lunatics?' I asked Paula, bemoaning my fate.

'He's very charming, I don't think you appreciate him fully,' and Paula began to go dreamy, which was a pose that didn't really suit her. They had in fact got on well in a purely platonic way. Gerald's natural sarcasm was an excellent foil for Paula's sharp wit, and both having the gift of mimicry, there were moments when no one was left untouched.

'Personally, I prefer the police force: at least they get you out of a jam, and not push you into one,' I answered with obvious truth. 'Mr Budden shares the same views, too,' I added, hearing his voice in the distance, now finding myself quite fond of him. The new situation had made us temporary buddies and I was satisfied that I was allied with at least one member of the household on this question of Gerald and his pets.

Paula grimaced. 'The man is insufferable. I can't stand him at any price. Do you know he wanders about attending to his necessities looking like a sort of elongated Gandhi in just a small towel – it's a harrowing sight for sensitive people.'

This was the third time I had been given this piece of information, but I had yet to see the offending vision. 'Well, it's his wife's job to reprimand him, not the landlady's. I wonder Jane hasn't taken it upon herself to drop a few hints, you know, about "germs" or "bad for the mind" or something; but you can't really blame his opinions this time. Of Gerald, I mean. Not everyone can appreciate the charm of a python as a sort of domestic pet, and by the time the monkeys are fetched home, there won't be a neighbour for miles around that we will be able to speak to either – and God knows who will get bitten.' It was an inglorious picture to say the least.

Paula gave a trifling laugh. 'Judging by the people around here, that would be no loss.' She had never quite got over the fact that anyone should think she was an inmate of a brothel and still felt vindictive about it.

We stopped our discussion to watch with interest the heavily proportioned figure walking up the road towards us and gasped together at the almost unrecognisable sight of Magda. Her once long, thickly curling hair shorn in a crude boyish crop, she walked with the cowed attitude of a sick animal and had a drawn look to her sallow face. The short hair, with thick black brows meeting over deep-set eyes, gave her face an unhealthy masculine look.

'Roger wondered where you were,' I called out, hoping this would please her, feeling a surge of pity and momentarily puzzled by this strange girl, not sure if I should remark, even kindly, on the new hairdo.

'Did he?' she answered apathetically, and without another word passed us and went indoors.

'What a ghastly hairstyle,' Paula was offended. 'Makes her look as though she is changing her sex.'

I agreed with Paula. 'I think she must be suffering over something, perhaps she is getting ready to go into a convent.'

'Aren't we all suffering,' Paula stated callously, 'and whether she is suffering or not, I do wish she would shave under her armpits. It's quite nauseating. It reminds me of the French, and with so many things on the market it's quite unnecessary,' our expert on cosmetics ended. Paula and unshaved armpits were natural enemies.

'I like it,' a voice said behind us. 'It's like me Ma's.'

Nelson ducked to miss the flat of my hand. 'Caught you!' he vibrated with mirth, pleased at this little contretemps.

'For a boy of your age you spend far too much

time not minding your own business.' Paula scowled at him in exasperation.

'I answered your telephone,' he said with importance, unaffected by reproaches. 'There's one of them little 'orrors on the golf links. I was just going down to look for 'im.' He had a piece of paper in his hand, which he pushed carefully onto a nail that was already sticking out of the gate: it had caused a major tear in Mr Budden's best jacket the night before and had not exactly endeared Nelson in the eyes of that gentleman. Nelson and Mr Budden were also natural enemies.

'Nelson, don't desecrate the gate again,' I ordered sternly.

'What's descecrate?' he asked. 'Sounds like something to eat.'

'Destroy – a word you evidently don't know the meaning of,' Paula explained, while I examined the crude notice, stating that we were now having a closing down sale of 'Spechully bread mice'.

'At least it's a step in the right direction,' I said, reading it out to Paula.

Two small flying figures and a dog raced from the back garden to the gate, with Mr Budden in pursuit. Scattering us, and gathering up Nelson with hectic shouts as they passed, they disappeared towards the park. Mr Budden, breathing in long heavy gulps, stopped at the corner of the house, realising he wasn't exactly dressed for a long chase – washed-out knee-length shorts and an ancient string vest. I noticed how hairy his legs were, and how bandy.

'I'll wring their so-and-so necks!' he swore furiously.

'What a lucky thing our picnic with my aunts wasn't arranged until this afternoon,' I murmured under my breath to Paula, having told her of the events she had missed on the previous day. I was convinced that if Mr Budden ever did give in his notice, he would never get another lodging with his crude habits and noisy child – which already showed signs of reaching Nelson's proportions. It was enough to kill the kind urge of any landlady.

'Do you mind,' Paula rebuked. 'Not on a Sunday please.' She had a flow of language which, when sorely tried, would equal Mr Budden's any day of the week, but for a moment that point was forgotten.

The telephone ringing again sent me in to answer it, leaving Paula to soothe the ruffled man and escort him away from the front garden, where his presence, I felt, would only give cause for further gossip, with the suggestion that she should tackle him about his habits: not recommended in a mixed household. Mrs Budden manoeuvred her pram out of the door and onto the lawn, where she could watch it from her window. The jelly baby slept.

'I told 'im to put some clothes on,' she explained to me apologetically as I passed, 'but he will try and get his body in the sun. He'll end up with pneumonia.'

I agreed, and we both laughed. Mrs Budden was busy now making arrangements for the christening of her child. Alfred was the chosen name. Mrs Williams, dressed as if she was about to attend church, smiling a little wanly, hurried out too.

‘Going to church?’ I enquired.

‘No dear, I’ve got a job to do.’

We didn’t mention Nelson’s previous misdemeanour. It was forgotten in the light of a new day.

The telephone revealed that yet another monkey had been spotted by a neighbour; it was in the woods behind the house. Should I go out and look for it, or wait for Nelson and send him? Wandering out, I noticed Paula and Mr Budden, having buried their rancour, were discussing amicably the advantages and complained that the Corporation were not good payers, and that he preferred to work for a private firm. They moved away to the back garden; their friendly tones killed any hopes I had had that Paula would tackle him about his offences. Especially the one about relieving himself behind the dustbins.

I saw with half interest, leaving the vicinity of my titled neighbour’s front garden and walking towards me, a cadaverous beanpole of a man in a black trilby, with the gloomy look of someone who was about to attend a funeral. For a moment I thought it must be Lord Booth masquerading in foreign clothes to involve himself in battle. Then I saw it was a stranger. Fixing me with the narrow calculating brown briefcase, he took out a pamphlet and thrust it firmly before me.

‘Do you want to be saved, and led through the paths of righteousness?’ It was a direct and dogmatic accusation, and startled me. Jehovah, I realised, intended to add his weight to my other burdens. I had always thought I had rather an innocent face, and was crestfallen at the bold, presumptuous and perhaps true statement that

I was going to seed. He noted the effects of his words with open satisfaction and followed up his advantage quickly.

'Jehovah can give you peace, put you on the right road to blessed eternity, to the only true way,' he told me. Before I had time to say I wasn't aware that I was in so much need, he went thundering onto other convictions, pressing a wad of electioneering pamphlets into my hand for inspection. Wondering if he was any good at handling monkeys, I peered into a magazine with an embarrassed show of feigned interest, not wishing to hurt.

'I'm a Catholic,' I piped up at last with utter conviction, grasping for a straw. The man drew back as if I had produced Edward's collection of doubtful postcards.

'Then you are in trouble,' he moaned. 'All the strife in the world today is caused by Catholics.'

I thought this a most unfair assumption. I had been led to understand that politics were the cause of all the trouble in the land – and according to our staunch Labour supporter, Mr Budden, it was the entire Conservative Party. He and my aunt would also have got on well together, I thought, wondering if it was a suitable idea to send him over to her hotel.

'She's deaf,' I said hurriedly, seeing my disciple's eyes wandering to the floral apparition of Mrs Budden busy rocking her pram, frightened that the booming voice would disturb the slumbers of her child. I looked about for rescue. Then Edward waltzed out of the house with his daily bundle of rubbish bound for the dustbin. A gaudy peacock showing off to catch his mates, his beard freshly combed spread in a fan of burning colour, he danced a couple of steps to an unintelligible tune, and looked remarkably unsaved, if not a little mad. I noticed him with joy.

'Who is that?' the inquiry was a shocked one.

'He – needs help.' I was gloriously malicious, determined to entangle Edward in the web and so escape myself. This would be a meeting which I felt sure would stem the flow of his convictions pretty rapidly. Edward, summing up the situation with a quick hostile glance, disappeared: it was obvious he had already experienced the wily ways of a Jehovah disciple.

'He's a Yogi, would you like to see him?' I inquired, determinedly revengeful, now wild at the sight of Edward's grinning face at an upstairs window and the rude gestures that accompanied it.

The beanpole digested my piece of information suspiciously and did not appear overjoyed at the prospects of tackling Edward. Feeling my tactics had failed, I wondered what other excuse I could find without being offensive to end this pilgrimage to save my soul. I stood a defiant and unpenitent sinner, refusing stubbornly the road to salvation offered me. Then, insidiously, as if the devil intended to play his part reaping a picture of wicked comparisons, we fell from the lofty pinnacles of salvation and commercialism took over.

'You can have this book for a subscription of only seven shillings and sixpence a year,' the man ended, compromisingly eager and pathetically watching me with anxiety. Was another straying lamb to escape?

I went quickly to fetch the money; it was a

cheap price to pay for freedom and the saving of one's soul. I paid the money and collected my first instalment of literature. But the devil, still playing persistently beside me, forced me to point over the fence to Mrs Briggs' house. 'That fellow's no good,' I remarked, reprieving Edward with this more mischievous idea in mind. 'Half his day is spent on his head, or sitting on nails, and nothing will budge him. And you would be wasting your time,' I added as an afterthought, 'he hasn't any spare money anyway.'

Thanking me courteously, the fire reviving in his eyes again, he made for Mrs Briggs' back gate, reorganising his pamphlets hastily. This was a moment I could not miss. I crept down behind the fence, filled with curiosity. What would he do for Mrs Briggs, and what would she do for him? I heard the knock, the opening of the door, and the news assuring Mrs Briggs that Jehovah embraced all religions including hers. There was a moment of frightening suspense, then up rose the familiar voice: 'No circulars or hawkers today, thank you. Au reevor.' The door slammed. There was a painful pause which even I felt, then the dragging tread of Jehovah's defeat down the path across the road to Mrs Brady's door. I chuckled. Mrs Briggs had got off lightly – I was a year's subscription out of pocket, I thought, a little ashamed of myself, for after all it took courage to stand alone and breathe aloud words of conviction to possible ridicule.

I forgot the incident quickly in my other worries, the most important of which I concluded, was the gathering up of animal life and strategic moves to keep my aunts at bay. This conclusion sent me scurrying to the kitchen to cut bread, wash tomatoes and lettuce, ready for a quick getaway on their arrival in the afternoon. I stopped a moment later with an armful of suspended lettuce: there was a noise that I had not heard before, a long drawn-out '*eeeeee*!' and a frantic squawking of chickens. Thinking that my life was governed by a series of sounds which left me treading gingerly between each one, my stamina considerably weakened, I waited to see what would follow.

'Mister, quick, bring your gun!' came the formidable command. It was Mrs Briggs, of course; a Mrs Briggs who obviously intended to carry out her day in violent action. Probably the fox was at her chickens again and I prayed that she had not yet discovered the temporary absence of the inmates of my summerhouse. Nevertheless, apprehensively curious as to why she would want a lethal weapon, I dropped the lettuce and flew upstairs to the men's room, which gave the best aerial view into Mrs Briggs' back garden. Roger and Magda were having a little light entertainment of reconciliation – light, I felt, after the attitude of eternal faithless indifference to the opposite sex which seemed to be part of Roger's character, and which no woman would survive in for very long. Excusing myself unfeelingly, I explained the situation and my curiosity as to what went on next door as I made for the window.

'This is the fourth interruption to my sleep I have had this morning,' Roger sulked to my indifferent back. 'Is there no privacy in this bloody house? Either it's that production of Mr Budden's manhood bawling, or Mrs Briggs' cockerel, or the dog barking, and now these demented chickens. Earlier this morning it seemed as though we were camped in the middle of a zoological park.'

'You must give and take,' I retorted, my eyes anxiously on the happenings next door. 'You might be surprised to know that Mrs Budden has complained about your scales on the trumpet.' Loyally I didn't tell him that Andy's scales had also called for a comment or two. 'She says she can stand the sound of your music, because she realises she has to, but those scales drive her up the wall and her migraine attacks are increasing. She is going to call in her MP.'

'I'm surprised she knows what scales are, illiterate as she is,' Roger scoffed, hauling down the flags of communism.

'My God!' I said, at the sight of Mr Briggs armed with a gun, marching with an air of national pride as if war had been declared, straight for the chicken run at the bottom of the garden. Their garden was a secluded mixture of shrubs, trees and greenhouses, and it was not easy at first glance to distinguish points of disturbance. Then I caught sight of the figure I was looking for: Mrs Briggs, armed with a long broom, standing in a threatening posture before the open door of the chicken house. Inside, on a hen roost, sucking eggs with blissful unconcern, was a monkey. Below him hens fled in agitation. A defeated cockerel sat stunned to silence.

'Put it down!' she yelled, mustering up some courage and threatening furiously with the broom. Then came the strange '*eeeee*!' again. Mister was now running.

'Don't shoot!' I yelled indignantly. All that fuss

as though it was a homicidal maniac, I grumbled, turning from my perch in concern, frightened that I would not be in time to save the monkey's life.

Roger was useless at a time like this. 'Ask her if she's got a bloody gun licence,' he remarked.

'Don't strain yourself to help,' I retorted icily to the inert body. 'One needs a man at a time like this. Where's Andy?' Rushing out I noticed vaguely my rubbish dump – just – painted in colours that I had never seen in the garden before.

'Try the girls' room,' Roger's voice called after me ambiguously, with a muffled laugh.

Roger's insinuation filled me with immediate jealousy. How dare Andy cavort like a tomcat with my female lodgers. I stood in the hall and screamed his name. Doors opened on all sides: the object of my screaming appeared from the front room and was immediately by my side. My rage melted at the sight of him, reassured by his quick answer to my call.

'One of the monkeys is over at Mrs Briggs' and about to get shot – can you rescue it for me?'

He followed me without a murmur of protest. We met an excited Edward – the news was spreading quickly about the house – and we ran, all three of us, to the back garden. Andy cleared the fence easily, falling at Mr Briggs' feet. Edward, not able to do the same, jerked me up to a viewing position with the frailest pair of arms I'd ever experienced. I was just in time to see Mr Briggs levelling the gun uncertainly, the dramatic effect spoilt by a collarless shirt, shoeless feet, braces and longjohns before Edward's arms collapsed and we landed in a heap. Olwen, with Paula beside her, was derisively urging her spouse to greater efforts. Mrs Budden, fussing over the welfare of all concerned, was asking if her baby should be taken to safety, to the twitterings of Mr Budden quoting from the Bible that Sunday should be a day of rest. We unravelled ourselves and could only picture the scene of dissension now deprived us. The gun went off.

'You missed!' came the disparaging comment of Mrs Briggs, the renewed noise of chickens in frantic terror, the deafening squeals of a now very frightened monkey and Andy booming out unrepeatable curses.

'Has someone been shot?' I asked Edward aghast, all ready for mourning the loss of Andy.

Andy's head and shoulders appeared above the fence; after a slight struggle he dropped beside us, pain and fury making his face haggard. His hand was bleeding profusely.

'Are you bitten?' I asked the obvious with deep feeling, my spirits chilling at the sight of his ashen face.

'My dear old soul,' Edward commiserated readily, 'thank God it wasn't me.' Olwen, sickening at the sight of blood, fled.

'Ay.' He turned to me bitterly. 'Where do you want this monkey?'

'Where's Jane?' Paula inquired hastily, and she too sickened and fled.

'Back to the garage,' I answered the hero with a shamed face. This round would go to the nurses I had to admit, following the furious man.

Across the wall, from an upstairs window, the Booths watched the pageant stealthily from behind lace curtains, while a torrent of abuse from the Briggses was a direct stab in the back.

Jane, drawn by the noise, and being told by Olwen that there was blood shed, rushed out, jubilant at the sight of a bleeding victim, and enveloped Andy in sympathetic arms. She led him away, without a glance in my direction; a willing victim to the healing porticos of her first-aid chest. This was a final blow. I had lost him, I told myself in anguish, to that sexless creature who had proved herself more efficient than I in a crisis. I was destined to be an old maid, a sour-faced landlady, aging quickly and not at all gracefully, without even a fortune to pacify me. I would be a second Mrs Williams, worn before my time and, shedding a few tears on the comforting, garlic-ridden but silky shoulder of Edward, I went back to make my picnic arrangements, throwing the things into the basket. Who cared what we ate?

More noise: the children had returned. Nelson had caught another monkey. He carried it proudly, unbitten and unafraid. He'd climbed the tallest tree in the park: he would, I thought, watching him put the animal back in the garage.

Ten to two found the children and me, outwardly calm, sitting at the gate and watching for the party that was to be our endurance test. The boys, finding that Nelson was not invited, were reluctant to come.

'Nelson must spend a day with his mother,' I insisted firmly. 'We mustn't be selfish you know, Nelson must be shared.'

'Nelson says . . .'

'I don't want to know what Nelson says,' I answered tartly, my nerves frayed. 'The fact remains that we have got to go out with our dear aunts, and what's more you have to behave yourselves. . . .'

The sight of the car with my Aunt Patience at the wheel stopped any further argumentative conversation.

The picnic, I felt, had not been a success. The boys had produced with pride a pair of adders, spliced in a lovers' knot, and it was a sorry party that returned home. My thoughts sped homeward before me. Was the object of my dreams languishing with rabies in the skinny arms of Jane, in her prize negligee with the come-hither rose? Who else had been bitten, perhaps fatally? Had Paula made any subtle progress with the police? And what was Nelson up to? These were my thoughts, the demented wanderings of a hard-pressed landlady, as I watched the sun set like a giant marshmallow swiftly into lonely blackness.

Chapter Eleven

My relations returned home, persuaded that my house was being run on conventional lines, but unfortunately convinced that my children were heading straight for a reformatory. They both recommended Eton or an ecclesiastical school as an antidote for their high spirits.

Andy passed me now with a still face – a deformity of pink lint and bandages carried with painful care, an uncomfortable reminder of yesterday. Nelson, too, nursed a small scratch, which he insisted was a monkey bite. I prayed that Gordon's farewell party, destined for the morrow, would soften the blows and mellow us all back to fireside friendship. Even our nursing talents had made a great endeavour to be present, managing to switch their night duty after a tussle with Matron, and were excited at the prospect of a free evening's gay debauchery – as they put it.

The escaping monkeys, like the holidaymakers, were exploring the delights of the town; and the local paper started a daily column following their routes and escapades, which brought me no consolation. They could afford to – after all it wasn't *they* who would have to pay the damages of possible disaster.

I sent a brief telegram to Gerald telling him to

return and collect his specimens, ending it with the word 'vital'. He arrived almost immediately, with the harrassed look of a father on holiday with a large and unruly family, all under five. I met him with a face that looked as though I had just received fatal news from the doctor.

Gerald, cursing my incompetence, stated that my terrible habit of trying to brighten the lives of both animals and humans usually ended unhappily for all concerned and set off at once to remedy the matter, to bring home whichever offenders had been caught and to pacify those irate citizens whose lives had been disrupted.

The prodigals returned, one by one, in slow procession. They greeted their foster father with recognisable cries of welcome and touching shows of affection. Touching, that was, to those of us who had not suffered either the galling indignities of chasing a monkey, which is always just out of reach, or its bites! Now the monkeys were once more safe, Gerald treated lightly the incidents ensuing from the escape.

'The bonds of true love,' he told me, in the pose of an analytical doctor, 'are strengthened, not severed, by a few disasters.'

'Not monkey bites,' I insisted, proving my facts with a dismal tale of a lost love.

'And,' he went on, 'the remedy for lodgers of Mr Budden's calibre' – a man who had the audacity to claim compensation for a bottle of aspirin to soothe his wife's frayed nerves – 'is simple – a week's notice would soon cut his capers down to size.'

The suggestion that I should give anyone notice brought fresh indignant protests from me and a summing up of Mr Budden's virtues into a picture which even I did not recognise. This provoked Gerry to suggest the Salvation Army as a suitable channel into which to direct my activities, although he thought the bonnet would hardly suit my type of beauty. Anyway, he told me, he had decided to leave after Gordon's party to take the monkeys to safer quarters. 'But don't worry,' he added, seeing the delight with which I received this news, 'I've decided to come back again promptly because I feel most strongly some sort of sensible support is needed round here. The house is a blatant pool of idiosyncrasies which obviously need attention – even the dog looks as though he needs a term at the psychiatrist's,' he ended, with a patronising smile.

Nelson, sucking noisily at his finger, concentrated on our conversation with a puckered brow. He was hoping desperately that someone would notice his suffering, and would not only commiserate with him but compensate him, for he had witnessed with interest a money transaction for a lampshade damaged by a mischievous monkey finger and could not get over it. The prospects of a quick financial gain were illuminating and innumerable, and he renewed his energies to draw attention to his suffering.

We were standing in the hall, a normal place for discussion as it allowed the free passage of everybody's comments, when the revealing study of Mrs Budden opening her door, out of gas and hunting for a shilling, her son sucking noisily on a large, pink nipple, drew the attention decidedly away from Nelson's finger. He glared at her threateningly, unperturbed by a sight which he had witnessed before and which had already exhausted all his comments. Her head, wrapped in a scarf over crumpled bumps, showed that she was preparing to be a beautiful lady – a state of affairs invariably brought on after a chat with Paula. Once she had fallen into temptation it usually took the whole day to accomplish, with some success.

'What a charming baby!' Gerald smiled up at the woman, recognising her from the apt description I had already given him of the female species in the house. 'I feel as though I am back in Africa!' he remarked in an undertone, but not quietly enough.

'I'm sure you must do, with all this lovely weather,' Mrs Budden was enthusiastic, fortunately completely missing the point of his remark. Her broad face beamed in gratitude at the praise of her baby. 'Isn't he?' she bloomed with motherly pride, taking the conversation back to the most important thing in her life. 'Exact image of his dad, too. Good as gold – like a lamb, he is!'

Her sincerity, I felt, excused the outrageous falsehood, while the lamb squinted at us from pale eyes, not leaving his ample source of supply.

'Look, look. Blood!' Nelson said, squeezing frantically to no advantage.

'Excuse me looks, dear.' She patted her head remembering her curlers, now acutely conscious of her state of dishabille in the presence of strange, and very attractive male company. 'Perming me hair up.' She explained her headgear, suddenly a little embarrassed, colouring under the keen, confident gaze before her. 'Must get ready for the party tomorrow, if Hubby says we can come. He's tottering on the brink, like. First it's "yes", and then it's "no". Proper difficult he's getting.'

'You'll look beautiful, I'm sure.' Gerald had a way with women. 'See you at the party, then. First dance is mine! That's a promise.'

'Delighted, I'm sure,' she glowed confusedly and, looking suddenly quite young and quite gay, she hoisted the bundle of pink flesh and soggy, sagging nappy over her shoulder and, forgetting the reason for her appearance in the first place, she traipsed gaily back into her room, murmuring about preparing her dress and a clean shirt, and other trivialities.

'Well you've got her on your side!' I remarked, a little sarcastically, when the door was closed, thinking it was surprising what a compliment from another man could do, lifting the drabbest of married women almost to prettiness. 'And that's more than I can say for her husband,' I couldn't help adding. Gerald and Mr Budden were enemies of circumstance.

'Rotten woman, butting in.' Nelson watched the shapeless body of Mrs Budden depart, bitterly. 'Lost me compensation, that's wot. Me finger's stopped bleedin' now. Shan't come to the party, if she's going to be there,' he said disagreeably. For the moment, Mrs Budden had replaced Mr Budden, and moved into the front rank of opposition.

'You are not invited,' I said unkindly. 'Grown-ups only.'

Nelson's spirits deflated immediately, but only for a moment for he was very resourceful.

'Well, I won't be missing much, I don't suppose.

It won't be as good as the parties me Pa gave with them waiters, an' gold plate, an' red lights. Reel posh dos!' He ended with a patronising 'you'll never beat that' attitude and a final 'I know when I'm not wanted – and anyway I like 'em wild beasts better than 'uman beings.' He moved off with proud suffering to the garage.

Gerald laughed. 'Well, I suppose a little compensation won't do "any bleedin' 'arm",' and putting his hand in his pocket, he rattled his change and followed the offended party.

It was to celebrate Gordon's departure that we finally gathered, the entire household united in a glow of tolerant good humour. Our little differences were forgotten in the general stimulating bustle of arrangements. The stacking of drinks and food, searching melody, the yellow candescent glimmer of lighted candles and finally, guests arriving all produced a softening mood of sentimentality. The gangling blasphemous bricklayer melted to the homely proportions of a second Mr Beetle, while Nelson was a child of infinite goodness. Only Andy and I were still remote, proving the sheer unreliability of Gerald's statements.

Nelson, in spite of his feigned disregard, had followed the day's arrangements with his usual concentration. He would not accept, like my children, that this was a grown-up world of celebration that not even he could transgress. He had come to terms with the situation at length, settling ungraciously for an early sip of beer and a generous supply of edibles and bottles of pop and he now sat stubbornly, with watchful eyes, on the candlelit stairs; a silent, wistful figure determined, if possible, not to miss a single thing.

From a darkened corner of oblivion, with half-closed eyes, I felt, with a curious tightness of my spirits, the dancers carving silhouettes of changing shadow. The silent, dejected figure of dominating stature, Andy, sitting also a little part, shifted my thoughts to uneasy wanderings, broken by the passing figures of familiar patterns; a cheerful Gordon in his best suit and really looking like the progeny of a lineage, swamped a glamorous Blanche with his attentions, twining himself about her and blocking the view of crystal blondness from every other man in the room.

But I was not to be left alone for long. Demanding hands hauled me up and I was whisked away by an intoxicated Edward on a journey of delightful twistings and garlic murmurings, which told me that I was undoubtedly the most experienced and luscious woman in the room. His dancing was like his paintings, a soft blending of one to the other, over which presided his special smells. A transient thought made me wonder if this gentle, almost womanly trait made him inadequate as a lover. The perception turned my mind to Roger, and I glanced to see what he was doing. He had started drinking early in the day and I imagined his movements would now be a hectic and unintentional drunken performance where his whole soul would be laid bare before us in an embarrassing way. But I was wrong, for Roger was enjoying himself quietly and comfortably sprawled on the low divan, the candlelight accentuating his darkness to blackness, and with all the confidence of a highly-prized Mongolian prince, he openly flaunted his desires to the visitors, wilting bits of femininity at his feet. Magda, rejected, watched from across the room with hatred. She had said she wouldn't come, teetering with indecision like Mr Budden, but unable to keep away, she had turned up at the last minute. My sympathy as usual went to her and I looked to see if Andy was still alone. Were all these men playing the same game? I asked myself, losing my confidence for a second, for up to now I had thought I looked pretty good in a new dress of black lace, and Jane's borrowed pink rose added a cunning splash of colour at my waist. Mrs Briggs' passing comment earlier, about somebody unnamed (Mr Beetle, I suspected), that 'love would find a way', comforted me at this moment not at all.

I saw with relief that Andy was alone, drinking in slow deliberation – perhaps his hand was throbbing, and unexpectedly I found myself hoping it was. My unfeeling thought recalled a remark I had overheard on a bus, by a woman whose husband was intent on adultery that 'she wished him dead, or something!' It was the 'something' that had left me puzzled, but I now understood quite clearly: a remedy that would render him dependently immobile – to me death would be too final.

I speculated, as we collided with Gerald, who was making the best of the situation with Paula: a tube of twisting molten gold, shimmying towards her partner. They were a pair in gay abandon. We twisted and lost them, and Olwen was before me. She was looking up into the eyes of a suave and balding stranger, originally brought onto the scene by Judy, now otherwise occupied with another stranger of equally dubious character. Judy seemed inexplicably to go for middle-aged roués, I thought curiously, and they were always married. I heard the voice of Olwen saying 'but darling' to an equally affected endearment.

The music stopped. I dropped out of Edward's arms into the privacy of a dark corner, and saw him march determinedly towards his wife in the mêlée: a figure draped in muted brown with a large and battered posy of lace flowers pinned insecurely across her bosom. The usually straggly hair was ordered back to a crisp bun by a tortoiseshell clip. The untinted powder, shading the tired face, made her look like an invalid, who, with unconquered spirit, had gallantly risen up from her deathbed to join us. She was immediately swallowed by a greedy Roger who added her to the collection about him, pressing his own glass of liquid into her hand with sudden touching concern while he rose to play a few faulty notes on his trumpet and collapsed again, back to the comforting closeness of feminine debris.

'Thank you ever so.' I heard her say modestly, with a delighted giggle.

I was glad Roger had thought to draw her into his circle, for the compliment had obviously pleased her and she deserved a lifting break. It was the first time I had heard her giggle. This was going to be some party, I decided, unashamedly eavesdropping. Roger was now spinning a tale of fabulous colour which I knew to be true: a memory of his service abroad. A Malayan girl with the gentle proportions of a small bird, incomparable attentions, hot nights, the air dizzy with the scent of blossom. I felt he must be quite tipsy, for this was hardly the news his present company wanted to hear. The two clinging blondes were already exchanging comradely glances mixed with revenge, while the faithful and unsophisticated, shining-eyed Mrs Williams cooed loyally: 'Now isn't that nice, Mr Roger, it must have been quite an experience.'

But I was not allowed to enjoy the reminiscences of a roving Romeo indefinitely, for Barry, sneaking up unobserved, was muttering to me with his face marked by unreasonable, frustrated jealousy at the sight of his capering wife. 'Look at that,' he fumed. 'Can you beat it? Rolling in that sexy way – a trollope, that's what she is.'

'Nonsense, Barry. Let her have fun,' I argued, amused at this typically unfair attitude that men reserve for women. 'Don't you ever take an interest in other women?' I went on, knowing all too well that he did and feeling that drink was making him unreasonable.

'Of course, but that's different.' He stubbed his cigarette out viciously, as if obliterating Paula. 'It's the principle of the thing,' he muttered miserably. 'I've half a mind to go and punch the fellow on the nose.'

'Which one?' I said, wondering if Gerald was going to involve himself in a rumpus.

'That bald-headed coot, did you see he touched her bottom as he passed. Flaunting herself, that's what she was doing, the tart!'

He rose and sat down again heavily, finishing his drink in a long desperate gulp. It was the wrong moment to appeal to me for sympathy, for

I enjoyed the shadowy play of people, the little drama within drama which somehow the gaiety seemed to accentuate. Anyway, I had my own problems. Should I steal over, the olive branch firmly out, and place myself beside Andy provocatively before someone else did?

Upstairs there was an accompaniment of syncopated rhythm, and anxious Nelson awaiting his mother's return. He had just enjoyed, with hilarious chortles, the vision of an intoxicated Jane, without spectacles, posturing on a thimbleful of gin, not quite sure which male she intended to swim for – Andy was now regarded as a 'medical case' and not a male, I was glad to say. Deciding on her old flame Edward, enticed out by the false creakings of what she thought was his door and feeling that this was the moment to surpass all others (even my brother's innocent attention), she cried out in an unsteady voice: 'Take me! I am yours!' and flung herself at the dim figure before her.

But Jane had the wrong Romeo – an ungraciously aging roué who had persistently chased Blanche and was the cause of many dissensions in Gordon's world of romance. Jane's squeals sent Edward gallantly to the rescue, thinking it was me, while a profusely apologetic debauchee slunk away to hide.

Mr Budden, an advertisement for carbolic soap and starch, was swilling beer contentedly at our improvised bar and keeping a firm hold on his missus, unrecognisably silent and refusing to dance, examining with bulging eyes what I am sure he felt were a Conservative rabble. A curly-haired Mrs Budden in a ruched dress of blue flowers, her head a little to one side, listened for the whimpering call of her baby, as her eyes followed the passing dancers with envy, resenting the hand that forced her to sit and had not allowed her the first dance with Gerald.

Now Blanche, spinning a silver web in a solo, made every man think of bed, and Roger, rising heavily, disappeared unobtrusively with both his blondes in the direction of the garden, leaving Mrs Williams to lend Barry a sympathetic ear, for I was too absorbed in my own moods to render aid.

Gerald and Paula followed the solo with a skit on bull-fighting, to the candles falling apart and dawn like a torch dimmed the occasion to a closing note. The sound dwindling to a breathless softness awoke me to the movement of Andy creeping off upstairs: the brush of a yielding hand rushed me into a panic of indecision, and I sat, my head bowed, inattentive to the murmurings about me. I was being drawn; drawn upstairs, powerless to resist the urge, for the same reasons a lot of others had attended the party. I rose: a landlady has a perfect right to see how an ailing lodger is, even at this hour. I excused myself untruthfully, as I felt my way across an array of inert bodies and fumbled for the stairs.

'Ah me, love will find a way,' came a flippant comment from the top step of the unlighted staircase. Was I never to have a moment's freedom from inquisitive humanity, I asked myself exasperated?

'Mind your own business, Nelson, and go to bed,' I retorted icily. 'It's a landlady's job to see how all her tenants are, especially if they are not well, so your cheeky insinuations are quite unnecessary.'

There was a loud disagreement as I brushed past to the small door standing alone. I knocked gently, and entered.

A solitary candle burning had brought peace to the little room.

'I was hoping you would come.'

The words were simple, spoken with infinite tenderness, and we were together at last, comfortingly together, bridging all the frustrating gaps in the soft tender swellings of mutual passion. I kissed the ill-fated hand with murmurs of regret, touched the sleeve neatly folded back to a straight line by the trim fingers of Jane, without jealousy, suspended for a fleeting moment on a precipice of impelling emotion, and then we were painfully drowning – painfully and tenderly.

Chapter Twelve

It had been a good party, I felt, a suitable farewell to our departing comrade. True, the curtains had caught fire as a candle toppled and fell, but it was soon extinguished by a resourceful guest. Of course Mrs Briggs had called the police – a fact that Roger had omitted to tell me at the time. He told me he had met them whilst walking his blondes out for fresh air, and trying to decide which one he would eventually palm off onto someone else (Barry looked the most suitable candidate). With a few well-chosen words Roger had sent the law about their business. Lady Booth stuck abusive notices on those cars that had dared to use her frontage as a carpark, while Miss Brady, sitting up in a darkened window, watched the flickering candlelight with suspicion and applauded the action of Mrs Briggs in calling the police. Nelson, a crashing bright light at 6am, stating he was financially embarrassed, was collecting empty bottles. More than one person threatened to murder him, as the bonds of tolerant friendship which had flourished so gaily the night before, were severed one by one. It would always be like this for me, I supposed. Hail and farewell, and the void would be filled by yet another stranger; now all that was left of

Gordon's reign was a dark circle of dried oil in the drive and a row of empty medicine bottles awaiting disposal. Gerald had left too, submerged by jungle noises and in exceptionally good spirits. He would be back – there was no doubt about that!

The same morning the Jehovah's disciple conscientiously called again to inquire how I was getting on with his book and to see if there were any questions I wanted to ask. As I had not given the book another thought I was overcome with panic, passed a few comments which I hoped would fit and managed to offload him onto Barry in one of his intellectual moods – the man left carrying two tranquillisers for a raging headache.

Gordon's room was now taken by a ferret-faced waiter and his wife, a veteran nagger with a rear like a hippopotamus: a kindly couple who cracked after one week under the strain of brass instruments and left, a little regretfully for they had enjoyed the company. The room was once more emptied and filled by strangers. Most of us were a little self-conscious at having new people trespassing in our well-worn grooves and studied the new occupants of Gordon's room with a somewhat reserved, but friendly speculation.

The new couple, although we only saw them briefly from time to time, in no way resembled anyone else in the house. Mr Higgins, a swarthy well-built little man of great dignity, treated his wife with old world courtliness, putting to shame the habits of almost every male in the house, leaving a wide opening for immediate womanly comparisons. Except for myself, heady with the champagne qualities of a new love, who had no reason for reproaches, and a doubtful Mrs Budden, her first ecstasies dulled a little by familiarity and the overstrain of a troublesome child, everyone was at the moment sitting on the fence.

Mrs Higgins appeared to accept the ardent attentions of her husband as if they were her rightful due; diluted blue eyes gazed at him fondly from a face lost in doughy roundness. The head of shining mustard-coloured ringlets, the comfortable body, a martyr to pastel blues, spreading without restraint, gaudy paste jewellery sparkling against the sloping shelf of a full bosom, her over-indulgence in make-up, all somehow matched his flourishing cavalier airs, as he escorted her up and down stairs and in and out of the dark Vauxhall parked resplendent in our drive, giving the place a tone of opulence that it had never received from Gordon's heap.

Nelson, Edward and the children, settling together like flies, surveyed the strangers' arrival with unending curiosity. The careful sorting of their belongings from a brand-new car, the delicate handling of certain items, stern rejection as offers of help were politely but firmly refused, were received with disappointment as Mrs Higgins, playing nervously with a shining ringlet, guarded her belongings. She was jealously protective of a tall, upright basket on which was a giveaway label 'Jamaica to Southampton', and which, in consequence, became the cause of much speculation among the onlookers. Nelson was certain it harboured contraband – opium was slowly rotting the villain in this week's comic – for an adult audience, I felt and the word was constantly on his lips as he discussed the potentialities. It was an American comic, and where he got it from nobody knew. Jane, reading it out of curiosity, said it had produced a night of excessively bad dreams and the seller of such literature ought to be prosecuted.

Edward was equally convinced that the basket held contraband, but of another sort, and I thought that if this inquisitive gathering of the clans didn't put the new people off, nothing would. But if we thought to thaw the occupants of Room 5 into chatty revelations, we were mistaken, for they minded their own business and closed their door firmly to intruders.

Then Edward started the investigation of one of his ideas which eventually involved everyone in the house and all because he said he heard sounds as if someone was being tortured. Catching him for the fourth time standing in the hall and obviously eavesdropping with intent, I couldn't help but reprove his actions. He carried me away swiftly to the seclusion of his room, with the offended face of a man heavily misjudged.

'I don't want to alarm you, but I have reason to suspect these new people,' he confided to me. 'Strange sounds. Their reticence to being sociable. It is just not natural when coming to this house. And that basket – you observed it no doubt – to my mind it gives a sinister tone!'

'It looked like crockery to me,' I said, spoiling Edward's dramatic effects with a few plain words.

'Why didn't they want me to touch it, then?' he asked. 'When I offered with all the geniality in the world to carry it to safety single-handed.' He poured two glasses of a solid-looking greenish liquid from a crystal decanter with a shaking hand; I wondered if I should refuse it, but as it hadn't come from beneath the kitchen sink I felt it would be worth the risk.

I looked around. The painting of my blonde giant was no more, removed to oblivion, and a new study of Olwen, decently draped in a white coverage, her arms raised as if in prayer, had replaced it. I was glad, for that was past history!

'Nelson and I, for once, have agreed on something,' he went on. 'There are occasions when he seems to have a natural insight into things, and his help then comes in very useful. Not that I have any brief for our fat boy's mind – but . . .' he paused.

'Go on,' I said, examining the green liquid I was about to swallow with a suspicious change of mind. Edward's recital sounded to me like the beginnings of a typical 'thought', exaggerated beyond the bounds of sanity, that he was so good at manufacturing.

'I've knocked several times since,' Edward reverted to the new people, 'on some pretext or other. I once cunningly suggested that I was the milkman, and had the door practically slammed in my face,' he ended in consternation.

I looked up at the harrowed speaker – he really meant it. I burst out laughing. 'Really, you are outrageous. Let them be secretive if they want to, what's wrong with that? It's a change in this house,' I added ruefully, thinking of the irritatingly knowing looks I had to endure from various quarters and the constant speculation on things to come that was part of everyday life.

'I shall certainly keep watch in spite of your

derision, and will inform the law at the slightest evidence of foul play.' Edward was offended.

'Please,' I begged, 'whatever you do, don't call the police. We'll be getting a dreadful name if this sort of thing goes on; we have just had them involved over the monkeys, not to mention the party and who knows what other complaints they have received that we know nothing about yet?'

'That's what the police get paid for – to protect the public.' He had obviously been indulging in comparisons with Nelson, who would never accept the fact that the house down the road was not entitled to a police raid every week in order to satisfy his curiosity.

'Yes, but we don't know yet if we do need protecting.'

'Wait and see; if you'd heard the sound I've heard you would think differently,' Edward prophesied. 'And if I hadn't actually seen that Mrs Budden's baby is safe, not that I want to see it, the little monster, I would have said that the sounds were the father strangling it.' And he left me to finish my drink alone with the sordid picture of Mr Budden strangling his offspring in my house, as he took up another position in the hall.

It was surprising how, once the suspicions of Edward and Nelson had started to circulate, the idea took root and gathered momentum. By evening Edward's surveillance activities had spread and affected the whole house, while behind their locked door the guilty pair sat on unaware of the upheaval they were causing.

I was eventually dragged out from behind my own locked door to Edward's room, to preside as the head of the house at a general meeting of my lodgers, feeling a spiritual affinity with the Prime Minister at the hasty reassembling of Parliament in a crisis.

In Edward's and Olwen's room imaginations had soared, as the supposed contents of the basket became wilder and wilder. Edward swore, after minute inspection of the stairs, that he had detected traces of something that certainly wasn't rust! Nelson, not to be outdone, announced pathetically that the dripping of fresh blood from the basket had sent him reeling to his room for a smoke, being forced to borrow a cigarette from the only generous member of the household as his own machine for making illicit cigarettes, cadged off Grandma Durrell, and broken down. Mrs Williams paled at the thought.

'That was a picture I should have liked to have seen – you swooning at anything!' I remarked with sarcasm.

There was a nervous titter all round.

The children, rather frightened at Nelson's declaration, likened the situation to a trunk murder and questioned Jane closely on exactly how a body could be carved up without detection. This set Mr Budden fearing for his wife's firstborn; silencing the weeping, terrified creature bluntly, he scanned the local paper, produced from his hip pocket, for fresh accommodation while Blanche and Judy, enjoying the situation to the full as they always did, and trained in the art of handling delicate interments, had to be forcibly stopped from leaping out to the front garden and severing the tyres of the Higgins' car with Edward's palette knife to foil any plans the culprits might have for a quick getaway.

Paula and Barry, quarrelling over Barry's lack of winter employment, gladly joined the discussion, pleased to forget their quarrel in someone else's predicament that might, after all, be rather an adventure. Roger, brought down protesting by an amused Andy, said that the house was going from bad to worse, and that since the night of the party his thoughts had been consistently in Malaya and now, with this interruption, the special Malayan dish he was trying out would be reduced to a ball of solid rice. Jane said she'd never rest in her bed till the cold-blooded murderers were brought to justice and really these days one just didn't know what would enter the house next.

Edward, having stirred up a hive of suspicion and counter-suspicion, now sat a little apart, a little superior, as though his manifestations were now materialising on a higher plane, while everybody turned to me, their landlady, for the final solution. I stood uncertainly before public opinion which was directed against my indecisive attitude to sit back and do nothing.

'A true Conservative,' stated Mr Budden categorically, hoping to rile me, as no new accommodation had come to light from the pages before him. 'And when she does make a move, it will no doubt be the wrong one – true to Conservative form.'

Roger, reflecting, agreed. The bickering went on.

Edward turned from his meditations at last, silencing his audience. He spoke directly to me: 'Nelson has seen blood. You must act now,' he declared, in the manner of a surgeon diagnosing the right disease and deciding on a cure.

'That's right,' said Nelson proudly, remarkably wholesome for one who had seen so much blood, glad of the newfound fellowship with Edward. Nelson's mother burst into fresh whimpering: 'It might 'ave been 'im. It might 'ave been my Nelson chopped up and stuffed into the basket.'

'Don't be ridiculous, Mrs Williams,' I said kindly. 'Why should anyone want to harm Nelson?'

'Yes, why indeed?' came a chorus of immediate comment, and the reasons why!

Edward raised his hand to quell the mob to another silence. 'You are the landlady,' Edward declared with a small apologetic smile. 'We, the tenants, demand you do something.'

'Before we are murdered brutally in our beds,' Jane added.

'You must go,' Edward ordered bossily. 'Make a small imaginary inquiry, firmly getting your foot in the door, then take a good swift look round,' he suggested thoughtfully, 'then . . .'

'I like that,' I interrupted indignantly. 'I've got to do all the dirty work and probably get slaughtered and end up in the basket with whatever is already in it!' I was gloomily distraught at the unpleasant job ahead of me.

'I don't think it'll come to that,' Edward consoled, 'but obviously, as you are the landlady, you are in the best position to enter their room. I've already tried and failed, as you know. I've done my bit.'

'Whenever there is anything unpleasant to do, I've got to do it because I'm the bloody landlady,'

I retorted exasperated. 'If it's something nice nobody asks me – I get trampled in the rush. And what's more I don't like at all the idea of prying into other people's lives.'

Olwen agreed with me. 'Leave it,' she said, 'and see what happens.'

'In fact,' I continued wrathfully, 'I don't think I can do it – it's against my principles, anyway,' I ended stubbornly, backing for the door and escape. At that moment a long drawn-out yelp chilled every face in the room.

'My God,' Edward exploded, 'if you don't return we'll work out an immediate rescue.' He thought my move was one of resigned investigation.

In that moment of acute stillness that followed Edward's remark we heard a loud knocking at the front door, which somehow seemed ominous in the circumstances. Nelson made a quick stampede to investigate and returned excitedly. 'A cop car!' he announced hoarsely. 'At our gate!' And everyone turned from Nelson to me.

Feeling dismayed, forced into a situation of no return and yet filled with the violent urge to laugh, I made my way unhappily out to investigate, trying to compose myself in the short distance across the hall, with the unpleasant sensation of a dozen pairs of eyes boring into my back. The shadow of a tall body blotted the mottled glass at the door.

'Do you wish to see someone?' I asked, opening the door with some misgivings.

'Just making some inquiries,' the blue-uniformed man replied, holding a notebook, not unlike Nelson's, in his hand. 'Have you some people here by the name of Higgins, newly arrived from Jamaica? Docked at Southampton, I believe.'

'You see!' Edward's voice came through to me in a storm of gasps from across the hall. 'There is something going on – I was convinced of it! Convinced!' he said with relish.

I hesitated uneasily, wondering if I should disclose our suspicions and feeling a sudden sympathetic fear for the culprits as I examined the cold face before me. 'It's nothing unpleasant, I hope, like – er – murder?' I blurted out inquisitively, unable to stop myself, forced on by the tense compelling breathing of the lodgers down my neck.

'Just a little matter.' He was non-committal, then he must have noticed my tenseness for his coldness suddenly turned to kindness. 'Don't be alarmed, it's not murder,' and a smile transformed his face.

Relieved, but still grudging the situation, I ran up the stairs two at a time to summon the Higginses below to face the law. The crowd had vanished tactfully and noiselessly, but I knew they would be listening. Reaching the Higgins' door I paused to listen: what were the guilty pair doing? I heard the low gentle murmur of Mr Higgins' question and the sound of his wife's answer.

'A policeman to see you,' I called out, knocking carelessly and loudly, adopting a nonchalant air. There was a complete and guilty silence; my heart sank. So Edward's assumptions had been right. I repeated the performance even more gaily and breathlessly awaited the answer. It came in the door opening a few inches to show the white and scared face of Mr Higgins. 'The police for you,' I repeated. 'It's all right,' I added, 'nothing serious, just a small matter – not a corpse or anything drastic.' I laughed nervously, desperately sorry now for the shocked little man, almost wishing I had warned him to escape. Mrs Higgins, looking like a badly-made Christmas decoration, shaking visibly, fell from behind the door and burst sobbing into my arms. Astonished, I staggered under the sudden weight.

'There, there,' I said through a mouthful of golden curls, wondering what the woman could possibly have done. Mr Higgins, patting his wife's shoulder with manly courage descended the stairs to face whatever was coming. Fresh tears welled up and slowly rolled down the rouged cheeks of the curvy bundle in my arms.

'We thought nobody would find out,' she explained the mystery between gulping sobs. 'We smuggled our Tinker through customs to save the quarantine.'

I knew by the infinite stillness that my lodgers were digesting the latest news. Then came the usual trickle of comment. 'Well, I never,' Edward said, 'you can't behave in a perfectly normal way to protect a pet without police interrogation. I shall despatch a note to the Chief of Police – who is he?'

'Gestapo state, that's what England's coming to, what we need are a few Communist riots.'

'I agree, bloody riots,' Nelson was quickly ready to draw blood. Mrs Williams was already showering sympathetic tears.

'Just because they are in uniform, doesn't give them the right to interfere with the working man's pleasure; someone ought to tell them so.'

Mrs Budden was in a strangely dictatorial mood, a Boadicea, her shield a nauseating pink child, held in an attitude of leadership.

'Me old woman's right; they are always interfering, I find, and what are the Conservatives going to do about it I'd like to know?' Mr Budden was bitter. His slight clashes with the local police force over minor offences had never been very successful.

'Why don't they investigate those coffins, instead of hounding innocent souls. Nelson's got enough criminal data on that place to sink a battleship.' Nelson beamed at Edward's extraordinary suggestion.

'Well said, me ol' bearded mate.' The chief instigators of every riot were bonded firmly together.

'Poor little innocent pup – carrying on as though it's a rabies infected monstrosity.'

'Scandalous I call it . . .'

The women drew together in fluttering sympathy, nevertheless examining the male form in the door in a way that only women can.

'The law is the law,' Barry sanely suggested, whilst trying to block the new attraction from Paula's view. He was quietly crushed by further insults, as British red tape and the police force rapidly fell from favour.

'Turncoats,' I muttered, leading Mrs Higgins to a chair.

'I never really wanted to see them go to prison. It's just the idea that was somehow exciting.' Edward sounded a little sad, as he explained his actions – to an accusing audience.

Nelson, unaffected, lied as usual. 'I knew their crime was innocent all the time, but I just didn't want to spoil yer fun,' he remarked casually and waited acclaim. There was none – we knew him too well.

The dog, the least affected of all, a scampering ball of white fur and yappings had to go.

There was now nothing to keep the Higgins from going back to their rightful home in the north of England and wait patiently for the six months' quarantine to pass with only a severe reprimand as a sour reminder and leaving me yet again with a vacant room. But I did not worry. I knew it would soon be filled.

Chapter Thirteen

When my next advertisement sent me a choice of two people I chose Harriet Amelia Greenfield, without hesitation, for here was the 'ideal tenant'. The paragon that my Aunt Patience had referred to, I decided, as I welcomed her with great respect and tucked her into the vacant room which had already seen three sets of tenants in its short life. Room 5 was certainly seeing a change of faces.

She was a gentle, delicate widow of great refinement, obviously a Conservative, which would in no way constitute a thorn for Mr Budden – she was too retiring. Here was an open background of indisputable education and breeding, a woman who had undoubtedly fallen on hard times with stiff dignity. There were no signs of hidden inhibitions in that fragile ladylike face, no possible indecent pregnancies here, or skeletons in the cupboard or gigantic sex problems, which seemed to prevail in the rest of the house. I regarded the rather sad silhouette of perpetual grey, smelling discreetly of lavender water, moving with an air which was the essence of sanity and respectability, with a new satisfaction.

My other lodgers regarded my attitude of obvious jubilation and respect towards the new member as a definite form of disloyalty to them.

Refusing to accept my unstinted praise, they harboured the sombre stranger with a slightly antagonistic tolerance mixed with human kindness. Nelson's mother alone was drawn towards the new tenant, seeing in her a kindred spirit of conformity. Unfortunately, she lacked the confidence to surmount the barriers of class distinction. Her servile greetings wrapped in an air of lonely hopefulness were not enough to gain a friendly footing. Mrs Greenfield made a pointed insistence on her full name, but she paid her rent promptly with few words.

She came and went in silence, as soothing as a warm bath after physical labour, as ineffectual as Mrs Williams' reprimands. The fleeting glimpses of her passing never failed to rouse me into self-congratulation on my newfound taste, selecting a lodger who not only did not gossip but who had the good taste not to discern people's characters at a glance, sifting the possible and impossible. This was another milestone in my landlady's career. Who could doubt it?

In quiet moments of introspection I examined the intricacies of the household. I seemed to be no richer, and the patient moanings of my bank manager, like a nagging tooth, reminded me of this fact. Discussing the situation with Mrs Briggs after a harrowing morning spent sorting out bills, she informed me that 'Bed and Breakfast' was the answer and that one twisted and screwed life at every angle, sneaking in a fast move to acquire wealth whenever possible if one wanted to watch the luxury of a mounting bank balance.

'I've been letting for years,' she told me. That

explained the unobtrusive trickle of people going in and out of her house. 'I know all the ins and outs, give you a tip or two,' she boasted, forgetting how many tips, good and bad, she had already given me. 'Hum, you've let yourself in for it, I know. They're mucking your house up too, I bet; you'll have to change your ways, my girl, anyone can see you are too lackadaisical. Blonde hair and blue eyes won't help you much when you're letting – them's only pitfalls,' was her sardonic reminder, with a look which suggest that I was in charge of a reformatory, and not doing my job properly. I left her: I was even more depressed at the knowledge that if I wanted the illusion of my first dreams to come about the whole house would have to be reorganised to bed and breakfast activities. It was as gloomy a proposition as breeding mice.

The summer was rushing indeniably to a close and once again the town, as though attacked with the severe hand of a barber's scissors, would simmer through a lonely winter and turn again to pander to her yearly diehards. I was thankful that I had made my niche, launching myself onto some sort of keel, before the market was flooded with rooms to let and the stampede for cheaper winter quarters began.

Mother, supported by Leslie, remembering her previous promises, arrived to stay, armed with a bundle of gardening tools, packets of seeds, and a small well-packed suitcase; sweets for the boys and Nelson, and some recipes in a cookery book of Bombay sweetmeats by Mimer Sing which she wished to discuss with Edward. Leslie had added a quantity of fresh liquor to the luggage to replenish the drink shelf, feeling, he said, that it would give my uncertified lunatic asylum the air of a stately home.

I had promised to take Nelson to the beach, and we should have to take our day out soon before the weather broke and we were dismally engulfed by autumn. It would also fulfil the promise I had made to Barry to spend a day of uninhibited luxury by the sea. For Barry, time had still remained remote; the brown bodies were still unattainable and reality brought him only the efficiency of Jane who increased his urges with helpful massage, guaranteed to relax a tired body. Paula seemed unable to satisfy them, and I refused to be more than sympathetic. The children were blasé over our excursion for they were going to spend the day with their father, a sober and righteous man, with whom I now seemed to have nothing in common except arguments over money, which I felt were usually my fault.

Waving goodbye to the children, and leaving Mother to a restful day of quiet reverie and pottering, we set off to the beach. Beside me walked a model of appreciative delight, carrying a small bag of necessary gear and spouting a lot of unnecessary chatter. The bus was packed with people, but we managed to lodge ourselves in with skilful determination. Remembering Edward's shudder, and his flow of deprecating speech at our suggestion that he take a day off from painting and join us, at what he called 'the revolting spectacle of sweating, seedy humanity, determined in a depraved and ghoulish way to enjoy themselves, making any venture to the town a contamination and nightmare', I was inclined to agree now, as the first discomfort of bodies jammed together in confined space on a hot day hit me. But Nelson, I could see, disregarding discomfort, was already beginning to enjoy himself – and after all it was his day, I acquiesced tolerantly.

Our conductor, a flower-like Adonis, with pale gold hair slicked back like a smooth curtain to hang straight, had already given Nelson an ambition in life – something, I regret to say, he had never shown before. He watched in admiration the traditional hat crushed to a volcanic peak, pushed well back on the smooth locks, the fair moustache growing sparsely on the top lip, and listened to the thin arias of song floating up, it seemed, from the very bottom of a flat belly, punctuated with 'Fares, please,' and other pleasantries. Being a woman I noticed, without Nelson's enthusiasm, that his fingernails were dirty.

We stopped for an unofficial moment at a wayside café to replenish an empty billycan, a move of independence that Mr Budden would have thoroughly applauded: after all it was a democratic country, I told myself, as a protesting murmur echoed from those passengers who were in a hurry. My own thoughts in solitary flight lingered with tender indulgences: the comforting arms of my lover; the boiler which seemed to be a menace of lighting and re-lighting; the grumblings of Roger and Edward and their coming to the undoubtable conclusion that we women were the worst offenders at bath-taking. I thought of the new lodger, Harriet, who would no doubt be taking tea with Mother and, possibly, a reserved Edward, who was still a little watchful. He had not yet weighed up this unknown quantity, he was prone to saying. And then I was back again to the growing completion of a perfect relationship with Andy, which had so far managed to survive the close proximity of an unpredictable household.

The bell donging smartly brought me back to Nelson, but it was not the troublemaker as I had suspected, but the return of Adonis with a steaming billycan. 'Next stop the cemetery,' he called out, renewing his contact with his passengers. 'Anyone for the cemetery,' he quipped pleasantly. 'Come along ladies and gentlemen, who is for long-sleep corner?' His audience shuddered, and the over-fifties glanced uneasily at the walled cemetery. He expected laughter but there was none, except from Nelson. The British, intensely reserved, deplore this sort of humour; the man gave his admiring audience of one an impudent wink from pink-rimmed eyes, undaunted at the lack of other appreciation, reshuffled his already wounded song, and blasted forth again, until we were at last regurgitated in the heart of the town without ceremony.

It was still pulsating with traffic, people, and sound: the last fling of a dying summer, of which we were now a part, fighting our way forward like the rest. The inevitable money-box rattled. I groaned. It was another flag day.

Nelson had begged to be allowed to see Paula and Olwen at work, a sight he said he would be much interested in because, in his opinion, he had 'never seen a more idle pair of birds in the 'ouse', a scandalous smirk of deprecation filling the broad face. A slim silhouette of pale turquoise elegance presided over a glass counter of exotic scents and entrancingly wrapped packages, and there was Paula persuading an aging novice that the contents of a particular small and expensive jar would bring back the long-lost youthful contours.

'Blooming liar,' Nelson whispered, outrageously truthful. Then came the comment that 'she was past 'elp anyway', and he and Paula exchanged slow subtle winks. Dragging him quickly away from where, obviously, a tense situation would arise within minutes if he was allowed to linger, and forfeiting a new lipstick I was intending to buy, I marched him determinedly to the nearest exit. We passed the shop where Olwen, sitting in a bed of shoes, a dark head bent over a slim foot, persuaded the owner it was a perfect fit. Suitably impressed by the array of footwear Nelson looked down at his rather stringy grey plimsolls with distaste, suggesting hopefully that he could do with a new pair himself. He examined my expression carefully for the sign of a generous whim. I firmly ignored the pleading look – I had forfeited my lipstick, so why not Nelson his shoes? We were once more fighting our way to the sea.

The promenade was a jungle of people, the sand a jam session of arms and legs through which here and there a yellow mirage beckoned. Storming the promenade, we surged forward again like gold prospectors, pausing for a second to view the attractions of the seaside through a jaundiced-looking telescope and lingered beside a brightly-coloured tent to applaud Punch belabouring a much misjudged dragon, while Judy, hiding her thoughts behind a mask of boredom, blinked an eye and suffered the audience. Nelson stayed longest and laughed the heartiest, then, remarking it was 'kid's stuff', he followed me reluctantly away, but revived instantly at the spectacle of a pink woman with blue hair and a body like a bolster, suspended on a giant pair of scales, whose weight was being carefully matched by a pyramid of iron discs expertly handled.

'Sixteen stone, lady, and every one a winner,' said the stout jovial fellow in a panama hat and cream linen jacket, stepping smartly forward to bring her down to earth. Nelson quickly took the chair, self-conscious and blushing, but determined to miss nothing, while the sixteen stone, screaming girlishly at the result, hid her face and fled to the comforting arms of her husband, a shame-faced man in a gaudy blazer. Trying to appear unconcerned, Nelson watched intently as the iron weights piled up against him. It was a tense moment: would he make it?

'Made it,' he yelled delightedly, as up he went.

'That will be sixpence, son, and a fine figure if I may say so,' said the man, his hand out, while the shrewd eyes were already looking for his next customer. Nelson, ignoring the result of his weight and reluctant to part with sixpence, was already standing posed like his namesake in Trafalgar Square for a quick photograph.

Then we saw Barry, a figure of rippling brownness against the shiny surface of the sea, and his working partner, proving that there was more than one attraction on the beach this summer. Feeling our way carefully through rows of prostrate bodies towards them, we selected a small basin of sand, which scarcely provided for Nelson's bulk. Removing first a broken bottle and an ice-cream wrapper, and myself deftly burying a condom, we pegged out a few square feet of solitude and settled unglamorously like a couple of squatters in an Indian bazaar.

Barry, hearing Nelson's shout which had a flavour of long-lost friends meeting unexpectedly in a remote part of the world, bubbled up with a gleaming smile of welcome and turned for a hasty consultation with his working partner, the male study of what an English summer can do for you if it's a good one – especially if you have the magnificent confidence of a Valentino enhanced by a silver medallion swinging on a string against a bronzed chest. Barry joined us, delighted.

'I'm so glad you made it,' he whispered, as if I was the only girl in the world, white teeth bewitchingly close to my ear as his eyes followed the passage of a couple of well-filled bikinis. 'Can only stay for a moment, so make the most of it!' he said suggestively, with a gaiety of spirit that never revealed itself in the house.

Grumbling again at the crowds, we changed into our swimming costumes; I manoeuvred myself into my bit of red coverage, as I watched with some amusement Nelson decorating himself swiftly in royal blue and red splendour. Shining like a young and well-fed porpoise, he leapt a couple of inert bodies, spreading sand in short, sharp spurts, while moans of indignant protest followed the unheeding, dancing figure headed for the sea, roaring to me to follow.

'Pity you had to bring that menace,' Barry said

with good-humoured unkindness, as we settled down on our ration of sand unpenetrated by the twangy quality of sea breeze, for it was a still, solid day drugged with heavy odours.

'I promised him a day by the sea,' I murmured, my eyes half closed and soaking in the trembling rays of warmth, like Mr Budden in his string vest. The unavoidably trained mind of a mother, always on the alert, hoped that Nelson was not going to provide the local paper with a column of seaside drama, but I decided that, in his home-knitted woollen, he was a landmark for all to see, and would not be providing the house with a funeral this summer – not if I could help it, anyway.

A slight friendly pressure on my hand told me that Barry demanded attention. 'Yes?' I answered.

'Maggie, dear Maggie' – Barry always called me Maggie – 'I can never really regard you in the light of an ordinary landlady. As Edward says, you're, well, different.'

'Can't you?' I said, happily, my mind now back at the house.

'I have something to tell you,' he hesitated.

'Go on – I'm not laughing, I'm listening even if I have got my eyes closed.' I joked gently, aware that at times my uproarious mirth would intimidate him.

'I've found the only girl in the world for me!' The whisper vibrated with emotion. 'And I intend to marry her!'

'What?' I said opening my eyes and sitting up. 'You must be mad. That's bigamy. Anyway, who is she? And what's the matter with Paula?' I asked stormily. I could see Barry was going to get himself into another muddle and then come to me for help. 'She can't be very much anyway, as you've never mentioned her before, and you can't have known her for long either,' I surmised, 'or you would have told me about her the last time we chatted.'

'It's you,' the words trembled from him.

'Well, that's different,' I said calmly, bursting forth in hearty laughter. 'I approve of the choice, if not the action. Anyway, how can you marry? You are already married,' I reasoned, suddenly indignant, hoping that Barry was not now, in a mad moment, going to try and involve me in bigamy, or worse.

'Wait and see,' he muttered darkly. A compelling shout from Barry's working companion made him hastily leave my side with a smothered curse.

'Come on, Mush. 'Ere a mo, I can't cope all day alone while you're coming the old seduction lark.' The cockney voice ruined the aura of a blonde god, and I collapsed back to my sunbathing pose, relieved that yet another unburdening of Barry's soul was temporarily averted as I subsided again for a moment of thought in peace. Above the unfamiliar noises of the crowd came the familiar robust yell of Nelson – as somebody got a ducking, no doubt. I snuggled into my small patch of sand. The children would probably be driving their father mad by now, I chuckled, and Mother, though enjoying her day of peaceful solitude, would surely by now be missing the presence of her grandchildren.

I raised my head to give a penetrating look of disapproval to the seedy-looking man on my right, who was thrashing his child merely because his nerves were frayed, feeling in sympathy with a neighbour who, reclining in a deckchair, had just said in a voice about to sleep 'ee but it's luvly 'ere', and was beginning to swallow his words.

The sound of deep breathing told me Barry was back. 'Now, where were we?' he asked, running a soft finger up my arm.

'You were trying to soft-soap me, and I had said, "No",' I replied lightly.

Barry sighed. 'Are we never to come to a better understanding?'

He already knew the answer – 'Not if it involves me in bigamy, and anyway I am otherwise engaged.'

'You're lucky,' he said. 'And he's lucky, too.'

I accepted the compliment with grace, but I had already forgotten him as his own words reminded me of the biting memory of Andy; an intense warmth tucked away deep within me, a comfort yet a threat. Curious, I thought with a sigh, how with a touch, a look and an intonation one was rocketed up to the dizzy heights of a starry sky, or plunged into a chasm of cold despair. At the moment privacy was our problem, for where can one find privacy in a house full of people effervescently alive, and hopelessly curious? 'That's life,' I said aloud, referring to my thoughts.

'I refuse to accept it,' Barry announced with absurd bravado. 'I shall fight every inch of the way to win you!'

'Is this another infamous proposal?' I asked teasingly.

Barry's face, whitening under the tan, told me

that he was serious. Any minute I thought, suppressing my laughter, a tranquilliser will appear.

'I must do something with my life,' he said gloomily, rather offended at my levity. 'This job will only last another few weeks, and what then?'

In spite of my mirth I appreciated his predicament. How many of us longed to do other things and were faced with a hundred different reasons for not doing them – lack of money, lack of education, lack of opportunity, lack of initiative.

Nelson's flat-footed, providential arrival saved any further discussion, and despatched an irritated Barry back to his floats. 'Some fun,' he panted, whipping up his small towel, blowing his nose, rubbing his rolling body, and repeating the whole process of annoying our neighbour with flying sand.

'That's better,' he stretched himself out, wriggling about like a well-fed puppy, giving the child who was still snivelling from its father's hand a vindictive look.

I studied the contours of Nelson's bone structure, blunted to circles of roundness, so different from his mother: Nelson was well insulated from the cold. The stubble hair was flattened to a dark smoothness; it was a different Nelson, more mature, but the voice was the same.

'I suppose yer didn't see me standin' on me 'ead?'

'No. It must have been a revolting sight,' I said callously.

'Thought yer didn't,' he sounded hurt. 'Yer was all caught up with 'im – drooling, positively drooling, 'e was. Wot was 'e saying anyway?' Nelson couldn't bear a conversation to flourish without him.

'We were just talking about things,' I remarked vaguely. Better not let Nelson get hold of the story of that proposal. 'You know, situations and so forth. You wouldn't understand if I did tell you.'

'I understand more than you think,' the pink mound rose indignantly and, producing a bottle of suntan lotion given to him by Paula, he poured a generous amount into his hand and beat it into his body. 'Yer can tell by people's mugs what they're talking about.'

'Can you? Then you must find life very interesting! And it's not "mugs", it's "expressions".'

''E's a fine chap, don't you think?' The question was deliberately artful.

'I suppose you could say that.' I was deliberately vague. Nelson and I were playing our usual game, the game which so often Mrs Briggs and I indulged in, when curiosity got the better of one.

'Ain't you betrothed to 'im yet?'

For sheer unadulterated curiosity Nelson and Mrs Briggs were united. I fumed. 'Mind your own business,' I retorted, looking at the body now exposing itself to the sun. The mischievous eyes were closed. 'Mind you don't get burnt. Remember what happened to Barry.'

Nelson kept his eyes closed. 'It's time yer got yerself married off.' His face was full of fatherly concern. 'Yes,' I thought. It was just the expression that preceded his telling Mrs Budden to drown her baby. 'Ma only said so last night, not that there's much to recommend the process,' he added in a very mature way, 'from what I can see.'

I couldn't help feeling that the comment was not something that his dad had said, but Edward or Roger, because both 'recommend' and 'process' were entirely new words spouted from the mouth of Nelson.

'Nelson, where's your father?' I asked in direct attack, feeling it was my turn, and using his and Mrs Briggs' tactics for a change.

'In prison. I've told yer before.' His reply was airy, a little impatient at my disbelief. He sat up to examine his toenails carefully, his breath caught up in a roll of rippling fat.

'I can't believe you, you take the matter too lightly.'

Nelson chuckled. 'All 'em bars. I wouldn't like it meself.'

'I only asked because I like your mother and I would like to see her happy. Perhaps we can send your father a food parcel or something, that is if he *is* in prison, though I very much doubt the fact.' I was certain that Nelson was a liar.

'Ten years, he got. Robbing a bank, it were.'

I gasped, genuinely horrified. Ten years, how ghastly! Perhaps he was speaking the truth. I watched Nelson's face closely, but not a flicker told me whether or not his father languished in prison. It struck me suddenly that Edward never mentioned his family, was reluctant to do so. Was he ashamed of them, or were they too being forcibly kept by the government, in the north perhaps? The intonation of Edward's speech automatically led me to believe he was from a northern county.

Squeaks of feminine laughter suggested that somewhere one of the Romeos played: it was not

Barry, he was too busy. I turned lazily to examine the cause: that idol of the bathing belles and matrons alike, Barry's mate. He was the object of many a lingering glance, a figure which had even dazzled Paula and occasioned her to breathe the facts over a midnight coffee. The description had held both Jane and me spellbound, and had inflicted Jane with the decision to spend a day by the sea when she could find time, for she did not care for the beach. Jane had now taken up dressmaking, for which she had quite a flair, and orders were piling up, so that the sound of a sewing machine buzzing all hours had added to her and our confusions. A seamstress with a mouthful of pins and a tape measure round her neck in no way blended with the starched efficiency of a hospital nurse, or the allure of black chiffon.

I looked around for Nelson: he was sublimely content, floating unconcernedly out to sea, lying back on a wooden float as if he was in bed. Barry was shouting at him, words of warning to which it was certain he turned a deaf ear.

Eventually the tide, sweeping up the beach with a ruffle of angry sound, swept us before it, and soon there was no beach. Like misplaced persons we were searching the promenade for a patch of privacy, and the day was gone; the sun sneaking away behind the hill and the slow trail of departing people made even Nelson think of home. Feeling that we had not spent our day in vain we helped Barry to stack his floats, the last job of the day, gathered up our wet things and returned home to see what that had to offer.

Chapter Fourteen

The flutter of Mother's silk gown in the bay window of the drawing-room suggested to me that she watched for our return, but it was not Mother and Mrs Greenfield taking tea in the window, as I had first suspected, but Mother and Mrs Budden. They were discussing babies, I supposed, or horoscopes, which seemed to preoccupy a lot of women. My own led me to believe, at least for today, that the future lay before me a clear path of sheer delight. I wondered if the children were home from their outing.

The door opened before we reached it, to the unusual sound of Mother speaking first.

'A disaster has struck the place,' she declared tragically, as if the house had collapsed and she was breaking the news from the top of a heap of rubble.

We stared at Mother in surprise. It wasn't like her to indulge in exhibitions we agreed, exchanging glances as she jostled us in with silent signs of warning to shut the door behind us with careful, noiseless precision. Mrs Budden sat on the wide window seat in the attitude of a collapsed jelly. This surely then was Doomsday!

'By Jove,' Barry said breathlessly. 'Not another crisis, I hope?'

'I had better tell you the worst,' said Mother.

'It's Harriet,' the green jelly interrupted, in a voice of outrage, giving way to tears, unable to wait for Mother's announcement.

'Harriet?' we exclaimed.

'You know, that woman upstairs with grey hair, a saint-like face and a mole on the left cheek,' Mother explained, as if we were a pack of imbeciles.

'Not our Harriet Amelia Greenfield?' I questioned, spinning out the words as though announcing her entry at a royal function. I noticed with some amusement and not a little trepidation that Harriet was now 'that woman', whereas before she had been a sweet soul, worthy of special attention and that unbelievably Mother was sharpening her claws.

'That's just it,' Mother declared with hauteur. 'We have all been misled, I fear, for she is – I hate to say it, dear, it sounds so bad – quite potty.'

There were further cries of disbelief.

'One doesn't want to spread false rumours,' she went on, 'but we have had a most illuminating and alarming day.'

There was complete agreement from the figure in the window seat, who resettled herself in a more comfortable position of endurance. The thought was impossible: all my dreams of Harriet tottered and collapsed.

'Yes, I am afraid so – mad as a hatter,' and Mother settled down to tell her story to what at first was a silent and paralysed audience. She hurried over her words and peered anxiously in the direction of Harriet's room as if expecting her to appear through the wall with the Sword of Damocles in her hand.

'Edward and I were having a warm beverage together, and discussing the best method of approach to that Malayan recipe that Roger was having a bit of difficulty with – it would keep going into a solid ball even when it was watched – when suddenly there was a deafening knock at the door. Not a usual normal knock, mind . . .'

'Yes, I know,' I said with long-suffering understanding. 'The sort of noise Nelson makes when he wants to be noticed.' Nelson smarted at my jibe.

'Anyway, let me continue,' said Mother. 'Edward opened the door, and who should be standing there but that woman,' she paused in a purely dramatic way, like an actress who has made her entrance and now waits for the applause. Mrs Greenfield, I felt, was now irrevocably cast as 'that woman', whose wants in future would be dismissed with a disapproving shrug. 'She had a shawl wrapped about her head, and looked most odd to say the least.'

'I know,' said Nelson. 'Like an Irish peasant – I've seen it in films.'

'Quite,' said Mother, who, I felt, had never seen an Irish peasant, in spite of her ancestry.

'Sounds more Russian to me,' Barry remarked.

'Perhaps she has Russian ancestors?' I suggested helpfully.

'Perhaps she is really a he, Russian bod, a spy disguised . . . Did it 'ave a wig on, did yer notice?' Nelson was delighted at his suggestion, and the prospect, he knew, that Edward would back him.

'Yes, go on Mother,' I demanded, silencing

Nelson with a look and feeling that the suggestions were on the point of getting ridiculous as usual.

Mother became all confidential: 'Well, at first I thought she had joined the local dramatic society and was rehearsing for a play. Then I wondered if she could possibly be going to a fancy dress ball and preparing herself early. Then I noticed she had a knobkerrie in her hand, and I began to think it all a bit queer . . .' We all looked concerned at the knobkerrie. 'However I kept my presence of mind and smiled sweetly as if nothing was wrong, as if it was the most natural thing in the world for an old lady to carry a knobkerrie . . .'

'Did it 'ave knobs on?' Nelson interrupted with concerned interest. 'The knobkerrie, I mean?'

'Silence!' I roared. 'Go on, Mother, and don't leave out any details.'

Although the family were prone to exaggeration, Mother could usually be relied upon to stick to the strictest truth.

'All I said was "Are you going out?" and Edward started to say "Fancy," having the same ideas as I had a moment before, and the next thing we knew she was pointing at us threateningly, and shouting "Will you stop talking about me on your radio programme? I can hear you quite plainly!" Poor Edward went as white as a sheet, and we both looked guilty, I know; though we couldn't have been more innocently employed.'

'Of course,' I said, burying my illusions of Harriet with large clods of dismal earth in acceptance of the tale.

'Are you sure it was a knobkerrie?' Barry asked, as seriously as if he were making a police inquiry.

'It seems a strange thing for an old lady to have, quite sinister in fact, I should say.'

'Does it 'ave a round end like a stone-age man's?'

'Shut up Nelson! Go on Mother.'

'My radio programme, if you please!' Mother's voice went on indignantly. 'As though I was some sort of common entertainer, indulging in vulgar exhibitions. You know I have never broadcasted in my life, and I don't intend to start now.' She ended with the defiant toss of her head like a circus pony.

'Of course not,' I agreed comfortingly. 'But go on.'

'Well, by now I began to feel decidedly uneasy. I could see there was something drastically wrong, and that she was not going to end the conversation there. Then Edward had the misfortune to laugh – a hollow little laugh, just to elevate the atmosphere, he said, though I'm convinced it was pure nerves. The next thing we knew she had turned on him: "And as for you," she shouted, "you and your mumbo jumbo, God will punish you in the proper manner, no doubt!" Edward looked quite ill, poor man.'

'Was it his painting or his dancing or . . .' I stopped, 'she referred to,' I went on, poking fun with sly innocence at Edward.

Mother was oblivious to the laughter underlying my remark. 'Now wasn't that an unkind thing for her to say?' she reflected sadly. 'Edward, who wouldn't hurt a fly, poor soul.'

'Sounds to me like a bad case of schizophrenia,' Barry announced seriously, airing his knowledge. 'She needs a spot of pethedrine or something similar – administered in the buttock is the best place, Mrs Durrell. A quick jab and it is all over.'

'Quite.' Mother agreed as if she already held an hypodermic in her hand.

'Why don't you two call in Jane,' I was inclined to laugh. 'She might have a better idea.'

Mother's expression squashed the levity in my suggestion. I could hardly believe, did not want to believe, that my paragon of all virtues had fallen so dismally off her pedestal. Could it have been drink, I asked myself, rummaging round for a suitable excuse so that it could be forgotten as a trifling incident. 'Perhaps she was a little high?' I suggested hopefully, desperate for a better solution than madness for my star lodger, bringing Harriet up for revision from where they had consigned her.

'No, my dear, she wasn't drunk, most definitely not. I thought so too at first, but I managed to smell her breath and there were no signs of alcohol on it whatsoever. Edward and I were unanimous on that point.'

'*We* saw a drunk,' Nelson remarked chattily, and had to be firmly silenced again.

'Continue, Mother,' I ordered.

'Well, we both fell against the door and closed it, and have been huddled like refugees before the Gestapo for the rest of the day. Edward had to creep to his room by the back way, if you please, and I have been terrified to go into the hall ever since.'

'Mother,' I asked sternly, 'are you sure you have not taken to gross exaggeration?'

'Mrs Budden has now confirmed my worst

suspicions.' Mother spoke in her 'I am not amused' tone.

'What happened to you?' We all turned to the reviving jelly, who was getting ready to take the centre of the scene. It must be serious, for she should be preparing an evening meal for her robust spouse at this hour. Any minute he would return home caked in dust, shouting for attention and food: for why had he wasted seven shillings and sixpence? Not for the sole purpose of free copulation: the working man must be fed!

The woman choked. 'It's dreadful, really dreadful.' She blossomed with artistic talent at a live audience of sympathetic faces, her immobile face shattered to lines of exaggerated despair. She looked remarkably like her child when deprived of its human nipple. I could hardly wait for the next instalment; the whole house was slowly going mad. Whose turn would it be next, and was it catching?

Mrs Budden now took up the tale, and Harriet's misdemeanours unfolded before us in a story of Hitler-like actions, seasoned with cockney criticisms that could only have originated from the belligerent tongue of Mr Budden, and lost no depth with repetition. It appeared that Harriet, like Gerald, also considered she was part owner of my property, to which she added a resentment of trespassers. She made her point quite clear, it seemed, with acid remarks; she rearranged the bathroom and lavatory for her own comfort; removed electric lightbulbs to oblivion, to endanger the lives of those who followed her to these quarters, demonstrating with a series of highly organised bangs to those who did not heed her warnings; she played with the mains and with goodness knows what else to follow. . . . All this had been accumulating over the past few days without my knowledge – it was unbelievable.

'And now,' the storyteller went on, 'she keeps saying "you know what's coming to you."'

Barry and I exchanged glances: yes, we all knew what came to Mrs Budden, but we refrained from mentioning the obvious now. Nelson's face split to a knowing grin, making it quite clear he had missed nothing.

'It were like a wicked prophecy,' she went on, blind to our smiles. 'It makes me that jumpy and twitchy wondering what is coming next. It's like tempting fate.'

'Don't worry, dear,' Barry soothed her with a half smile. 'I'll soon get that right. Try this with your cup of char.' He handed her a brown lozenge. She took it without enthusiasm.

'My 'ubby says either she goes or we go; but where will we find anywhere to go? Mr Budden's a difficult man, you know,' and the green jelly wept. We knew that, too.

Consoling the creature, I escorted her back to her quarters, promising to look into the matter. But what could I do about a senile brain, I asked myself feelingly, as I listened with relief to a lifeless sound from Harriet's room and returned downstairs to Mother. Nelson and Barry departed after a military consultation, expecting to be attacked at any moment.

'Where is she now?' I inquired of Mother, 'there was no sound from her room that I could hear.'

'She must be in her room, I haven't seen her go out. And let's hope she stays there.' Mother was belligerent now, and showing belated signs of battle. I grinned at her.

'It's madness. We can't have everybody cowering in various parts of the house just because Harriet appears to be a little bit kinky . . .'

Voices in the hall made us both stop and listen fearfully, but it was only Paula and Olwen expanding after an inhibited day of stock phrases.

'The consequences of harbouring a lunatic might be disastrous,' Mother contemplated.

I was thinking that I would have enjoyed the spectacle of Mother and Edward fleeing before a knobkerrie. My grin grew larger. We listened again to the arrival of the bricklayer demanding his rights. Mother shuddered: 'That man!'

'That's life,' I said. 'Life in the raw as seen by a landlady in a sunny seaside town.'

'I wonder if I should return to Leslie's, dear,' Mother said too brightly, cunningly starting an elaboration of reasons why. 'I have a feeling that perhaps he needs me, and that all is not well with the new dog . . .' She faltered in her embroidery, realising by my calm expression that her little plan to impress was failing.

I waved Mother's excuses aside, refusing to pander to retreat. 'Perhaps it is something to do with the moon. Where's my book on the mind-madness and all that sort of thing?'

'We might all be done away with in our beds, that's what,' Mother murmured with all the sad poignancy of a last post as if somebody had already been laid to rest. 'Especially as you have the silly and dangerous habit of leaving all the doors and windows unlocked.'

'Oh, that,' I said carelessly.

'I shall have to resume my precautions of looking under my bed at night while I am in this house, and I had just decided that perhaps it was not necessary.'

I tried to brush Mother's fears away with colourful descriptions of a house full of saner elements, possessing the milk of human kindness.

'Nevertheless I feel distinctly nervous now,' she insisted firmly. 'In fact this consolidates my opinions of the other day that this is turning into a thoroughly unreliable household.'

'Just because of one case of slight eccentricity there is no need to tar all the others,' I complained. 'Now take Roger, for instance . . .'

There was a quick interruption: 'I was not at all sure about that fellow in the first place,' Mother confessed. 'I mean he has landed you with that queer-looking girl mooning about the place. She has been here today looking for you, walking barefoot like some male aborigine with twigs in her hair.'

I accepted the unusual description of Magda with complete calm, for I felt sure it was one of Leslie's.

'And then there's his friend who seems to be no better, as far as I can see, with a one-track mind that always leads to his trombone.'

This I could not accept, but I thought it wise to remain silent.

'Though I must say he is good with the children,' she softened a little towards Andy as she gave the matter thought. 'You've had smugglers, too . . .'

'You can hardly call them smugglers!' It was my turn to interrupt – Mother was going too far.

'The police had to come didn't they? Well, that's enough if the law was forced to call; the principle of the thing is the same whether it is opium or some other minor thing. It's obvious that you attract the weirdest sort of people. How do you know you will not in time harbour a vicious murderer, a sex maniac, or a white slave trafficker?' Mother was back with her old fears. 'And the bank manager's face looked none too hopeful when he discussed you either.'

'Oh, that old fusser,' I remarked, scornfully disloyal, for without him I would not have survived so far.

'I'd advise you, dear, to keep in with him.'

'I do,' I said hastily, 'but I shall avoid him in future.'

But Mother was still living with her fears. 'You might end up in the newspaper,' she went on nervously. 'Once you get into one of these vice rings I am told it is difficult to escape. They keep you half-naked, deliberately, so that you cannot escape.'

'Really?' I couldn't help wondering where Mother received her inside information. 'I suppose if I am going to attract lunatics I shall attract them wherever I am,' I reasoned, sensibly enough, with not quite the same gloomy interpretations as my mother. 'Anyway, I don't think the vice ring would be interested in someone who has had children. It's virgins they are after, I expect, and they won't find one of those in this house I shouldn't think, at whatever shining angle the halo is worn.'

'Really, you do talk rubbish sometimes.'

'Yes, I know,' I acknowledged gloomily, 'it's part of my charm.'

'I should leave others to decide that,' the remark was crushing. 'No, the trouble is being alone. When people find out it's only a woman they have to deal with they take advantage. I soon found that out when I became a widow.'

I had no doubt she was right. 'But,' I prophesised gaily, 'consolation lies in the fact that there must be hundreds of women being taken advantage of all over England, and some more pleasantly than others, I'm sure,' I ended on the whimsical note of Mrs Williams.

'Quite,' said Mother, missing my implications.

'Have the children arrived back yet?' My maternal instinct was back with me.

'Yes, indeed, as happy as larks but with an exhausted father. I can't think why, when men have to look after children for more than five minutes, they behave as though they've done twenty-four hours of hard physical labour.'

'Typical of men – some men,' I added hastily, quoting my Aunt Patience for a moment.

'Exactly,' said Mother, 'now you know why I have remained a widow!'

Mother and Aunt Patience both shared the same views of the male population: there was only one man as far as Mother was concerned and that was Father, and none at all for Aunt Patience.

'And where are the little angels now?' I inquired, hoping that they were happily occupied.

'Having another tea with that Andy man. I must repeat that is one thing in his favour, he is good with children – any man who is good with animals or children must have a special quality somewhere,' she ended generously and then spoilt it all by adding, 'even if it is not apparent.' But I wasn't listening as I flew upstairs with the odd stir that climbing the stairs now instilled in me.

The evening had passed uneventfully. There were no more stirrings from Mrs Greenfield and I decided to wait and see before I tackled her about her curious behaviour. The next day was also quiet, and Mother began to breathe more freely again, and to walk without gazing behind her as if expecting a surreptitious blow. In fact she became so brave as to visit Edward in his den, spend an hour upstairs unravelling Mrs Williams' crochet – a vest for Nelson who insisted on having one like Mr Budden's – who wasn't finding the pattern easy; she even announced her intention of strolling a few minutes in the garden in the seclusion of the apple trees.

We gathered together again, a trifle self-consciously perhaps, as our optimism grew, and we felt it had all been an illusion, brought on by the unusual heat. Harriet must have had a day on the bottle; there was no other explanation.

It was just after Mother had taken her walk, and had been forced to retrace her steps at great speed, frightened by the crunching of footsteps down the garden path next door (for her dread of getting involved in our suburban machinations had risen to gigantic proportions by now). She had just entered the safety of our house remarking 'that was a near one', when we both noticed with fascination a large envelope being slowly thrust under the door. For one awful moment I thought it was Edward's pornographic pictures, and that he was now having a brainstorm, but picking it up quickly I recognised the huge scrawling handwriting that indicated Harriet's presence behind the closed door.

The note was addressed to Mrs Durrell and underneath the message said: 'If you will return the scarf you have stolen from my suitcase I will not inform the police.' The signature was a grand flourish of swirling letters.

'Mother,' I grinned, 'it's for you, a small offering from one of your admirers, and not Mr Beetle either.' I gave it to her and stood back to watch the result of Harriet's fresh attack.

'Really?' Mother remarked with interest, taking the envelope, 'now who could it be, I wonder?' she said, examining the scrawl in a friendly way. There was a long pause, while the significance of the message struck her. In a series of gasps, leading to a final explosion of vindictive and penetrating comment, words came that I had never heard Mother use before.

'I do wish you wouldn't upset the lodgers, Mother,' I complained. 'It's as bad as having Gerald in the house, I must say.'

'I'll ring my solicitor at once, the old lunatic.'

'Come on, out with it. Where's the scarf?' I teased. 'Don't tell me you are going to cause a scandal in your old age, and get taken in for petty theft.'

'Indeed,' Mother drew herself up to her full five foot, with worthy indignation. 'I've never heard of such a piece of cheek, the woman's an obvious lunatic. I've a good mind to go up now and give her a piece of my mind.'

'I wonder if she still has that knobkerrie?' I reminded Mother pointedly. 'But do go, Mother,' I urged, still teasing her, for I knew exactly what Mother's peace of mind constituted: kindly words with a gentle apologetic smile as if she were really the culprit. She would most probably return really believing that she had the scarf, or that some other poor innocent was to blame.

Mrs Budden entered stealthily, not waiting for an answer to her knock. The jelly-look had gone. We were faced with a dilapidated flower garden, a fluttering smock with three buttons missing which did not stir the imagination to romantic heights. Her normally pallid face was flushed unnaturally and she was breathing hard. In fact, I reflected, both she and Mother wore the same expressions.

'Anything the matter?' I inquired, my mind already occupied with the reason.

'It's that woman again: she tied a rope across the landing and I nearly broke my neck.'

I drew her quickly away from the door into the kitchen, automatically putting on the kettle. I knew this was only the beginning. Mother followed clucking, with a noise that would outdo the Briggses broody hen.

'Perhaps it's Nelson?' The suggestion, though unfair, held less sinister implications, I felt. For once Mrs Budden refused to blame Nelson.

'This is serious, Margo,' Mother broke forth, sounding like Edward. 'Action is called for.'

'I quite agree,' Edward had entered the scene. 'The whole place is knotted in rope,' he remarked wonderingly.

'Mother is having trouble, too, but in a different way.'

'And what's she doing with all those bulbs, anyway?' he asked thoughtfully.

A door slammed somewhere upstairs. Mother and Mrs Budden exchanged significant glances and then came Nelson's delighted inquiry: 'Anyone 'anging themselves today?' as he joined us.

'This is no time for fatuous remarks, my dear boy.' Edward was stern.

'She's an obvious 'omosexual maniac,' Nelson diagnosed the case.

'You've got the wrong word,' I remarked, laughing.

'You must give her notice at once,' Mother was quite decisive, now that she didn't have to take immediate action herself.

I exclaimed in consternation. If there was one thing I dreaded, it was having to give anybody notice – a fact which Mother, Edward, Gerald, all of them, failed to appreciate. Mrs Budden agreed with Mother. There was no need to ask Edward's advice. He had given his views in strong terms lasting over a solid period of two days at the first upheaval, and since managed to remain dormant for the ensuing quiet period while his suggestion proved itself to be necessary. The house was unanimously behind him; only Mrs Williams, who felt she was about to lose a friend, however remote, suffered at the possible consequences of Edward's suggestion. Nelson, feeling the situation was akin to coffins, filled his notebook with more extensive scribbles gleefully.

'She has paid her rent, so far,' I reasoned

unhappily, cringing before three pairs of accusing eyes. I was hopeful for reprieve, pinning my faith now in what seemed to be Harriet's one remaining virtue. And after all if some other member of the household had tied rope across the stairs no one would have considered it an act of sheer lunacy – inconsiderate, maybe, but not lunacy. 'I can't really believe she is taking electric light-bulbs, though,' I told Mrs Budden firmly, feeling that this was a pure fabrication from a Labour supporter to belittle the Conservative party; for my first impression that Harriet would constitute no thorn in the already bleeding wound of Labour's imposing presence was after all proving to be a false judgment.

'Well, it's true,' she defended her accusations cockily. 'Wait and see for yourself.' People grow like their dogs, but Mrs Budden grows like Mr Budden, I thought pityingly.

'Don't worry, dear,' Mother put a kindly hand on the heaving shoulder. 'Margo will have to settle the matter immediately, and put our minds at rest.'

'Right!' I stood up bravely, exhausted by their persistent nagging. 'I'll go and tackle the woman now.' Secretly I hoped she was out as I marched upstairs, unravelling rope as I went, feeling more than ever before like having a swig from Edward's bottle of homemade sustaining liquor, and not feeling at all like having it out. I knocked on Harriet's door; a sinking sensation welled up in my stomach. I had a frightening premonition that I would end up as the landlady with the most ulcerated stomach in Bournemouth.

'Anybody there?' I called softly as though I was

on a visit to the vestry. The silence that greeted my call was a moment of sheer relief. Thanking God for small mercies, in one of my moments of prayer I was apt to indulge in, I was just about to turn away when the door opened and the figure of Harriet was before me in an attitude of positive disapproval. She wore her usual grey garb, and a black shawl hung about her shoulders, a dismal suggestion of mourning. Were there Russian or Irish strains in that sallow face? The hair was her own, I decided, going from the hair to the face and back again.

'Somebody, I'm not saying who, but somebody has stolen my plug,' she announced loudly involving me in theft and flinging out her arms widely, her voice cracking with bitter emotion at the event.

'What plug?' The sickness had left my stomach and attacked my legs.

'From my basin, of course – idiot,' she replied, giving a sudden merry laugh, in which I found an irrepressible urge to join.

'Perhaps Mother's got it?' I found the remark irresistibly on my lips.

'That's just what I thought,' she agreed in a matter of fact way, a brooding look rising easily to her face again. 'She's making a collection of my things – it's really too mean of her.' Falling on her bed in an attitude of despair, Harriet began to sob bitterly, producing real tears, so that I could not fail to be impressed by this dramatic portrayal of distress. I wished I had held my tongue, completely nonplussed at this watery turn of events. I looked round for the knobkerrie, which was all that was needed to confirm my worst dread. The knobkerrie, I felt, would be a final symbol of insanity, but I could not see the badge of thuggery.

'There, there,' I said, closing the door on the curious rabble which I knew would be in the hall by now, gingerly treading the room patting her shoulder heartily. 'No one has anything of yours, I assure you, and as you are the only one with a key to your room your things must be quite safe.' I fidgeted awkwardly, trying to find the right words. 'So you must refrain from accusing people.' I was getting bolder for the noise of an inquisitive house on the alert had put me on my mettle. 'Mother is most annoyed at your accusations. You won't be so naughty again?' I asked hopefully, examining the room about me curiously as if I had never seen it before. What other mysteries had she got hidden in this den of lavender water smells, to reveal at a later date?

'Nobody cares about me,' she lifted a grey and tearful face; a pathetic picture of self-pity which plunged me into a mood of sympathetic retreat.

I could not possibly give this sorrowful creature notice, I argued to myself, retiring quickly with promises of greater attention, falling over not the knobkerrie but an umbrella and a little sheepish at my cowardly reactions I shut the door behind me. Harriet had decidedly won the first battle.

Mrs Budden, with Mother, Edward and Nelson, met me at the last step, all agog for news, not catching the final conclusion of my visit. All the doors were now, curiously, ajar. 'Well?' they said sternly in unison.

'Well what?' I asked innocently.

'What have you done about that woman?'

Mother demanded, sticking to the point, and not in the mood to be trifled with. 'Are we to continue to be slandered and accused of theft, the whole house living in a state of nervous tension – or if they are not now they very soon will be!'

'I had a few straight words with her,' I lied. 'And I don't think we shall have any more trouble, though I didn't actually get around to giving her notice,' I said vaguely, apologetically, avoiding more than three pairs of accusing eyes.

'Had I known,' Mother proclaimed royally, 'that you were inviting me precisely at the same time that you were beginning to cater for lunatics, I would not have accepted your invitation with such alacrity, and . . .' She paused, watching with disapproval the retreating ungainly figure of Mrs Budden hastening away attentively at the demanding yells of her child. 'She really ought to do something to tidy herself up. She looks as though she is expecting another happy event, dressed like that,' Mother observed, her mind wandering mercifully from the major problem of the moment.

'She is,' I said without thinking, so relieved to be off the topic of Harriet. 'She told me so when she paid the rent,' I faltered.

Mother was horrified. 'It's preposterous,' she said. 'But, of course, it's that monster's fault, there is no doubt about that.'

'No,' I said, 'no doubt.'

'No doubt at all,' came a chorus.

'Now is your chance, dear, to kill two birds with one stone,' Mother egged me on. 'Tackle her about her husband's low behaviour, wandering about in a towel, and that sort of thing.'

'And I understand,' said Edward in a very low voice, 'he has been indiscreet against the dustbins.'

'Really! It's not to be tolerated, you'll have the health authorities around your neck before you know where you are, and what a disgrace that would be!'

'That's what Mrs Briggs is always saying,' Nelson said.

Suddenly I felt inadequate to deal with the fresh events: Mrs Budden, Mrs Greenfield, or Mr Budden. 'I'll deal with everything tomorrow. Harriet has had her warning, the Buddens will get theirs; must be fair you know,' I said with a sudden spurt of energy, caused by the mental vision of Nelson wheeling me to the 'home'. A new day, a clean start; I was relieved to have found such a happy solution of appeasement.

Mother, momentarily satisfied with my meek acquiesence, expanded generally – she was never ruffled for very long. 'I'm so glad you are going to take a sensible view of the matter, and deal with it accordingly. It only needs a little courage.' There was a long hopeful pause. 'But I still have a premonition, dear, that Leslie needs me.' She spoke as kindly as she could, breaking the news of her intended departure tactfully but firmly, and she went to pack.

Harriet Amelia Greenfield stayed – for the moment.

Gerald returned to compete with Harriet for pride of ownership, and added his views to the general clamour to rehabilitate Harriet. He brought several technical books, which we all studied, on problems of the brain, deciding eventually that as Harriet didn't fit into any special category she must be 'on the change'; but Jane disputed the fact. 'She's too old for such capers,' she said. The knobkerrie proved nothing – it was either stolen or a much-loved relic of her past.

Nelson developed chickenpox which swept the house in an epidemic, taking the stage from Harriet's involvements; only Jane, Harriet and I survived. Jane, once again delighted at the scope for her talents, arranged wards, hung sheets solid with disinfectant at all the doors to stop the spreading of germs. Nelson and the children, recovering first, played a game called the Great Plague, until every nerve in the house was reduced to an irreparable shred and I longed for the peaceful, bygone days when I roamed the empty building and looked forward to the future and the fortune I was going to make, as I waited for the incubation period to reveal yet another spotty face.

A baby-sized knitted bear, strangled in a life-like way, hanging limply from the first floor had upset Olwen and Paula, rising from their sick-beds. Harriet was blamed for the scene of destruction, but it was, after all, the work of the children. Reports filtered through that Leslie and Doris were wed at last, much to Mother's delight.

Chapter Fifteen

The epidemic over, we hardened, quickly, back into our various grooves, as Jane removed all traces of chickenpox and exchanged disinfectant odours for more palatable scents.

The hint of coldness in the air and the leaves turning the colour of toast, warned us that summer was finally over. The visitors had already left, filtering home to their first fires, and the locals, sighing with relief, spread their elbows in a gesture of release and prepared to enjoy the deserted town.

After the first upheaval of Harriet's accusations which nominated each one of us in turn, and sent us oscillating between anger and amusement, we fell into a state of acceptance, sometimes uneasily, as we reflected a trifle sardonically that 'it was only Harriet having one of her turns' to acrimonious announcements, angry gestures and accepted with grace the electric lightbulbs that vanished without trace from vulnerable parts of the house.

Even Mother, recuperating quietly at Leslie's, took courage as if by telepathy and telephoned to say that she had quite recovered her nerve and she now felt that she would be able to call again without feeling her blood pressure rising to dangerous heights. Taking stock in quiet retrospect of

Harriet who, in spite of her outrageous behaviour, seemed to be harmless after all, she had decided that 'we must all do our best to help her over an obviously difficult period, poor soul.' Then, showing a streak of her old fighting spirit, she announced that on no account could she accept inhumane behaviour and never before had she felt so uncharitable towards a human being.

Chuckling at Mother's righteous indignation, I carefully glossed over the latest episodes, as if describing a light farce at the local theatre, for I did not wish to destroy her tide of rising courage. I refrained from illuminating the now obvious fact that it seemed to be only her presence that inflamed Harriet to an abusive literary career: for with Mother's exit at least the pointed incriminating notes had stopped, and the knobkerrie, too, seemed to have momentarily disappeared.

Mother, still further reassured by my obvious good humour, giving her the feeling that things weren't so bad after all, promised again to return at an opportune moment and finish tidying the garden.

Brother Gerald said that during his lying in state with chickenpox, listening for hours to the strange inhuman noises of my lodgers, he too, like Mother in semi-retirement, had found plenty of time for reflection. In his opinion the sounds were equivalent to any Brazilian jungle – though he admitted honestly to my retaliatory attack that he had yet to see such a place but the simile was beside the point; any halfwit could see that what my boarding house needed was not, as he first suspected, the firm hand of a landlord, but the rather more subtle influences of Freud's or

Groddeck's theories. He thought the next few months of living in their midst was going to be an interesting experience, parallel to the anthropological study of a rare tribe, which would probably make any future safari look like a church outing by comparison and I could now consider we had a resident psychiatrist, free of charge, in our midst. A hollow laugh was all I could produce, but at least, so far, we were still free of animals.

With the change of weather and the consequent kindling of fires all over the house, Edward had disclosed a new trait in his character – the haunting fear of a blazing house and the slightest suspicious whiff of an acrid smell would send him careering madly to investigate the cause, which usually happened to be behind a locked door with the occupant out. After the second door had collapsed, under force, in the first week of fires, I felt it necessary to lodge a firm but friendly complaint and hand excuses over for Gerald's analysis. Our analyst, happy to oblige, reading from the pages of a four-inch Groddeck, gave no mercy: the diagnosis was quite unrepeatable and it sent a sheepish Edward to his room for solitude, swearing that when the next fire occurred he would let the house go to blazes.

Nelson, too, astonished us all by insisting on going to the local church one Sunday, and marshalling the boys to follow – upsetting his mother who felt she was now under an obligation to the vicar and had nothing to wear for such an occasion. He came home bulging with reforms and the attitude of a saint, and the silence from his natterings became as alarming as Harriet's threats had been. Finding him sitting alone in the summerhouse, amidst the remnants of monkey droppings one chilly evening soon after, his chubby chin tucked in chubby hands, gazing after a salmon pink sunset belted in silver cloud with an expression touching his eyes which I had never seen there before, I was reduced immediately to one of my usual apprehensive investigations. From the closed window above came the smothered sound of a gramophone and the familiar Negro call pleading for Bill Bailey to return home.

'Why don't she wrap up – it's ruinin' me thoughts,' he remarked plaintively, referring to the singer and aware of my close inspection.

'What's up, Nelson?' I inquired with concern, noting the new furrows creasing the normally smooth plump cushion between his eyes. Could his mother have deprived him of something important? Perhaps there was bad news from the jail – if so, which one?

'Something worrying you?' I asked heartily, hoping to lift the atmosphere with a boisterous appeal.

'Them colours,' he spoke softly, 'sheer 'ideous beauty of them bleedin' colours. Couldn't 'ave done a better job meself – I wonder 'ow he did it . . .'

'Who?' I asked, puzzled.

'God, o' course!' he said, surprised, throwing me a pained look as if I should have known the answer. 'Yer know – what that ol' geezer stands up in that ol' box an' spouts about. The Almightily: surely you've 'eard 'bout 'im – does good, gives the ol' lolly away to the poor, and lots of other good things besides – does magic too, changes things. And they crucified ’im for that – just fancy ’orror – those nails . . .’

‘Nelson! Are you sickening for another illness?’ I asked, concerned, touching his arm. It was a solid arm, and no amount of dieting, I reflected, would make the slightest difference. Measles, perhaps? I felt his forehead for signs of a temperature.

‘Nope!’ He was scornful. ‘It’s them ’orrors I keep thinkin’ about . . .’

‘How many children’s diseases have you had?’ I was insistent.

‘Only venereal,’ he answered. I refrained from pursuing the subject further. Nelson would go to his grave with a lie on his lips I felt sure, however reformed.

‘Listen to that music,’ I said, trying to break this depressing spell of religion, to Nelson’s further declaration of an early childhood spent in twisted agonies in a hospital bed with every childhood disease ending with more of his observations in the last pew of a cold church.

‘Doesn’t it make you want to dance, be gay, laugh, make money?’ I paused, wondering what else I could suggest to tempt.

‘And cry, maybe?’

The question was penetratingly grown-up and, shocked, I watched him turn away with a kindly smile as he looked back in the direction of the softening sky, deepening gently to night.

The distraction of a window opening made us both look skywards. Harriet swung above in leisurely sinister greeting; her hair loose, swept wildly down towards us and if she had flown out on a broomstick I would not have been surprised. Our eyes met.

'Nobody bothers about me,' she moaned, giving us a frown of unjustified hatred. How long, I wondered, would it be before Harriet qualified for medical attention? She stepped back, and disappeared: the window fell with a heavy thud and I awaited Nelson's reprisal of derisive remarks – a perfectly normal procedure.

'Poor soul,' he spouted piously. 'She must be on the change.' He sounded so like an imitation of my mother that I looked at him intently to see if he was having one of his little jokes, but there were no wrinkles about the eyes, no half-moon grin. I felt a chill – this, then, was serious. Nelson would be taking Holy Orders next and life would be deprived of an old world jester: so this was what bereavement was, I thought, as I stood in the twilight and contemplated the calamity that had befallen our peak of healthy comedy.

An owl hooted, circled noiselessly and melted into the blackening trees behind the house. It was a bad omen, I felt, and tried to ignore it.

'Ah well!' Nelson rose with the tremulous sigh of his mother. 'I'd better get in an' give me Ma an 'elping 'and – and you'd best get in too, yer might catch yer death – poor ol' soul.'

I felt decrepit, a hundred years old.

'Yes, all right Nelson,' I acquiesced meekly, deflated and, walking as if I was already on a stick, I made my way indoors. If this was the result of Nelson going to church – away with it!

My children, it seemed, had come out unscathed: I found them squatting before their uncle listening with avid delight to a descriptive dissection of Mr Budden's anatomy.

The drawing-room was light, with a blazing fire and, through the round of the window outside stood black and shadowless. I drew to the warmth of the glowing coals listening to Gerald, engrossed in his conversation with Jane before an admiring audience of two boys and a dog. They were sitting under the hard, public bar glow of an unshaded light of maximum strength – Gerald deplored what he called dismal hooded contraptions so that even lifting a glass of spirits became a battle of wits. They were now discussing the domestic life of the gorilla as compared to human environment.

'How right you are, my dear.' Jane was agreeing that Mr Budden was the nearest thing to a missing link in our circle. She was hanging grimly on Gerald's every word, her narrow body posed in a sexy way, trying to reveal a saucy bosom, as she twisted her small mouth in a babyish pout. Any minute now, I decided, Jane, under Gerald's influence, would be sitting in a frosty garden with a magnifying glass examining nature. In some ways, I mused, this might be a restraining influence for since the night of the party and her unfortunate encounter with the debauchee, she considered herself not only a connoisseur of the physical arts, but a woman of great experience. She had become a little blasé, hinted at affairs of the heart, dropping a Freudian phrase here and there with a tragic little droop of skinny shoulder, giving a cynical laugh – carefully adjusted when men were mentioned – mourning her lot in incessant dark colours, accentuating her thin features with long swinging earrings.

I squatted down now beside Jane, feeling that we might just as well be sitting in the local pub as far as the lights were concerned, for I preferred soft lights to lounge in; and waited for a lapse in the conversation to put my worldly word in. But I waited in vain for my chance, for we were interrupted by the absorbing spectacle of a displaced Barry hugging a newspaper to his bosom and demanding attention.

He had been in this collapsed state for a few days now, submerged in a mood of desperate despair. The season over, Barry's beach job had automatically ended and, once again, he had taken temporary employment at a bakers until the day when his searching brought him that remunerative post with dazzling prospects: very gallantly, I thought, for a baker's round now became the source of daily bread, much to Paula's shame. But Barry's destiny did not include a baker's round, for after a momentous week he collapsed under the strain and disappeared into the protective cover of a brown blanket, as a tortoise would hide on sensing danger.

We had rallied forward to console the forlorn apparition and finally managed to persuade him to telephone the bakery and explain that he was temperamentally unsuited to the monotonies of a bread round, but would finish his term of office – 'with honesty and dignity' as Gerald put it – and collect any money due.

Unfortunately the bakery foreman, faced with Barry's problems at the wrong moment, did not take a lenient or sympathetic view; rude words were exchanged, and a heated discussion started which aggravated a trivial situation to such vast proportions that Barry's temper, already simmering unpleasantly, broke out in a trembling rage. He threw off his blanket, dressed feverishly in his best suit, swallowed a handful of tranquillisers, and cramming his trilby on at a wolfish angle, with a forced gaiety which rang hollow, he had marched out to the bakery to resume his job, spite the unfeeling foreman, and claim the week's wages he was convinced he was owed – with our encouraging cheers behind him and a rabbit's paw in his pocket.

But Barry had never made the bakery, how, he still doesn't know. But some hours later, he told us, in a frightened voice, he found himself idling down on the promenade beside an empty beach, the sea pondering sullenly at his feet as he waited patiently for the other Corporation workers to arrive. He didn't know, he said, just how the realisation came, but suddenly, like the breaking of a bad dream, he had remembered with horror that he should be at the bakery, not the beach. Fumbling for a cigarette to soothe his nerves, unable to steady his shaking body, he returned home a frightened man, desperate to discuss the strange occurrence with everybody.

Tucking him cosily into bed, with genuine sympathy mixed with laughter, and accompanied by Nelson's uproarious sniggers (he had yet to experience his reforming visits to church), we telephoned Paula, who was not a bit amused. I summoned the doctor, a long-suffering, pale-looking man whose professional touch was tinged with wry humour as he gently told anecdotes, a twinkle lighting the keen blue eyes behind their spectacles, of other victims of tranquillisers – train journeys completed without knowledge, patients in wakeful comas. Surely this would shake Barry's unquenchable faith in pills, we asked ourselves? The prostrate Barry, delighted at the doctor's full attention, rallied sufficiently to bandy medical terms with knowledgeable abandon, prescribed his own treatment before the unsuspecting medico could get his second wind, and generally felt a lot better for the encounter.

After the doctor's departure I had telephoned the bakery with a murmur of helpful suggestions from the rear and explained the situation to the foreman as best I could. 'Blimey, I always thought 'e wasn't right in the 'ead,' the foreman said rudely, 'if yer ask me.'

I wasn't asking him, so I rang off equally rudely and put the finishing touches to Barry's career in the bread trade. Barry had now lapsed back, inconsolable again not at the loss of the unpalatable job, but at the indignity of the whole situation. He lay huddled, Red Indian fashion, surrounded by detective novels, pored for hours over his football coupons as a possible way of escape, and muddled out his troubles to unsatisfactory conclusions. Paula saw her ultimate ambition of being the wife of a business magnate, entertaining at glittering tables, lighted by crystal chandeliers, diminishing, with certainty, to a life spent in one room with the everlasting worry of bills to pay and not enough money to pay with, let alone to squander on luxuries.

When Barry had recovered enough to descend the stairs we all welcomed him affectionately. His face was rather drawn, and his suntan turning a bilious yellow gave him a melancholy jaundiced appearance, which concerned Jane and gave her the solace of being needed yet again and made me feel that, in spite of everything, Barry's need was perhaps the most urgent in the house.

Gerald, welcoming yet another interesting specimen, attacked Barry's problems in a way he never attacked his own, as though partaking of one of Mother's most delicious curries. This brought out Edward, who would never miss an evening of idle gossip – he was never far away. He was mellowed at this precise moment, not only by a glow of self-appreciation at the final achievement – a real alcoholic mess contrived by his own hands – but by the gentle sippings which he had revelled in all day, unable to leave the satisfying results of his own labour. Olwen followed reprovingly, her face impassive as a slab of marble.

We were a small band of Salvation Army strength, drawn together in one cause, to thrash out the important problem of Barry's career in the unfolding *Times* before us, as he pointed with a hand that still shook to columns of opportunity that could be his with a bit of luck.

Nelson knocked with great reserve, as though entering a room of sickness; so different from the usual succession of noisy thumps. He wore a Dutch apron draped about his vast middle and begged politely to borrow six eggs – he was making his mother a birthday cake, he told us solemnly, as she would be thirty-five tomorrow. Pleased at a firm little audience of admirers, he entered willingly into the discussion of Barry's future, like an old man who had been through it all before. Placing a stout fatherly arm about the drooping woolly figure, he told him in a sagacious voice that he felt sure he would make good in the end. And he personally had the greatest faith in his ability. Then, collecting up his six eggs from the kitchen, he left with the lordly air of a royal chef: I wondered idly if the girls in green were also missing Nelson, with his frantic wolf whistles that sent them into a flutter of delight. Could Nelson's acquiescence to a church sermon be just a pose for our benefit to hide a more significant situation as yet unrevealed, I wondered, suddenly suspicious – again, time would tell, no doubt.

I followed Nelson out, picking up a thick sweater hanging across a chair as I went; leaving the vibrant atmosphere of friendly argument punctuated by the rich chuckle of Gerald and the rolling high-pitched noise of Edward. Barry's laughter at the moment, only managed with great difficulty, had the hollow note of an empty can; Jane, not having the capacity for deep laughter, occasionally made a strangled noise worthy of an hysterical Pekingese. I hoped that Gerald would not be so carried away by his own enthusiasm that he would forget that he was putting the children to bed and attending to their bedtime wants, for I was going to take the first steps out into the jazzy world of my two lodgers upstairs and sweat out a night of hot music.

Only one light burned in the hall – the other was missing. Harriet, a grey mouse, rustled past us down the stairs and averted her face without a greeting, closing the front door with the usual disturbing protest. Mrs Budden, sneaking a look from a scarcely open door, nervously whispered for less noise because the baby slumbered; a pig-like vibrato told us that it was not only the baby who took a nap. Across the way, lifting the atmosphere created by a frightened Mrs Budden, a pleasant singing voice trilled from the bathroom. A rich smell of luxury bath-oils filled the length of the corridor, making it clear that Paula was refreshing herself extravagantly after a tiring day's work of sales talk.

I passed from the scent of apple-blossom into the earthy upheaval of the men's room. They were gathering up their instruments with accustomed movements, polishing a dull spot and arranging their gear with tender concern. I watched the two men with deep interest: thoughts far removed from those of a commercial landlady. They were vastly different in character, yet perfectly harmonised, bonded together in this common obsession. Which was the stronger basic character? I was biased of course, for Roger's swarthy oriental-featured face, passively gloomy, attracted me not at all; though for some he personified male attraction. He had grown away from Madga now, leaving her floundering like a bird with a broken wing, and again sought his woman, almost ruthlessly, but still with a gloomy disinterested air as if he did not really enjoy it. I wondered about the first wife, a neurotic by all his accounts, but then human nature tended to slander a discarded love.

My thoughts were not allowed to linger on the fascinating intricacies of Roger's life, as Andy, with a glance at the clock, suggested that we should be going, with the boyish eagerness of an anticipated pleasure.

'Art thou coming now?' he questioned softly, picking up his trombone and smiling with his eyes. I nodded without a word, feeling as though a sudden midnight noise had jolted me to watchful wakefulness; an emotion which I am sure Mrs Briggs would have placed in the category of 'them's only pitfalls', or perhaps the scarlet wonderings of a Jezebel.

'Yes, we had better get going,' Roger remarked, while I noticed the difference in the two voices: the toneless cultured smoothness of Roger and Andy's, deep, yet almost rough.

We left the room together, and fumbled our way to the stairs as I cursed Harriet audibly, for the darkness meant that yet another electric light-bulb had to be found before someone fell and broke a limb.

'Hell, what a stink!' Roger broke out, as Paula revealed herself, a statue in red velvet; the heavy smell of crushed blossoms drenched us. A house-coat and the perfume of which, being a woman, I thoroughly approved. She and I exchanged light words to Roger's aspersions about over-scented females. Paula's haughty retort was drowned by Mr Budden's sudden roar for silence and from Nelson's room a smell of burning had brought Edward galloping up to investigate; his phobia outweighed any other emotions through the winter months and I felt that summer must be a lean time for this submerged passion.

I soothed him quickly, reminding him that Nelson was venturing into the realms of cake-making, but Edward, disbelieving my theory, said no cake-maker ever produced a smell like that, even an amateur and he flung himself at the door demanding to be let in.

Laughingly, we left him arguing with an indignant cook, shut the front door on the uproar and made our way out beneath the inky sky, a dark mantle, where the first stars, like fairy lights, spread above our heads. Two figures, ministering angels, home from a long shift at the hospital, hailed us merrily. I advised them to join the throng busy arranging Barry's salvation and, linking my arm through Andy's in a gesture of gay affection, I experienced a moment of supreme contentment as we threaded our way crisply towards the town's nightlife. Being a landlady had its moments.

Then we were in a new haunt, a room below ground level, scarcely lit, enveloped by a stifling fog of smoky perspiration and brassy noise, as a white band beat a hot rhythm, trespassing the path of the negro in a vain attempt to capture the secrets of the original. For the most part they looked a seedy bunch, their sweating faces pallid shifting masks in the gloom; before them jiving couples twisted to keep the beat. Clinging against the wall, standing crowds rocked, appreciatively moaned and applauded wildly.

I found myself alone, for Roger and Andy, fighting their way through the crowd towards the nucleus of sound, were now strangers, melting into a mood in which I played no part. Feeling very much alone and forgotten, I edged my way shyly forward, shuffling like a cripple through the tightly packed audience, manoeuvred back and forth by enthusiastic bodies stamping in ecstasy, and shouting 'great, great', as the clarinet wandered sweetly into a lonely rift, and died as the drums, breaking the spell, rolled like a burst of thunder. There was a roar of approval.

Then Andy was up there playing, and the growl of his trombone split the other sounds. Pride stirred me, excitingly now for the first time I heard the hidden melody. So this was what it was all about, this was the thing that had touched so many, compellingly ruthless, to fire the imagination.

I was so close I could have touched Andy: his damp body stripped, shirtless, loosely swaying, moved me sweetly. Involuntarily I put my hand out to regain contact, and stopped: he did not need me now, I thought, a little stunned, and a twinge of jealousy rose mercilessly. I felt hot and sticky and alone for a sickening moment, but the trombone spun an enticing golden sound, and the music that was a religion to some seduced me, caught me up in a rolling wave of intoxication. I found myself applauding with the rest through my silent tears.

The hours stilled. Night slipped away unnoticed. The crowds disappeared listlessly, and we returned home with the dark before dawn to another world of still sleeping shadows. I was subdued, troubled, walking alone, trying vainly to collect myself and step back from the brink to safety, with the harsh question nagging, could I endure the one solitary thing that now divided me from completeness with Andy, immersed in this demanding musical barrier that few women, I realised, however hard they tried, could ever really cross? We were in love, but would I survive,

I wondered doubtfully, at this moment fighting to save myself the bitter experience of an affection that could surely only play a second fiddle to a trombone.

Fortunately if one lives close to the lives of other people one is not allowed to smoulder alone indefinitely and I found myself quickly drawn back into the fold of my household, my own problems tempered down and softened in consequence. For who could wallow in self-pity for long with Harriet at the door, or a pitiful Barry bemoaning his disastrous career and Nelson proclaiming openly now that he was in love with the last girl in the lime green crocodile – a suet pudding with golden curls and blue eyes – and church reform was buried for ever?

Chapter Sixteen

Waking up like a sleep-walker to the needs of my lodgers, I found the major problem of Barry's career was temporarily solved. He was now on the dole, much more cheerful, and writing away enthusiastically for jobs; letters to which the more literary types amongst us added a word or two, or gave our references willingly. He kept his best suit carefully pressed for the summons which surely, by the law of averages, would not be deprived him, filled in his football coupons and wandered from room to room once more absorbing himself in his uneasy private life, which the promises of the beach had dimmed a little.

I could not rejoice in any way for Harriet, for though we had also discussed her needs with endless energy there seemed to be no clear solution for her mental disturbance. Gerald, after spending some time dashing between Barry's troubles and Harriet's, following the trail of electric light-bulbs without success, gave the latter up as a lost cause, convinced that she was in that curious state that some women seem to get into after the age of forty. He was agreed with heartily by all those who had not the slightest idea what the symptoms of a woman of over forty were: the over-forties remained silent.

'Either you will have to have her forcibly removed or we shall have to go on wearing a martyr's crown until she drops dead, and hope that your nerves and everybody else's will stand the strain,' Gerald remarked, exasperated and disappointed that the brown bag which Edward discovered secreted in the dustbin after dark by Harriet held an empty bottle of cough syrup and not incriminating glass.

'The latter is to be our fate,' I declared apologetically. I couldn't give her notice, for she continued to pay rent meticulously and took great care that her rent book was in order. Sometimes she seemed to want to reach us, reminding me of a trapped wild bird frantic to escape, for so often the angry shouting seemed to be seeking attention, bemoaning desperate states of health and lack of care but she withdrew immediately into sullen refusal when a face turned to her in friendly impatience. I waited with some interest for Mother's next visit, to see what effect it would have on our wayward Harriet and if the epistles would start again.

Gerald, confident that he was a sobering influence and that in Groddeck lay all the answers, even if not immediately accessible, watched over us tenderly, rather as though he was privileged to watch the birth of some rare mammal. He was constantly advising me on the best ways of handling humanity and securing any rent overdue. He taught Nelson the rudiments of biology, played the women with charming unconcern, ate garlic and outdid everybody else's smells and pored over his reptiles in equal rapture to his other activities. Then, following the subject closest to his heart, like Jane he returned inevitably to the core of his interest, persuading us into lengthy expeditions to the countryside, regardless of the icy weather, to find that suitable estate in which to start a zoo. I found myself following eagerly, for I watched with open concern a furry thing follow the reptiles to the kitchen and Nelson wishing that he had mice to sell for fodder again.

Once more we retraced the old familiar roads, cut by frosty threads of startling whiteness. We found the large mansion still empty. We paced the sunken garden, a pillage of dead leaves and greeny dampness, until hippos wallowed comfortably before our eyes. The sun shone as our visions transferred themselves into an animal paradise, only to be brought back to cold reality; a north wind that broke the silence to rustling wilderness, with the very big governing factor, lack of sufficient money, which even the ingenious ideas of my brother, the lodgers, or Nelson's mercenary brain could not overcome.

One week we returned home from such a venture of hectic searching, Gerald, Andy, Nelson and the children, with Jane and Blanche now tolerating each other in a common cause, their mutual regard for Gerald. We were a chilly band of mortals once more glad to get back to the warmth of our hearths, for it was October now. We envied the more courageous members who had refused to come with us.

Mrs Budden's baby, Alfred, coddled in his luxurious black pram, was parked in the hall and bellowing mightily; he stopped when he saw us swarming in, blue and panting, our breath patterned by a white mist, lifting a big red face to give us a reproachful greeting from sodden eyes. 'Little beast' – it was a nasal comment from Edward, who welcomed our return in the hall with an inquiry as to whether or not our day had been blessed, not only with a suitable property but with a cheap one. He had been unable to accompany us, though willing in spirit he added hypocritically, for he was nursing his first cold of the winter in a bad-tempered way; a blue nose sniffling into a large hankie soaked in eucalyptus, and swearing he had caught a dose of something from Judy who had collapsed and retired to her bed the night before. Edward's nasal grumblings sent Blanche up to see how her room-mate was faring after a day of neglect, while I, ignoring Edward's terse comments, now smiled at the baby in a completely motherly way.

'He's got a face just like 'is bleeding father – and I wouldn't trust 'im an inch either.' Nelson was examining the baby with extreme distaste.

'He's been bellowing all day,' Edward told us. 'Made my cold fifty times worse, and I've lost all powers of concentration now.'

'Where are the bloody parents?' Gerald asked, blowing warmth into his hands. 'That's what gets me, the parents who have children and then don't bother with them.'

Edward gave him a significant look amounting to agreement. Nelson, as usual, caught the look. 'Sex again,' he remarked cheerfully, 'yer can't get away from it.'

There was a snigger and Gerald's hand came out and clouted Nelson across the back of his head, an action which, if my mother had seen it, would have brought a hail of criticism: she considered the head a most vulnerable part of a boy's anatomy and one that should never been tampered with. He leapt as if he had been hit with a red hot poker, startling Alfred into a fresh uproar.

'That's what comes of giving him biology lessons,' I remarked acidly.

'Grannie said you weren't to do that,' Gerry rebuked his uncle.

'It's bad for the brains' – Nicholas was already making for the inside door, putting a safe distance between himself and any blows that were going, confirming his grandmother's famous speech on blows to the head.

Roger, haggard and unshaven, appeared at the top of the stairs. 'Will somebody strangle that personification of the devil?' he asked, looking us all over as if expecting a volunteer to step forward. The baby was not popular; it was understandable under the circumstances, for Roger was studying for an important art exam and was absorbed in working on a collection of paintings which seemed to have no connection at all to the titles, and I felt faithlessly that they would not place him very high on the list of modern painters. He opened his mouth to repeat his demand when, to our horror, Mr Budden's door flew open and he stood before us. An unforgettable figure of aggressiveness, goose pimples and towel, we got a long view of his bandy legs covered in black hair and grotesque pink body accumulating in flabbiness to square ungainly hips and rounded breasts like a woman. Mother was right, but it was not only his legs that were a trifle ugly.

'Anyone want to argue the bloody point?' he

said raising his fist in a pugilistic fashion, his face purple and his eyes standing out of his head.

Johnny, who had had a wonderful, uninhibited day in Dorset, cocked his leg in sudden fright and christened the big black baby carriage. We fell back, silent and horrified at our indiscretions, now that we were caught. Was there going to be a fight? And if so with whom? It seemed as if there was more than one candidate for a punch up.

'Oh dear me, time for another dose,' Edward excused himself weakly, giving a little cough, having been caught in the act of slander and not spoiling for a fight. The baby had stopped crying at his father's voice and watched the scene with a decidedly cunning eye.

'I thought not,' Mr Budden sneered, looking us all over as if he contemplated buying from a pile of rotting vegetables. He walked silently like royalty through our uncheering midst, gathered up his child in a clumsy swoop, knocking Alfred's head against the bannisters as he turned, and marched back up the stairs breathing heavily. Roger melted before the dragon; he was no St George. Alfred started on an automatic protest at his parent's rough handling, sensed the danger value, and decided silence was a better move, and closed his mouth hurriedly. He was learning fast, even at that age, and he squeezed out two silent and very big tears. With a noise that vibrated through the house and outdid any of Harriet's, the offended parent closed his door behind him and we heard the beginnings of an intimate family brawl.

'My God, the uncouth sod, give him notice! I

told you to do that before, now you see what you've done by not listening. We are all going to be victimised by that picture of how not to have a baby,' Gerald said.

'Quite,' said Edward from a crack in the door.

'I should 'ave tripped 'em with me foot,' Nelson suggested, sad at the chance he had missed.

'An absolute beast,' Jane said, her face pink.

'His legs were interesting, though – all hairy like a caterpillar's,' was Gerry's comparison.

Johnny, expecting the usual chorus of boisterous yells at the polluting of the mighty pram, cowered waiting punishment and revived delightedly at the unexpected as Nelson bent and patted him gently. 'Well done,' he whispered, 'I couldn't 'ave done it better meself.'

Roger's head appeared over the bannister. 'Perhaps I can finish my painting now,' he remarked, an unusually slow grin spreading across his face. 'I must say it was quite a funny sight watching him storm through your midst like a Japanese general, unseated at an opportune moment by the enemy – I noticed there wasn't one brave enough to tackle him,' and he backed hurriedly out of sight as a noise behind the Budden's door suggested Mr Budden's possible reappearance.

'He really hasn't a leg to stand on, you know,' Edward remarked peevishly, 'Whereas I have.'

'Who? Mr Budden or Roger?' I inquired.

'Roger, of course. The racket that issues from that room really leaves him without a reason for a legitimate complaint.' He looked at Andy apologetically.

'You cannot compare the perpetual crying of a baby to the melodious strains of wind instruments,' I insisted tenderly, rushing in quickly to defend the room where my heart lay, noting Andy's wry look.

'That's a matter of opinion.'

'Personally I think those two are mad as well,' Gerald remarked with conviction, forgetting one offender was in our midst. 'But it's all beside the point, the question is – are you going to give that uncouth man notice or not?'

As so often I found one event seemed to set off a whole chain of events, and I was saved from making an immediate decision by just that. A yelp of help from Nicholas who, stoking up the drawing-room fire to furnace-like proportions while we were arguing the point in the hall, had started a fire of some magnitude, which in seconds roared up the chimney throwing out showers of hot sparks, and soot falling like burning coals was already spreading threateningly across the hearth. The roar told us that the chimney was well alight.

Edward, struck to rigid horror with the first news that the unbelievable had happened, quickly transposed himself to a model of 'I told you so' and rescue. 'My God,' he announced, 'lucky I'm here to deal with it for the rest of you don't realise the dangers of fire.' Completely forgetting his ailments he took charge in the tones of a regimental sergeant major suffering from adenoids, showing a side of his nature that we had never suspected. He barked our orders in rapid succession. 'Women and children to safety on the lawn. You, Gerald, warn the house.'

I tried to point out that after all it was only a chimney fire, but was silenced, rudely.

Feeling rather foolish I marshalled the children and the dog onto the front lawn. I could hear Gerald warning the first floor that we were all about to go to perdition and Andy rushing to preserve his trombone and records, Jane her medicine chest. Oaths and protests followed. Edward, armed with a packet of salt, was all ready to fight his way to the rooftops where a smoke screen spread above us. Flames leapt merrily out from the chimney, sending out a shower of sparks like a fireworks display. The neighbours had already gathered and I tried to ignore what I considered their vulgar curiosity. Lady Booth, swallowing her pride, for she never mixed with Mrs Briggs, was now standing shoulder to shoulder with her. Curiously our fire had made them comrades in arms.

They glared at me as if I was a public menace. Mrs Briggs, as usual, spoke first: 'One spark and we shall be up,' she complained, but almost as if she enjoyed the spectacle and was trying to terrify her neighbour in an underhand retaliatory way. This observation, as intended, sent Lady Booth into fresh cries of panic, for if there was one thing she dreaded it was an all-consuming fire.

Mr Beetle, observing the disturbance, was already on his way to save us, puffing up like a small engine, his jaw wobbling and arms outstretched to catch the first victim. 'I thought things had been too quiet,' he panted. 'I do hope Mrs Durrell is not in the blaze.'

'Everything is under control,' I remarked haughtily, my hauteur dissolving into a sheepish grin as a string of fugitives, headed by Mr Budden carrying his baby, left the house looking as though they were following Moses to the promised land. Blanche appeared at the window.

'Save her, save her!' Mr Beetle shouted excitedly.

'Beauty before age,' Nelson remarked.

'Judy feels too bad to get up, so I'll just hang around for a while to see what happens,' she called down, giggling at the sight of us all gathered together on the lawn.

Then all eyes turned to the roof, where Edward, like a tropical bird with whiskers, had appeared. Still clutching his packet of salt, he was clambering cautiously across the grey slates to a series of sympathetic 'Ahs' from the ground. He made towards the chimney where the flames were licking up to a frightening height. I burst out laughing, in one of my doubtful bouts of humour. We lost him for a moment in a gust of black smoke. There was a gasp of horror from the onlookers, accentuated by Mrs Briggs: 'He's gone in, that's what, poor creature.' Then Edward re-appeared, safe from behind the chimney. A small cheer went up. 'More salt,' he hollered, 'bring more salt.'

'What's he saying?' I shouted, hoping my fire insurance was not overdue.

'What's he want salt for?' Mr Beetle inquired with great interest.

'He's not cooking up there, is he?' Lady Booth spoke anxiously.

'It's an old-fashioned fire-extinguisher,' Harriet said in a remarkably sane way, standing with the tragic air of Joan of Arc.

'I think 'e's 'aving a fit, poor man, overcome by the 'eat, no doubt.'

'Better send for the ambulance.'

'Can't find any salt,' Gerald shouted, appearing at the window beside Blanche, 'we've used it all, it seems.'

'Is he going to save her?' Mr Beetle was agitated by the possible fate of the blonde in the window.

'Seduce her, more likely,' Roger smirked.

''Ear, 'ear,' was Nelson's contribution.

'We haven't any more,' I called up to Edward who was hanging over the eaves now, as though he was examining them for the best place to build a nest.

'Imbeciles!' he roared, dragging us all into the picture of wrath. 'Then get the Fire Brigade.'

'I've sent for the Fire Brigade,' a croaky voice announced dramatically behind us. Miss Brady, shrouded in a blue shawl, was hurriedly crossing the road.

'Thank God, we are saved,' Lady Booth burst into tears, and leant for comfort into the welcoming arms of Mr Beetle, whose short figure, unable to bear the welcome burden, called loudly for Lord Booth, who never appeared.

'Crikey, there'll be some mess to clear up now, mark my words,' Mrs Briggs announced in a pleased voice, as a frantic ringing of a bell and people popping out all over the road told us that the fire engine was speeding to our rescue. Within minutes the shining model of civilised efficiency had put out the blaze that Edward's courage had failed to quench, and there was only the mess to clear.

Edward, extremely happy, having at last experienced the fire he had subconsciously longed for, I firmly believed, told and re-told his story to all those who had not been present to witness his own little rooftop charade.

'I knew we'd have a fire one day,' he kept saying. 'I had a premonition,' and at last, hoarse from his own recitals, he remembered that after all he did have a cold, and clutching his throat he announced pathetically that he thought the episode had brought on pneumonia. He rushed to the nurses' sanctuary for medical aid – we noticed this with some amusement, for Blanche and Judy never kept more than cotton wool.

Going upstairs after the excitement had died down, to see how Judy's illness fared, I found her alone, lying in bed with a pallor and limpness that frightened me. 'Shall I call the doctor?' I suggested, really concerned.

Judy weakly protested that Blanche was doing all that was necessary. 'Sorry to have missed the fire – I heard that Edward excelled himself,' she managed a small smile, attempting a lively note.

I regaled her briefly with a few of the finer points, poked up the fire into a more cheerful blaze and went to find Blanche and insist that the doctor was called. Jane would have had her patient in hospital long ago, but this was one room, however provocative the situation, where Jane never trespassed. I followed laughter, and traced Blanche to Edward's room, where she was taking his temperature for the second time, in a most unprofessional manner, while discussing hairstyles with Olwen.

If Edward had a choice of nurse, he usually preferred a blonde one, so he was now of course reclining back and enjoying the soft hand, re-living the fire with Paula and Barry who had just returned from a day of visiting relatives.

Taking Blanche's attention away from a disappointed Edward I drew her into a private corner to discuss Judy's illness. The matter was soon made clear, in a calm clinical way, a tone that only a nurse could produce. Judy, unknown to us, had become pregnant and, terrified of the consequences, had procured an abortion. Where, was a mystery. The word which I had treated so casually, slipped over lightly in the dictionary before and which had played no part in my life up till now, had suddenly become reality and one for concern.

Mother, hearing exaggerated gossip about a few charred remains, not waiting to pack a suitcase, arrived holding a large phial of sal volatile beneath her nose, strongly supported by Leslie with a bottle of brandy. Finding the house still standing she recovered slightly, and entered almost gaily in her relief, though not without a few apprehensive glances in the direction of Harriet's room. Mother found me, not sitting in the midst of a smoking ruin smelling of anti-burn lotion and mourning my losses, but pacing the floor with this entirely new problem. She examined the scene of the fire intently, rebuked me for endangering the lives of the household, turning a deaf ear to the fact that it was her darling grandchild who had started the fire, while Leslie, finding our death by fire a false alarm, wandered off to have a celebratory drink with Edward, leaving me to wither under one of Mother's stern looks.

'And what else is going on?' she asked.

'What do you mean?' I said evasively, avoiding those direct blue eyes.

'I can tell from your face, dear there is more going on here than meets the eye. I thought I heard the murmur of illness – not another epidemic, I hope, that you are trying to keep from me?'

So hesitatingly, wondering if Mother had ever heard the dread word, I told her of Judy's plight. Mother, much to my surprise, not only knew the word, but seemed to know a great deal about the subject, learned, she said, in the days of her youth when starting a nursing career. She was nevertheless aghast at what she called the follies of youth. 'This is what comes of playing with fire,' she pronounced gravely, 'and why the unmarried mothers' home seems to be full all year round. It makes me quite certain that you must either close this house at once, or in future let me interview your prospective tenants. Doris, Leslie and I have decided that you seem to attract every worst situation. You have been in this house less than a year and murder alone has only been avoided by a miracle. Now this sort of thing' – she avoided the contaminating word – 'can hardly give the house a good moral tone. The doctor had better be called in immediately if you are to avoid a funeral.'

I agreed, feeling as though the world's problems were personally at my door. I asked the doctor to call, and he came quickly, the same slight figure of efficiency. No expression crossed his face during his visit, but as he left he turned to me as I hovered worriedly in the hall and remarked in a matter-of-fact voice: 'You do pick 'em, don't you?'

I agreed, blushing guiltily. It was no use contradicting him, for I certainly did.

'Another twenty-four hours and she would have been dead,' he said cheerfully. 'I shall send an ambulance immediately to collect her.'

Was this the right moment to introduce Harriet to the doctor? Perhaps not. Sighing, I decided Mother was right. In future I would let her choose the lodgers.

Chapter Seventeen

Mother had her chance to put her new resolution into action almost immediately by the sudden departure of Judy and Blanche to new hospitals, no longer mere pot-carriers but nurses of some standing. Exams had been passed with flying colours, disproving the theory that their role as nursing sisters was entirely superfluous. Jane, green-eyed, refused to believe that exam papers had not been tampered with or examiners seduced, and muttered disparaging comments about the present day standards of nursing. There were the usual farewells, the usual party, while Mother subsequently busied herself, with Leslie's help, concocting a suitable notice, and put it in the local paper under the column of 'Rooms to Let'.

It was a foregone conclusion that my family, however disapproving, in their great anxiety to see me as a success, would intervene kindly when they thought necessary.

The period of waiting for the results of Mother's labour was trying. Mrs Greenfield had temporarily forgotten her latest grievance – the frustrating spectacle of someone else and not her being carried away by an ambulance. The sight of Mother revived her irritations.

'I see,' she announced knocking and entering with ceremony, 'that you have allowed that woman here again.' Her eyes filled with the light challenge, flickered past me to Mother, innocently waiting a possible new tenant to materialise, the first answer to her call. The usual sound of music hung about the hall.

'Mrs Greenfield, I hope you are not going to cause trouble,' I answered coldly, trying to keep calm, for this was obviously the wrong moment to start a brawl with Mother's prospective lodger actually on the way.

'Me cause trouble!' She looked genuinely astonished. 'It's they that cause trouble,' she said bitterly. 'Rob me in broad daylight, talk about me – but do I get sympathy, oh no, other people can be carried off comfortably in ambulances . . .' She paused, deeply offended at the memory.

Edward, as usual, came to the rescue. Opening his door he bounded up the stairs with a 'No time to lose.'

'They are at it again!' she shrieked, immediately alert, and rushed after Edward. The rattle of the lavatory door told me that Edward was safe.

This convinced me that it was certainly the wrong moment for personal introductions of Harriet to a new tenant, for one had to get slowly acclimatised to understand her oddities. I turned to hear Mother say in a resolute voice: 'I shall stick it out dear, and I shall continue to look under my bed as usual.'

Then she was rising with an exclamation of pleasure and refusal to acknowledge the uproar going on upstairs, with Harriet demanding that

Edward leave her things alone. A tall, dark stranger had entered the gate.

'Ah, here he is,' said Mother. 'Just what your horoscope said, and what a nice looking young man; I knew success would be ours in the end,' she added cheerfully, preparing to bustle out. The noise upstairs was subsiding.

My interest rose as I took stock quickly of that handsome, almost smooth face, the easy swinging body. A splendid blazer and trim grey flannels. Healthy, too, obviously unperturbed by the east winds biting across the house.

'He's all yours,' I said affectionately as I made way for Mother. 'My turn will come later,' and I settled down to await the results of Mother's first business venture with great interest.

Jane popped in to say that she thoroughly approved of Mother's companion, and she hoped that our *bête humaine*, Mr Budden, or that screwy Harriet, wouldn't frighten him away; and she had managed to silence the music-lovers temporarily. We chortled together like a couple of old crones at the great possibilities of the stranger, listened on tenterhooks to Mother enticing a new body into our web, refraining from the urge we both felt for a closer investigation. Just as we were beginning to feel we couldn't stand the strain a moment longer, Mother reappeared in our midst, all smiles.

'I have let your room, which you will be pleased to know, and to a perfect gentleman.'

Jane and I exchanged satisfied glances.

'Good, good,' breathed Jane.

'Is he a bachelor, married, or divorced?' I asked all the important questions.

'Divorced, in my opinion,' said Nelson, cheekily popping his head round the door then disappearing again.

'I've no idea,' said Mother, with a little disparaging look at my vulgar curiosity. 'But even Harriet quailed before that smile and returned quietly to her room, though Edward looked a trifle sour, I must say.'

'Perhaps he is jealous.' It was a reasonable assumption.

'I do hope Edward is not going to be prejudiced of such a charming young man.' Jane was already teetering on the precipice of romance. 'And such a charming voice too . . .' It seemed that Mother was on the same precipice.

We praised Mother's efforts at letting wholeheartedly, and questioned her for more details on this new and perfect male who was about to establish himself among us. Mother, relishing the discussion on her find, fell into easy raptures, in which the words 'genuine', 'honest', 'handsome', all played a great part – ending with the bright observation that he had a good set of teeth: she knew how fussy I am about men's teeth.

'But did you mention rent?' I wanted to know, not really worried, mesmerised by the tale of his other charms.

Mother's face dropped. 'I quite forgot about that, but I am sure you will have no trouble. Honesty is written all over him.'

'I hope so, but I very much doubt it,' said a sour voice, and Edward had entered our discussion.

'He likes children and animals, that is enough,' Mother reasoned, 'and happily Margo's horoscope said that a dark stranger would make his presence felt in a satisfactory way,' she concluded. Our conversation ended there.

Percival Johnson certainly made his presence felt as he settled in our midst. Mother's whole-hearted praise, and his own ingratiating, almost Latin charm, graced with an Oxford accent, opened every female door to him – even the formidable Harriet – and outshone any of Gerald's previous manoeuvres. He carried shopping-bags for old and young alike, he listened with a personal cosy tenderness to each one: their health, their operations, their finances, uttering murmurs of sympathy: 'I say, how awful my dear', or 'My dear, how you have suffered', or the infallible 'You look charming, just charming'.

Even Nelson's mother, usually so remote, blossomed forth unbelievably, charmed by his good looks and his gentle but manly ways. She made early morning tea for him, carrying it reverently to his door, blushing like a teenager at the sound of his well-bred voice bidding her to enter. Nelson, taking an instant dislike to his mother's charmer, referred to him rudely as 'the gaffer', and thought up every possible device to inflict discomfort. For once Nelson had a solid block of male humanity behind him; for my male lodgers, in a unanimous body, detested the newcomer and smouldering tempers were fanned into spiteful sarcasm as they watched the simpering adulations of their wilting womenfolk. But Percival was impervious to male criticism. He treated them all as jolly good fellows, with hearty backslapping and friendliness that made his victims grind their teeth.

Weekend morning slumbers were disturbed by

the sound of a broom energetically stirring the dust on the front path and the air vibrated with a tenor thrashing its way through an Ivor Novello musical as Percy reorganised the garden with deplorable good health, talked sweetly to old ladies on their way to church or shopping and tickled Pekingese in what some people would call a sickening way.

Percy's career was somewhat remote. He spent long hours in his room, or sporting himself with great decorum with the ladies of the house. His explanation was that he was an ex-school teacher, but working on a thesis at this moment, and the government gave him a grant so as to enable him to have complete freedom with his work. I felt that with the old school blazer, a badge blazing colour with a Latin motto, we could not doubt him. When I tentatively inquired for the rent on several occasions he replied discreetly, in a tone that indicated the suggestion of rent was in really bad taste and that at any moment the post would bring the much-awaited bundle of money, and I, apologising profusely at my lack of taste, retired back to an unsuspecting waiting game.

Disintegration swept the house as the weeks passed. Gerald, openly hostile, stormed out with his box of reptiles under his arm, stating that in his opinion Percival was a lecherous-looking swine, and he preferred the unpolluted atmosphere of Manchester Zoo to the ordeal of having to sit around and listen to a pack of perfectly nauseating silly women drooling on about an over-affected, greasy-haired Romeo, and what Mother and I and any other fatuous female saw in him he couldn't imagine. Mother, highly indignant, fell to defend her prize lodger, saying hotly that words like 'ponce' should never be uttered and, in any case, Gerald had no business taking away a man's character like that as she had so often told both him and Leslie (whose disparaging descriptions were even worse than Gerald's). She turned to Edward to uphold her, but Edward, whose bad humour was now bubbling up like an acid bath, came out with words that forced Mother to seclusion. And the storm grew.

Barry, discovering Paula supplying the 'loafer' with hand-cream and hair-lotion, aided and abetted by Jane, threatened to write to the Education Authorities about what he called the misuse of government grants. Roger and Andy, testing the newcomer out, to find that sickly Ivor Novello songs were all he could aspire to, dismissed him as a moronic, unmusical bounder. Mr Budden, catching Mrs Budden in her pink kimono entertaining Percy to a quiet tea-party, did not wait for explanations but gave her such a backhander that I was, as head of the house, forced to intervene at the cries and soothe the tears of Mrs Budden and Mr Budden's temper; while Percival, behaving like a martyr, moved over to Jane's room for sympathy.

Then I began to feel a little uneasy by the repeated absence of rent, and was swayed by the men's animosity, feeling that my friendship with Andy might snap under the strain if I continued in the wholehearted support of Percival. Just suppose the men were right, and the fellow was the living image of all the uncomplimentary remarks that had been so rudely uttered about him? What a fool I should look as landlady. My wavering suspicions were instantly dispelled by the sudden picture of Percival carrying Mrs Williams' washing out for hanging, which took me completely off my guard, and I found myself shame-faced, dismissing the disturbing thoughts, until the passing of the postman again empty-handed made my optimism of rent sink dismally.

After a week or so living in a self-torture of suspicion and counter-suspicion and the growing dislike of the sickly adoration of Percival by my own sex, he suddenly produced a fiancée, with four children aged under six. She was a Wagnerian blonde, solid fat vibrating joyfully under tight clothes. A transparent lacy blouse scarcely held the contours of a buxom bosom, her hair was tied back with a black velvet ribbon and she watched Percival with big blue eyes. The episode caused a fresh stir, and his faithful followers found themselves tottering on the brink of disloyalty with shock – readjustment was hard. I heard with alarm the slam of Mrs Greenfield's door for the first time in weeks: the men were openly jubilant, and Mother and I read the tea leaves trying to fathom out whether or not the future held any further surprises for us. In the coming weeks the blousy lady was a constant visitor, and the love affair began to unsettle even Percival's most staunch supporters. Harriet went back to moaning that nobody loved her. Even Mother had second thoughts: she and Nelson had been an unwitting observer of what she described as an undisciplined and silly love scene – 'right in the window too, you will really have to have a quiet word with him. It will be putting ideas into the children's heads if you don't, though I must say I think he will be an admirable husband and father.' Nelson, undisturbed, told me he had 'enjoyed the scene of undiluted raptures.'

I kept silent about the rent and the five-pound note I had lent him for a desperate need – it was a birthday present from Andy and I was saving it for Christmas, looming up ahead. 'There is your security,' and Percival pointed to his wireless, as the money changed hands. Now, I hardly liked to intrude on his privacy and certainly not to mention the sordid business of unpaid debts, while the sound of loving frivolities floated out to all of us and another packet of cigarettes was borrowed and not returned.

Anyway other problems were brewing up which dimmed my interest temporarily in Percival's activities. Roger's past had caught us up. Magda's private volcano, rumbling a slow warning for so long, finally erupted, dragging me against my will into its thickly flowing lava in a never-to-be-forgotten night when I floundered at the ebbtide of someone else's doom. I was spending an evening of solitude, browsing over the memorable pages of a much-loved book when I should have been sorting out my rent books, when at a late hour the door burst open and a distraught Magda fell into my arms, plunging me into a mixed story of unfathomable origin.

Tempered with the shaking of slow incessant tears, a strange confidence in my ability to comprehend and heal, and the pleading urge to remain close, filled me with a nauseous taste of fear as the facts stood blatantly clear, that Magda was ill and needed help. Mental, physical, or both, I was not sure. Disentangling myself from her muscular arms, with a faint revulsion that made me inwardly shudder, I laid the weeping protesting figure on the spare divan and set the kettle for a cup of tea, promising halfheartedly that if she would return to her own lodging house in the morning I would come with the doctor. Silently cursing Roger's philanderings, I settled down to wait the call of the boiling kettle with gloomy thoughts on what I was sure was going to be an all-night vigil of some magnitude. I thought with concern of the possible loss of my doctor's good wishes, for he would be getting very tired of professional summonses and we might in the end be forced to have a bugle-call for Harriet, in which the doctor would undoubtedly have to feature. Even before the kettle boiled I heard the welcome noise of sonorous breathing, shuddering to a listless sighing silence, to start again in a mechanical repetition. Throwing a blanket over the sleeper, with cold thankfulness, I stole away back to my book with a restless awareness.

I heard the stumbling capitulation of a prodigal husband's return – Mr Budden. He had made a smouldering exit after demanding an answer to the question as to why a piece of steak sold at an exorbitant price should reach his dining table as raw hide: Mrs Budden had had no answer. Percival, cheery after obvious amorous entertainment, bid his blonde reluctantly to be gone. Andy hesitated before my door: I let him go in silent longing, for there was always tomorrow. The inquisitive creakings of Harriet's long dark shadow. With a concert of twanging bed springs the vision of Nelson's mound in happy slumber blotted out my wakefulness; but only for a moment it seemed.

I woke to the insistent feel of a hard cheek against mine, the soft rub of stubble growth. For an awkward moment I thought it was Percival, then the voice of Magda crooning to me, mixed with passion and material comparisons, told me otherwise; I was smothered by the clasp of strong arms and a heavy body. Nauseated I shook myself free of these sickly attentions, and leapt up in more haste than any episode in the house had caused me to do so far, to stand in an agitated icy silence. Uncomfortable prickles of shocking distaste, mingling with pity, shook me as I remembered odd remarks of Magda's, sensuous insinuations, remarks that at the time I had shrugged off lightly with fatuous retaliation. Paula was right, the girl was changing her sex, or something. One thing was certain, she was bordering on a catastrophe in a much more alarming way than Harriet.

But this should have been some other landlady's worry, not mine, I grumbled to myself as I stumbled away without a word to the kitchen to put the kettle on again; debating on whether to call upstairs for help, to administer a strong sedative in the manner of Jane, if I could find one. When I returned with three aspirins and a pot of tea, the cause of my anxiety was sleeping soundly. Feeling that the capacity to laugh had left me permanently, I crept stealthily to the shelter of another room, determined that Roger should share the burden of his ex-love at the first possible moment. I fell into a restless sleep, awakening at every sound: in the morning she was gone.

Reluctantly remembering my promise I rose early and telephoned the doctor, to Percival singing 'Where the bee sucks, there suck I', and apologetically explained the situation. As usual he answered in the helpful tolerant voice where his true thoughts were undetectable, and left me with a series of suggestions and the unpalatable job of visiting my patient and awaiting the arrival of a psychiatrist.

Thankful that I could despatch my children on their way to the seat of learning, I rushed upstairs to call the resident nurse, deciding, in spite of last night's resolutions, that Roger would hardly be of any use and would most probably cringe from such a drastic encounter, which it would be almost a cruelty to enforce. The sewing machine idle at such an early hour, I found Jane closeted by all the bits that constituted a very full life, sitting before a bright fire and watching with greedy eyes a thick slice of bread darkening to glowing brownness with the aid of a four-pronged fork.

'I am thinking about Percival,' she told me.

The black nightdress, bought in those first hectic days of Jane's transformation, now seemed to me ordinary, in comparison with other events.

I unfolded the story of my plight, refusing to prolong a discussion on Percival and tear to shreds the strawberry blonde who would one day be his wife. Jane listened with the deep concentration of a Red Indian chief plotting a scalping, as the toast blackened smokily (which would provoke Edward into another voyage of discovery as soon as the smell penetrated below) while the small eyes, curiously naked without their glasses, screwed themselves into pin-points of interest. Dropping the charred bread with careful precision into the hearth, Jane spoke with that slightly superior air of righteousness that could reduce one's inside to a nagging irritation and a desire to haggle.

'Of course I shall come with you, it's my job; even if I deplore the basic cause. I well remember a similar case, perfectly ghastly. I was a probationer at the time, three operations, and hey presto!' She dropped her pose and quickly prepared herself for a journey of mercy, while I gratefully apologised for my rudeness at our last meeting, a difference of opinion over Percival, which had parted us with Jane dangling a threat of notice to my retreating back. She accepted my apology with kindly patronage, her eyes closing to a smug smile behind their lenses once more. I refused Percival's congenial offer that he should join us and accepted hurried directions from an unrepentant Roger. Together we hurried out across the town, our difference of opinion forgotten.

Behind the high hedge of laurel and dark scrawny clusters of pine, high before us stood a shadowy building of red brick and small, heavily curtained windows. Somewhere in the interior of boiled cabbage smells and grilled kippers, Magda made her home and waited for us, I thought fearfully, as we climbed the steep incline. The place exceeded Roger's murky descriptions and was the personification of dreariness, especially reserved for lodging houses. A dank silence slipped out to meet us as we opened the door and stepped inside. A notice told us to 'close the door and keep quiet'. I wished that I was back home amongst my own noises: the scales ringing from a trombone; Nelson's small repertoire of song repeated like a cracked disc; even Harriet's hefty defiance, were all preferable to this silent gloomy dump. With Roger's directions still clear in mind we made our way almost stealthily through a maze of dark brown paints, up towards a coffin-shaped room on the top floor. My own house, I felt, was a palace in comparison, rich in human elements, big windows, clear paint and bright lights, which Harriet's darkening hand failed to diminish.

'This is definitely it,' I said, peering at the figure 10. I knocked intrepidly. The reply came immediately: a heavy shuffling of a weighty body in quick movement, and the violent wrenching of a door opening, and Magda was before us. She held a razor to her wet face, and her chin was cut in several places. I felt quite sick, more with the implications than with the sight.

'Go away, I hate you,' she hissed, her eyes bright with hatred.

I fell back astounded. Where was the changing lover of last night? I turned to Jane for reassurance. The now brisk attitude of Jane warned me she was going into action.

'Hello, dear,' she said brightly. 'Everything all right?'

Magda turned and gave her the full force of her menacing gaze.

Downstairs there was knocking, doors opening, voices, and a light tread creaked its way up towards us. The psychiatrist had made his entrance.

'Shall I take over?' inquired a deep, understanding voice from a figure radiating quiet composure.

We almost pushed him forward and fled.

'Let's get back to good old Harriet,' I sang fatuously to Jane. The thought was like a sweet dream, and we made for home with Jane in full agreement. 'For after all,' she said, 'I am a clinical nurse, not a mental one.'

I agreed, with a firm resolution that if there was any trouble in future with my tenants' friends they would have to deal with it on their own – I was most definitely on strike.

At home we were greeted by a surprising picture of wide dimensions in a bowler hat, sitting in the porch on a kitchen chair, and who I presumed with casual unconcern was a passer-by who had been taken ill and brought into rest by the kindly hands of one of my tenants – obviously Percival. I passed with a small smile of sympathetic understanding, but behind the closed front door inside the hall a cluster of gossipers told me otherwise.

'There is a bailiff in the porch,' Edward whispered hoarsely as if death stalked.

'Are we all going to be turned shamefully onto the street?' Mrs Budden, clutching her child with motherly ferocity, wanted to know, getting ready to give us a piece of her own brand of hysterics.

I stood amazed, connecting the word bailiff with unpaid bills, furniture forcibly removed and deep shame. It was an experience I had never been through before, but some of my friends had.

'Who let him in?' I demanded indignantly. Everybody looked at Percival. 'Saboteur!' I shouted to the look of apology. 'And who gave him a chair?' Everybody glared at Percival again. Another look of shame followed.

'I tried to keep him out,' Edward explained, 'but the fellow was quite determined. Said you hadn't paid your rates, or something.'

'Indeed!' I remarked haughtily, retracing my steps to do battle, amazed at the fellow's impertinence, my dislike of the local authority mounting.

The man was still sitting like a cardboard statue, and I was glad that he had not been given a more comfortable chair, as I confronted him with ladylike indignation for an explanation. He was a big man, with a clownish figure not unlike Nelson's, but his face did not bear the stamp of good-humoured roguishness. The incongruous dusty bowler was as symbolic of his trade as the three balls of a pawnbroker's sign, and somehow changed the situation back to comedy. The clown lived again for me as I eyed the headgear with appreciation.

'On whose authority are you here?' I inquired, ready to laugh.

'Town 'all. 'Ere I've come, and 'ere I stay: you've 'ad your warning about them rates – plenty I've no doubt.'

'Are you a real live bailiff?' I inquired curiously, filled with morbid interest, never having seen the species before, unconsciously letting my opinion of his distasteful job creep into my voice while at the same time showing him my most charming feline smile. Surely somewhere in that soft armour of flesh lay a heart of pure solid gold, susceptible to a woman's smile.

'Well, I'm not a dead one, I'm sure,' he remarked. I was discouraged to find that my smile had fallen on a stony surface. I withdrew it immediately, to a look of pity.

'You will get your money in due course, a slight misunderstanding, no doubt,' I said as I remembered with a sneaking horror the final demand which I had dismissed casually as unimportant.

''Ere I come, and 'ere I stay,' the man went on stubbornly.

'I shall write to the Prime Minister and complain,' I told him grandly, bringing the full fruits of my superior education down on the rounded bowler.

'And my MP,' I said, wondering who my MP was, while a chorus of suggestions supplied me with at least four different names from different parties.

''Ere I come, and 'ere I stay. I'm not budging,' said the bailiff, as if the safety of the world depended on his immovable ability.

'Where's my cheque book?' I demanded angrily to the waiting crowd. Eager hands found it for me, and with a flourish of writing I dismissed him and his sordid intentions, and turned indoors in dignified retreat, only to be warned by telephone that Magda had disappeared while awaiting the ambulance to take her to hospital and if she arrived at my door, the worried voice said, I was to hold her and ring for help. Fortunately we heard no more.

The next day, while I was still recovering from the shock of Magda and the bailiff, Mrs Williams, who clung to her beliefs and taking Percival his usual cup of tea, shattered us all by announcing that he had disappeared; lock, stock, but without his wireless. Her mournful declarations and our cries of disbelief were soon followed by the police. The truth was out!

Mother's young gentleman was a young man of many energetic roles, who it seemed kept one step ahead of the law. He had a wife and children somewhere in the north; he was wanted for alimony, larceny and fraud (and he had just escaped bigamy, I thought bitterly, by the skin of his teeth).

The news spread about the house at great speed and the women mourned together while a slow grin of malicious delight spread from man to man. Mother, extremely downcast, kept repeating: 'And I thought he was such a gentleman – but only at first, of course,' she excused herself. 'After that odious live scene I began to have severe doubts, but I did not want to cause false alarm.'

Having digested fully the escapades of Percy – it took time, for this was my first fraud – I remembered the wireless: at least he had one honest inclination. I rushed upstairs to claim it and to examine my room, half afraid that my investigations might uncover something even more sinister. I opened the door of Percy's room and entered a little apprehensively. The room was in order and the wireless was there, but alas, stamped clearly on the back, were the words 'For Hire'.

'Gerald's right, he's a thieving swine!' I shouted.

'I told you so,' came Edward's pleased voice

behind me. 'The fellow was an irrepressible rogue.'

I opened the cupboard gingerly, and a pile of unwashed milk bottles fell out and sprawled across the carpet. Sadly I closed the door. Edward put a comforting arm about me, and together we went down to Mother and a delegation who were sitting as if it were the day of judgment and the gates of heaven were closed to them.

Edward, though sad at my loss, could not contain his glee at the unmasking of the impostor, and left us to discuss the situation with his equally gleeful compatriots. Passing Harriet moping on the stairs, her face hidden in her hands and a shawl dangling about her shoes, he paused for a moment to sympathise, then at the suggestion that something might be missing from her room she perked up, the old glint returned to her eyes and she stood up hurriedly and vanished up the stairs.

'I must say,' I turned to Mother, 'Edward does seem to have got the hang of coping with Harriet.'

'He has proved himself to be a trustworthy and good man,' Mother declared. Then her thoughts returned to Percy and she went on: 'You know Margo, I can't help wondering how all the other landladies in Bournemouth get on?'

As we didn't know any other landladies, except Mrs Briggs who would never have allowed such a thing to happen over her threshold, we could make no comparisons.

'But this is the first really bad case, isn't it?'

'Well, yes,' Mother agreed unwillingly, 'if you don't take into account Harriet's peculiarities and the smugglers, though I can understand them smuggling in a pet and all that sort of thing. But this out-and-out deception of Percival's is beyond me . . . I can't think what went wrong.'

'The trouble is, Mother, you are still influenced by my horoscope.'

Mother's face changed expression. 'And I don't think much of your daily paper either,' she went on, reminded of our false prophecy. 'I think you should write a note to say that your forecast by the stars was entirely wrong.'

'I shall change my paper,' I said, grinning. 'I know what – I can always start an advice bureau if all else fails!' I was delighted at my sudden brainwave. 'Advise the lovelorn or sex starved, or . . .'

'I hardly think, dear,' Mother interrupted coldly, 'that drunk or sober, you are the person to give advice.'

'Well, I think I am,' I argued stubbornly. 'Half my life is spent sorting out my lodgers' lives, anyway, so I might as well stick an official board up and get paid for it.'

'Sh! quiet! Not before the children,' Mother said with agitation at the sound of Nelson careering indoors followed by Nicholas and Gerry.

'It's God's truth,' Nelson gasped excitedly and obviously impressed, 'that Percy is a bleedin' thief an' abortionist? An' do rabbits breed like flies? 'Cause me an' me mates are thinking of keepin' some?'

'Yes, to the second question, and yes – almost – to the first, but the word is bigamist,' I answered dizzily, 'and the final answer is No. See what I mean?' I turned to Mother.

'Don't disillusion the children,' Mother

remarked, and turned to embrace her grandchildren.

Chapter Eighteen

Jane, who was behaving as though a major operation was afoot, exchanged her sloping ceilings and the warmth of the eaves for another room, one which she maintained still held the fascinating aroma of a tragedy – Percy's. I was unable to share her spiritual liaison with Percy's ghost. Having removed the dirty milk bottles and returned the wireless to the rental people, I now found that Percy's personality dissolved into nothing: the strawberry-blonde and her retinue of children we had never seen again.

Mother, undaunted by her previous experience in the precarious field of a landlady, resettled in our midst for twenty-four hours to re-let Jane's more spacious quarters to a dilapidated pyramid of a woman and her son, a gangling youth with a crooked mouth who roamed the house aimlessly in a melancholy air of detachment undisturbed by the busy fingers of his mother practising millinery to the exclusion of all else, and her spasmodic appearance in her fantastic creations with the sweeping confidence of a Dior model.

Christmas greeted us with the soft sparkle of light snow; the sun as yellow as a young chick and fires crackling up at the first match to keep a sensitive Edward on the alert and the excited noise of the young, determined to live a full Christmas. Christmas spirit is infectious, and we dawdled into a pleasurable and lazy day, but as usual after every calm, chaos seemed to follow,

In this instance it was the new lodger. The listless, limping boy was lapsed into a last deathly coma of a chronic epileptic, laying bare his secret; plunging us in a cold horrified moment to the hectic activities of an emergency ward. Edward and Nelson conspiratorially stated that they were not surprised, they had long since had their suspicions, and a furious Harriet proclaimed loudly that she considered the scene an exhibition of thoroughly bad taste created by that weird boy Robin to gain attention. The sight of the much coveted ambulance arriving sent her scuttling off her soap-box to remove electric lightbulbs as a reprisal, making Robin's last journey of descent, slung in a blanket, down narrow attic stairs and round dark corners, a terrifying feat of acrobatic manoeuvres and crude noises.

We shed a tear of pity, not for Robin, strangely, but for the silent white-faced woman behind. Robin was buried in a shroud of gloom with a single mourner. There were no flowers. Then it was a new year, and he was forgotten by all except his mother and mine, who swore that on her visits she felt his spiritual presence about the place with friendly oppressiveness.

Another short period of calm, then once again I was dislodged from complacency into a disturbing element of familiar things on the change. Roger's decision and preparation to travel to London for fresh studies in the artistic world; Edward talking about cheap villas in Spain; Harriet disappearing as quietly as she had arrived – one frosty morning – a week's rent pushed beneath the door to pay her debts. No one saw her go.

Jane, settling into the life of a full-time seamstress, forgot her other hobbies, submerged in pins, patterns, material and machine needles. A new Barry, unusually gay with the definite promise of a remunerative career, united with a jubilant Paula, glamorous and untarnished now, all past predicaments forgotten.

There were the more gloomy prospects of the Buddens with a new large and bawling baby: Mrs Budden's rapidly increasing size left us in no doubt.

Gerald, off on safari and busy packing would undoubtedly return with a load of animals guaranteed to disrupt my life and that of the rest of the town.

Then the final blow of change: Mrs Williams and Nelson leaving. Mrs Williams announced her intentions breaking the news by intimate confidences – her first.

'We're goin' 'ome,' she murmured, apologising for her action. 'Of course we're truly sorry to go. Nelson's been so 'appy 'ere – enjoyed 'imself 'e 'as,' a tender smile illuminated the eyes and spread the mouth up sweetly. 'Yer understand dearie, 'ome to 'ome like.'

'Has he?' I smiled, letting a mocking note of disbelief creep into my voice as I remembered a dazed Mr Budden, Edward's face distorted in the apoplexy of a blue rage, a black notebook stuffed with slanderous secrets, in the pages of which I felt sure none of us had failed to feature, along with coffins and other memories. The remaining relics, a pebble-dashed corner, still cratered but no longer pebbled, were all living signs of Nelson's enjoyment. But the portrait of a true comedian without artifice enticed me to the winning post.

'We shall miss him,' I said impulsively and found to my surprise the statement was true. 'Perhaps he could visit us sometimes?' It was a dangerous suggestion, considering everything.

'Nelson would love that, I'm sure,' the answer was both pleased and doubtful. 'We don't want to go reely, it's so peaceful 'ere,' she hesitated, fishing for a suitable phrase to illustrate her disclosures.

Peaceful? It was my turn to be doubtful.

'But it's 'im, see, me 'ubby . . .'As an 'old on me, 'e 'as even at a distance.'

'Has he?' I asked, filled with a sudden hopeful and vulgar curiosity for there was still the ghost of prison to lay.

'Matrimonial bonds,' the explanation was tinged with regretful submission. For Mrs Williams the loyalties of convention were hard to break. 'Marriage is not all 'oney for some,' her mouth dropped.

'I know,' I agreed feelingly, thinking of the pregnant martyr upstairs.

'Yer see, me 'ubby likes 'is drink, and 'is women – a violent man 'e can be. It's 'is temper, see. 'E administers a back 'and at the slightest provocation,' she added tellingly to my intent ear. 'But I'm not saying naught against 'im, mind,' she hastened to assure me. ''E's a fine figure of a man for all that, it's just sometimes 'e goes too far, 'e reely does.'

'Does he?' I inquired hospitably.

'I told 'im so often, violence doesn't pay, me lad, and you'll lift your 'and once too often . . .'

'And did he?'

''E did. And paid the penalty.' It was a statement without malice. 'Mucked up the 'ouse, 'e did and all – blood all over the place!' A gruelling shadow of disappointment leapt to her face: 'Broke me best crocks . . . But 'e's promised to reform.' Doubtful reflection crept into the quiet voice, obviously not quite satisfied with his promise. Her faith in her partner was apparently a little shaky.

'But who did he do?' I asked, unable to bear the suspense, for Mrs Williams bore no visible scars from broken crockery and Nelson was untouched by his father's hand, I felt sure.

'Assault, nearly murder it were,' she reminisced sadly.

I exclaimed loudly, producing a gasp of sufficient respect.

'Yep, ups with me best plate and brings it down over 'er 'ead. "There" 'e said, "take that ya naggin' ol' cow", most ungentlemanly 'e were, twenty stitches she 'ad, and the blood made me 'eave; spouted like one of 'em fountains in Trafalgar Square, near killed 'er 'e did. 'E never could stand the naggin' sort, mind.'

'Was this the other woman?' I inquired, suitably awed at her fate.

'No, me Ma, dearie. 'E never treated 'is women like that, proper posh 'e is with them,' it was an envious reflection. 'Shows off like, puts 'is best foot forward, a proper Nelson 'e is.'

'I'm sure,' I agreed. There was an undertone of amusement in my voice, which I tried to conceal under the dramatic circumstances, for I felt this to be an understatement.

Dragging a crumbled and grimy letter from the seclusion of her mauve cardigan, she unfolded it carefully and read me the few lines of complete illiteracy, ending with an exaggerated endearment and a promise of such magnitude that Mr Williams was obviously going to spend the rest of his life doing penance 'outside'.

'Learnt 'is lesson, 'e 'as, by now I expect,' she observed re-reading the golden promise, and hid the mauled letter away again.

'I'm so glad for your sake. You must keep him to his promises, mustn't you?' How, would be her problem!

She nodded determinedly, but I could still see the small flicker of doubt clouding the lustreless pale eyes. 'Things will be different when we get 'ome this time, I'm sure.' She was hungry now for my confirmation.

'Of course they will,' I agreed warmly. 'You'll be like a couple of old lovebirds, I'm sure.'

She looked really pleased. 'Do ya really think so?'

'I most certainly do,' I lied. Mrs Williams brimmed with gratitude.

I pictured the scene clearly; a small house where war consistently raged, fanned by the nagging disapproval of mother-in-law, a stirring disruption in their midst. Mr Williams, uncouth, resentful of his lot, driven on the surge of lusty impulse to dangerous limits, seeking solace and the necessity to build up his manhood again to a swaggering confidence in the reassuring arms of other women, dominating his wife, depicting and despising her weakness, the enduring capacity for everlasting faithfulness, reconciliatory moments of transparent endurance. Nelson would bounce through the wreckage unperturbed, taking for granted the frail woman of steel-like qualities, who endeavoured to smooth turbulent waters with cockney philosophy. It was ''ome to 'ome' with a difference.

'But that's not the only thing that changed me mind,' Mrs Williams confided, softening into girlish prettiness, breaking my sordid imaginations of her background.

'Isn't it?' I inquired, seeing her as she once had been, young, pretty and gay, before she was whisked away to the nuptial couch on the arms of hopeful illusion. She paused for so long I thought she had decided not to tell me.

'It's 'im that was upstairs. Ya know, Mr Percy,' she blurted out, twisting her hands together nervously, a little embarrassed now by her own desire to reveal all. ''E advised me, 'e did.'

I wondered what possible advice that rogue could have given her, sensing with compassion her acute struggle to speak of the departed. I urged her to continue.

''E was a reel gentleman for all that,' she ended defensively, as if she had read my uncomplimentary thoughts about Percy. I had forgotten that the Mrs Williamses of this world were beings of tough loyalty.

'You liked Percy, didn't you?' I asked, remembering the early morning tea sessions, feeling a quick and new comradeship towards this careworn woman.

''E understood me, 'e did, for all his 'oity-toity ways of speaking. 'E got into me 'eart, 'e did.'

'Yes,' I agreed. I understood.

''E said to me, mightily solemn like a judge – except that 'e were lying back in repose on the divan, "Daisy, me girl" 'e said, "Ya must go back to ya ol' man. A fellow is lost without a good woman behind him, especially one that makes tea like you do." 'E spoke to me reel posh.'

'Don't you like the others here?' I asked, wondering if Percy alone had won such wholehearted affection. She answered unhesitatingly.

'Kindness itself,' she murmured, listing each one, adding a special touch of praise here and there. 'Mrs Greenfield is a lady, for all that she's barmy,' she ended, bracketing her opinion of Harriet with: 'And your brother, 'e's a beautiful boy, a reel toff.'

It was the first time I had heard Gerald described as beautiful. I let that remark go without comment.

'Well dearie, I must go an' sort me things out; such a lot to do, Nelson's collected this and that, yer know 'ow it is,' she explained. 'Lawks me paws are real mucky,' she confessed in sudden shame, catching sight of her hands. 'Not white and posh like Mrs Paula's.' We had a moment of envious rapture together over white and slim hands and beautifully manicured nails. ''Elped me, she 'as, no end with me looks; proper advice bureau she is,' Mrs Williams giggled. 'Given me a special jar of them vitamin creams too, it's ever so kind of 'er, I must say.'

I agreed.

'And some 'ints to preserve me looks.' She

patted her worn face. 'Told me 'ow to get me face fixed too, with all them colours, surprise me 'ubby I will.' The words were a challenge I agreed. 'An' most important, she said, I must never use water on me vulnerable skin parts – that was 'er advice . . .'

'It's just a question of spending ten minutes a day,' I added in the voice of a beauty consultant. I knew the routine well.

'Just fancy, no water an' only ten minutes an' yer can emerge lookin' like 'er!'

'Yes.' I agreed. I did not contradict her cheerful convictions though I knew that Paula spent all of an hour to get her face on, and water was replaced by an array of most expensive cleansing liquids.

I stood and watched the shabby figure leave, her head held hopefully high. Hope built on promises: Percy's attentions and Paula's creams. I thought of her one shoddy suitcase, and a few faded clothes: her load was a heavy one; her light in life would shine according to her husband's word, and joy was held in a precarious balance. Somehow I felt I was losing an ally.

Then I thought of Andy – suppose he left on this surge of household movement? Only marriage would be the ultimate end of such an affair.

Suddenly I could bear it no longer: I was to be left with a carcass, an empty house to be filled once again with strangers; left with a dog that cocked its leg at inconvenient times and two children to lead to the paths of righteousness; a hovering family convinced of my incapability and lack of talent in the art of discerning character.

How could I tell whether the menacing face with the stance of a criminal was as gentle as a newborn babe and would pay his rent diligently; the sallow-faced boy an epileptic; the white-haired lady who could be anybody's grandmother was bordering on lunacy; an old school tie and Oxford accent covered a self-made bigamist with other criminal tendencies; that a perfectly sane girl would end up in a strait-jacket? How could one turn aside, in the sobering light of dawn, the Mrs Buddens of this world, with their everlasting bulges and washing lines of perpetual nappies, or Nelson, a bulky satyr?

There would be another spring, another summer. Christmas, a new year, and the rigmarole would repeat itself with painful precision. Lodgers would mark my life like milestones.